Perfect Host

Felicity Cloake is a journalist and food writer from London. She writes for the *Daily Mail*, the *Metro* and *Fire & Knives* magazine and has a weekly column in the *Guardian*. She was named Food Journalist of the Year and won the New Media of the Year Award at the 2011 Guild of Food Writers Awards. Her first book, *Perfect*, is available in Penguin.

www.felicitycloake.com

Perfect Host

162 Easy Recipes for Feeding People and Having Fun

FELICITY CLOAKE

PHOTOGRAPHY
BY JOE WOODHOUSE

PENGUIN
FIG TREE

FIG TREE
an imprint of
PENGUIN BOOKS

For my parents

FIG TREE

Published by the Penguin Group
Penguin Books Ltd, 80 Strand, London WC2R 0RL, England
Penguin Group (USA) Inc., 375 Hudson Street, New York, New York 10014, USA
Penguin Group (Canada), 90 Eglinton Avenue East, Suite 700, Toronto, Ontario, Canada M4P 2Y3
(a division of Pearson Penguin Canada Inc.)
Penguin Ireland, 25 St Stephen's Green, Dublin 2, Ireland (a division of Penguin Books Ltd)
Penguin Group (Australia), 707 Collins Street, Melbourne,
Victoria 3008, Australia (a division of Pearson Australia Group Pty Ltd)
Penguin Books India Pvt Ltd, 11 Community Centre,
Panchsheel Park, New Delhi – 110 017, India
Penguin Group (NZ), 67 Apollo Drive, Rosedale, Auckland 0632, New Zealand
(a division of Pearson New Zealand Ltd)
Penguin Books (South Africa) (Pty) Ltd, Block D, Rosebank Office Park,
181 Jan Smuts Avenue, Parktown North, Gauteng 2193, South Africa

Penguin Books Ltd, Registered Offices: 80 Strand, London WC2R 0RL, England

www.penguin.com

First published 2013
001

Set in Gill Sans, Inscription
Designed and typeset by Nina Farrell
Printed in China

A CIP catalogue record for this book is available from the British Library

ISBN: 978–0–241–14569–2

ALWAYS LEARNING   PEARSON

Contents

Introduction

Feeding the people we love – or those we hope we might come to love in the future but presently just fancy, or even those we simply want to suck up to – is a pretty fundamental part of what it means to be human. Communal gluttony plays a significant part in almost every major religious and social milestone life can throw at us, from the christening cake to the boozy wake – which could say something about the sacred nature of food, or, alternatively, might simply suggest that as a species, we're irredeemably greedy. (And hurrah for that.)

Grandly picking up the bill at a fancy restaurant has a certain big-shot thrill about it, but if you enjoy cooking, then rustling up a feast for friends and family is a positively gleeful experience. Planning the menu, choosing drinks, decorating the table, seeing people happily wolfing down your food as they chat: it might be a bit of work, but trust me, even if you singe the sausages, or forget to turn the oven on for pudding, they'll love you for it.

I'm not going to pretend that entertaining is as easy as ordering a pizza, but, on the upside, it's certainly an awful lot more fun. Remember that hosting is only as much work as you make it: if you've just got time to pick up some good bread and cheese after work, and make a couple of salads, so be it. Everyone will have their mouths too full of focaccia to complain. The point is that you're feeding them, surely the most joyous thing one human can do for another: you've spent time and energy on their dinner – and that's love, that is.

'Entertaining' sounds horribly prim – this isn't a book about linen folding and fish knives, because I certainly don't know anyone who bothers with things like that: I doubt even Hyacinth Bucket knows her way around a napkin mitre these days. Rather than placing your guests on their best behaviour, the aim of a host should be to put them at their ease; which means good food, good conversation – and if they want to put their elbows on the table then you're not about to stop them, dammit.

One of the best things about hosting anything, from a picnic to Christmas dinner, is that you're in charge: if you don't like fruit cake, or turkey, then don't serve it. No one ever mentions the fact that, although it's always a treat to be cooked for, cooking yourself means you can be as selfish as you like. Desperate to pig out on that salted caramel ice cream you saw in a magazine, or keen to give whisky and food matching a whirl? This is your opportunity to do so – and be thanked for it into the bargain.

Lastly, chat flows more easily when it's fed with food and lubricated with drink – people put down their phones, leave Twitter to its own devices, and actually talk to each other. I really, really like food, but even I'd admit it's not the most important part of a dinner party: the guests are. Make them comfortable, feed them, water them, then sit back and let the magic happen.

The basics

I'm going to assume that, if you're reading a book on hosting, you're in possession of a basic kitchen. You don't need much more to entertain friends than you do to feed yourself, but a few things will make life easier. A food processor, although a big investment, will pay for itself in time, especially if you shell out a bit more for a sturdy model that will be with you for years to come. At least one very large saucepan or casserole comes in extremely handy for cooking for large numbers, so you don't have to divide everything between different pans, and a big mixing bowl is an essential – 'pound' shops (they all take liberties with the concept as far as I can tell) do cheap plastic and metal numbers that fit the bill nicely, even if they're not quite fit for the table.

Essentials

* Heavy-based frying pan (worth spending money on: you'll be forever burning things in cheap versions)
* 1 large and 1 small saucepan, with lids – and more sizes in between if you can run to them
* Heatproof bowl that fits over one of the saucepans to make a bain-marie
* Ovenproof casserole
* Roasting tin
* Wooden spoon
* Large serving spoon
* Whisk
* Mixing bowl
* Large sieve (this can also stand in for a colander and a steamer)

* Good, heavy knife
* Knife sharpener, used every time you wash the knife
* Chopping board (at least 2, so your strawberries don't honk of garlic)
* Vegetable peeler
* Tin opener
* Corkscrew and bottle opener
* Measuring jug
* Scales (preferably electronic)
* Grater
* Blender – stick blenders are pretty cheap, and don't take up much space
* Pastry brush

Not essential but very useful

* Digital thermometer
* Pestle and mortar
* Loaf tin
* Muffin tin
* Tart tin
* Cooling rack
* Rolling pin (if you don't have one, you can use a wine bottle)

* Ladle
* Silicone tongs
* Measuring spoons
* Steamer
* Silicone spatula
* Griddle pan

Larder

You'll also find life a lot easier if you build up a small larder of commonly used ingredients, replacing each as you finish it, rather than waiting until you need it again. If you've got the space, keeping a good selection of the following will mean you have to do a lot less last-minute shopping.

* Tinned tomatoes
* Anchovies
* Basmati rice
* Pasta
* Couscous
* Tinned or dried beans and pulses – e.g. chickpeas, lentils, etc.
* Jarred fruit (frozen berries are also good for last-minute puddings)

* Good stock cubes
* Garlic
* Onions
* Lemons
* Eggs
* Parmesan or other pungent hard cheese

Seasoning and spices

These are the ones I use the most often, but you'll quickly build up a more extensive library.

* Chilli flakes
* Smoked paprika
* Nutmeg

* Bay leaves
* Vanilla pods
* Sea salt and black peppercorns

Cooking and condiments

* Olive oil, both ordinary and extra virgin
* Groundnut or vegetable oil
* White and red wine vinegar
* Dijon mustard
* English mustard powder

* Worcestershire sauce
* Soy sauce
* Tabasco or other hot sauce
* Grated horseradish

Sweet and baking

* Honey
* Dark chocolate
* Dried fruit: currants, apricots, mixed peel
* Flaked almonds
* Plain flour
* Caster sugar
* Baking powder

* Dried yeast
* Gelatine sheets

Freezer

* Shortcrust pastry
* Peas and spinach

* Bacon or pancetta
* Breadcrumbs

If you can keep them alive, a herb garden is also an incredibly useful resource. In my fantasy world, I'd choose flat-leaf parsley, chives, rosemary, mint, basil, tarragon and thyme (I don't know anyone who's managed to cultivate coriander successfully in this country, so I'd have to reluctantly leave that one to the professionals).

Some general points on hosting

This sounds obvious, but it's so important that I'm going to say it anyway: planning ahead is the one and only key to successful entertaining. We all love the idea of coming home half an hour before our guests are due and knocking up a clever couple of courses from the larder before wafting off to get changed, but in reality, for most of us, that would be a nightmare scenario. I certainly have thrown together a decent-ish dinner of pasta and ice cream sundaes for last-minute arrivals, but I can't pretend I enjoyed the process. Even if you thrive on stress, your guests won't: it's hardly relaxing being caught up in a whirlwind of frenetic activity.

Such plotting should start early: if you don't know your guests well, it's always safest to check they don't have any particular dietary requirements before you get carried away with devising the menu. I generally ask about these, plus any violent likes or dislikes, when inviting people: although, like many gluttons, I've got little patience with fussy eaters, I don't want to risk my wrists shucking two dozen oysters if one of the party is going to sit miserably eating bread and shallot vinaigrette as the rest of us pig out.

When menu planning, it's tempting just to go for things you might like to eat without much thought for how they might work together: even the most enthusiastic dairy devotee might struggle to polish off smoked mackerel pâté, macaroni cheese and crème brûlée in quick succession. The same goes for nibbles and canapés at a party: sticky sausages, sausage rolls and salami will be meat overkill. Bear in mind that keeping things seasonal is not only cheaper and tastier, but also gives your gig more of a sense of occasion: a summer party devoted to gorging yourselves on asparagus and strawberries is ridiculously simple to prepare, yet feels like a real treat.

Don't feel you need to take it all on from scratch, though: it's better to do one course really well and buy in the rest than kill yourself trying to produce three different recipes. After all, most French hosts wouldn't dream of making their own duck rillettes or *tarte aux pommes* when the local baker or *traiteur* does such a good job, and they're born gastronomes (or so the story goes). You can also make life easier for yourself by choosing food that guests can dig right into at the table, rather than anything that needs 'plating up', *Masterchef* style. Not only is it easier for you, but passing things round makes for less food waste and more conversation.

When you write your shopping list, check the recipe for any special equipment you might need, so you don't end up trying to make a soufflé without a whisk, or muffins in a fairy cake tin, and give yourself a few days' notice, in case you find you need to make a special detour to a cookware shop for said item. And you should always make lists: geeky they may be, but they're more reliable than a memory, and it's very satisfying ticking things off. (I take a pen to the shops with me for that very purpose. Really.)

Timing and tidying

That great American epicure James Beard was never wiser than when he observed that 'there is nothing quite so satisfying as that lull before the first ring of the doorbell'. The idea is that you should have completed most of the cooking and preparation well before your guests arrive, which is why you won't find many recipes that need much last-minute attention in this book. I firmly believe that steak and chips is a pleasure best left to the experts.

And while we're on the subject of professionals, take a tip from them with regard to that mysterious thing called, rather unintelligibly, *mise en place*. In English, this basically means having everything in place before you begin cooking: chop your vegetables, make your stock, measure out your seasonings, and cover and refrigerate if necessary until you're ready to start. No frantic scrabbling around for the cornflour while the gravy bubbles over, and a neat and clean work surface to impress your guests, should any of them stray into the kitchen.

This is particularly important if, like me, you are blessed, or cursed, with an open-plan flat: although most of my friends know me well enough not to expect the kitchen to be sparkling clean when they arrive, it's still not pleasant to be confronted with a pile of dirty saucepans on the floor. If you don't have time to wash them up, stick a tea towel over them or shove them into the microwave or a cupboard *in extremis* – just remember where you put them, or you could be confronted with a nasty surprise a few weeks later.

Clearing up as you go along is, obviously, a very good idea, but don't take it too far: unless you're recycling crockery and cutlery, leave the washing-up until everyone has left, or people will feel, quite rightly, that you're more interested in clean plates than you are in them. Nothing breaks up a party like someone sweeping empty glasses from the table from beneath people's noses, even if you shriek, 'You're very welcome to stay!' over your shoulder as you disappear into the kitchen: it reminds people that they've got to go home eventually, and that's a horribly sobering thought. It's the hosting equivalent of turning up the lights at pub closing time.

Although I wouldn't go as far as to claim that I enjoy tackling the devastation left in the wake of a party of any kind, if a good friend or partner sticks around to help, it can actually be rather fun – and, in my experience, certainly less painful after a few glasses of wine than it will be the next morning. Stick on some music and get to work, both on the washing-up and the inevitable gossip run-down.

Atmosphere

I've made the bold claim that, when it comes to entertaining, the atmosphere matters more than the food (oddly, the opposite is true when eating alone) – but, if you're not blessed with the goddess-like powers, or the multi-million-pound home, of Nigella Lawson, working out how to create that elusive buzz can be a mystery.

Let me reassure you that, unless you've got a problem with the drains, it's nothing to do with scented candles or pot pourri – indeed the answer largely lies within yourself. At the very real risk of sounding like I've been possessed by Martha Stewart, hosting is largely a matter of making your guests feel welcome, so when they arrive, make sure you're around to have a quick chat, rather than letting them in and then disappearing back into the kitchen, leaving them to pour their own drink. (Again, it all comes back to organization: if the main course is happily simmering away in the oven, and the table is already laid, then you're free to be a good host.)

Even if it's all gone wrong, and you've got some emergency remedial work to attend to, take the time to introduce your guests to the assembled company if they're not already bosom friends. A couple of minutes spent getting the conversation going will reap rewards later, when they're all chatting away so happily that they quite forget you promised the food would only be half an hour at most.

To that end, if you have people over for dinner, whether you're doing a starter or not, always provide some nibbles, however basic: although going overboard will spoil people's appetites, a few nuts or crisps should go some way to ensuring that the early arrivals aren't completely blotto by the time the last stragglers escape from work, and will buy you a bit of time in the kitchen if required.

Don't rush the meal either: this isn't a speed-eating competition, and although no one wants so much time between courses that they're ravenous again, equally, if you speed through three in an hour, your guests will be left sitting like beached whales for the rest of the evening. Once the food's on the table, adopt the mantra of the Royal Family and never apologize, never explain. You may notice it's slightly overcooked, or a little under-seasoned, but in all likelihood your guests won't, and such observations are very off-putting. Brazen it out instead.

Make sure the physical setting is as comfortable as possible: lamps or candles rather than an overhead bulb if it's dark, and soft seating: it doesn't matter if it's a packing case or an Eames chair, as long as it's well padded, so invest in some cushions. They're very easy to make yourself or, for the less craftily minded, Ikea do absurdly cheap examples that can be stowed in a cupboard if they cramp your normal style. Give the bathroom or cloakroom a quick once-over if you suspect your standards of cleanliness might differ from those of your guests, and, rather than bothering to tidy any rooms you're not using, simply shut the doors. (Note, this does not work if you have nosy guests who insist on a full, *Come Dine with Me* style tour.)

Crafting the perfect cocktail

Nothing to do with stirring or muddling – when it comes to the success of a party, a well-mixed guest list is even more important than strong drink. Although it's fun to have lots of old friends over, the liveliest evenings always seem to occur when you shake things up a bit and introduce some fresh blood into the group. A couple from work, some school friends, that nice man you sometimes play tennis with and his girlfriend – when people don't know each other, conversation tends to turn to larger, more interesting subjects than so-and-so's love life and 'remember that time when …'

There are limits, though: just as two cheesy dishes, however delicious on their own, would be too much in one meal, some people work better alone than together. If one of your friends is religious, for example, and your sister delights in regurgitating the work of Richard Dawkins, they're probably best kept apart if you don't want things to end with tears and fisticuffs. The newly and unhappily single might not enjoy tea with the recently engaged, and, as Fi Kirkpatrick wisely advises in her hilarious *Debrett's New Guide to Easy Entertaining*, 'don't invite people if you know they actively dislike one another or are having a clandestine affair with the other half of one of the couples present'.

Some thoughts on drink

Wine

The oil in the cogs of every great event: alcoholic or not, drinks are almost as important as the food, so plan them alongside. If you haven't got a clue what goes with what (and, let's be honest, no one's born with it), a friendly wine merchant, should you have one nearby, is an invaluable source of interesting recommendations: tell them how much you want to spend at the outset, and you'll neatly avoid drinking next month's rent over pudding. If you don't, there are a number of handy guides online to help you: I've listed a few at the back of the book.

Broadly speaking, one aims to match the weight of the food with the weight of the wine. Nothing to do with scales: simply that rich, full-flavoured foods, like stews, curries and game, demand equally weighty, full-bodied wines, whether red or white. More delicate or plain fare, fish, white meat, steamed vegetables and anything with subtle flavours, should be matched with a lighter wine. Oily or fatty foods, from fried fish to cheese and pâtés, are often served with acidic wines like Riesling, to 'cut through' the richness, and sweet foods should be served with sweet wine – anything else will seem unpleasantly tart in comparison.

The only really hard and fast rule, however, is to avoid serving a powerfully tannic red wine with oily fish like mackerel or sardines, because the two tend to taste extremely unpleasant together. Lighter red wines – say a Beaujolais, or Pinot Noir – can work fine with fish, though, despite James Bond's snooty dismissal of the idea in *From Russia with Love*. ('Red wine with fish?' he remarks, when the baddie Donald 'Red' Grant reveals his true colours after dinner. 'Well, that should have told me something.')

As a rough guide, there are six glasses of wine in every bottle (although as the evening progresses, this may mysteriously decrease) and many guides recommend you should expect your guests to put away three glasses each in the course of a dinner party – and one drink an hour at a stand-up party (!). I'll leave it up to you to decide whether your friends are above- or below-average consumers, but adjust these figures accordingly. Unless you're very hard up, it's always better to over- rather than under-cater, because drinks don't go off, and the worst that can happen is that you've got a few extra bottles of wine to get through afterwards, which is at the better end of hardship.

It's quite acceptable to ask guests to bring a bottle: indeed, unless you're fraternizing with the elderly or very grand, most people expect it, especially at a dinner or house party. If you're cooking something specific, feel free to indicate what kind of drinks might be appropriate – a vague suggestion of grape or character ('crisp white') will probably go down better than a specific request for a bottle of Dom Perignon to accompany the griddled prawns.

Some wines, particularly those from the New World, will come with a handy back label telling you a bit about the wine – if it's been oaked, some tasting notes, what temperature it's best served at – but the French, in their infinite wisdom, generally prefer to allow us the fun of guessing.

Here's a basic guide to what to chill, and for how long:

* Sparkling and sweet wines should be served well chilled: 6–8°C.

* Light, crisp whites, e.g. dry sherries, Sauvignon Blanc, Pinot Grigio, Vinho Verde, should be served chilled: 10°C.

* Full-bodied or oaked whites, e.g. Chardonnay, Viognier, should be served chilled: 12°C–14°C.

* Light reds, e.g. Beaujolais, lighter Valpolicellas, some Pinot Noirs, should be served chilled: 12°C (honestly, try it).

* Fuller-bodied reds, e.g. Rioja, Shiraz, Barolo, claret, should be served at room temperature: 18°C.

Most wines don't need decanting – the custom dates from a time when they were sold unfiltered. Nowadays, you're unlikely to find much sediment in anything but older vintages and ports – but if you have a nice decanter and want to use it, there's little harm in doing so (be careful with very old and delicate examples, though, which should only be decanted just before serving).

Glasswise, I tend to use the same ones for both red and white wine, because I never seem to have quite enough to go round, but generally speaking, reds are served in larger glasses than white to allow more contact with the air, which helps to develop the flavour. Sparkling wine should be served in narrow flutes, to preserve the bubbles – the traditional champagne saucers are thus completely unfit for the purpose, but that said, I love the look of them, and would gladly serve cheaper fizz from them if I could lay my paws on some. Glasses with stems allow you to swirl the contents more easily, and stop you warming up the contents with your hands – but (and this may be important, depending on your friends) they're much easier to knock over with an expansive hand gesture. Bear this in mind.

Wine should be stored at a constant, relatively cool temperature – which makes the kitchen probably the worst place for it. Find somewhere without an oven or a frequently opened window: a cupboard, perhaps, or a garage.

Cider and beer

Proper cider (by which I don't mean the stuff that claims to be better served over ice, presumably to disguise its noxious flavour) is the ideal partner for cheese, especially nutty Cheddars and Alpine Gruyères and Beauforts – try sweeter ciders with blue cheese. It also makes a fine companion for chicken, ham, sausages, roast pork and anything creamy, from *moules à la Normande* to a risotto. Basically, if you can imagine cooking an ingredient in cider, then it will eat well with it too.

A few years ago, I was treated to an entire Christmas dinner paired with beer, courtesy of an organization called the Beer Academy, which exists to 'enlighten, educate and enthuse' people about beer – a noble cause if ever I heard one. From an English wheat beer with the smoked salmon to a wonderfully rich and fruity Belgian Trappist ale with Christmas pud, everything worked perfectly – although sadly I couldn't persuade my mum to let me replicate it on the big day.

The principles are just the same as matching wine and food. If you're eating something delicately flavoured, like fish or white meat, choose a lighter beer, like a lager or blonde ale. Richer, heavier brews will work better with stronger flavours, like cheese, sausages and red meat (just think of a steak and ale pie), while spicy foods, as any curry lover will know, are perfect with a hoppy IPA. For puddings, sweeter, more treacly Belgian dubbels or tripels, fruit beers, sweet stouts, barley wines and porters are all a good bet.

Oysters, following no logic at all, are delicious with stout. Who knows why, but the combination is a time-honoured one, and has a pleasingly Victorian feel to it.

Spirits and food

A rare choice for a reason, as I discovered to my cost when I invited people round for vodka and blini – the evening turned out to be much shorter than anticipated. However, spirits can make good matches for individual courses or nibbles: very cold vodka and smoked fish or roe before dinner, whisky with smoked fish or meat (or, with sweeter, more full-bodied examples, dark chocolate and nuts), Armagnac with Roquefort, prunes or foie gras – just think about the flavours involved and play around a bit, especially at the end of the evening. The worst that can happen is that you fall over.

Soft drinks

Even if you're a hundred per cent certain that all your guests are voracious boozers, it's always wise to lay in a soft option, just in case. (The newly pregnant, for example, will usually come up with an unconvincing excuse about antibiotics at the last minute.) This is particularly important at drinks parties, where people might want to linger without impairing their ability to get up the next morning.

I find a good-quality cordial is a handy thing to keep in the cupboard for just such eventualities – if it doesn't get drunk, it will keep until next time. At dinner parties, a big jug of iced tap water, garnished with some thin slices of citrus fruit (orange or lime look more exotic than the classic lemon), or even cucumber or mint, is absolutely vital, and you should keep it topped up at all times. As an enthusiastic glugger of water myself, it's annoying as a guest to sit there parched, waiting for a break in the conversation so you can offer to go and refill the carafe yourself.

The end of the affair

All good things must come to an end – but we all have at least one friend who fails to get the message that it's 1 a.m. on a work night, and however much you love them, you'd prefer to be in bed. Alone. I'd dearly like to be direct about these things, and if you're brave enough, it's usually the best way: such people are often impervious to even the least subtle of hints. Asking if anyone would like a taxi calling 'because they can be slow at this time of night' should get the ball rolling without bringing the evening to too abrupt a close, and enquiring about the last train, because, although they're more than welcome to stay longer, you don't want them to have to shell out for a cab is another option, albeit one apt to backfire with wealthier or drunker friends.

Once one person goes, others usually get the message. If not, you might have to adopt the strong-arm tactic of a friend of mine, clasp them in a friendly fashion, and steer them gently in the direction of the door, still chatting merrily as you do so. Failing that, chuck them a sleeping bag and leave them to it.

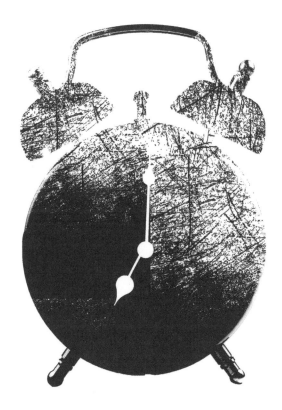

Breakfast & brunch

The idea of entertaining before noon might well strike horror into the heart of any right-thinking person – even those sinisterly chirpy 'morning people' (always self-proclaimed with a certain puzzling smugness) baulk at inviting a lot of grumpy night owls to sit around the table and yawn into their food. However, there are some occasions when it cannot be avoided. Weekend guests, for example, often demand more than a cup of tea before vacating the premises, and then, for the romantically footloose and fancy-free, there's the unexpected overnighter, who might well appreciate sustenance in return for their phone number.

I like, occasionally, to invite people for Sunday brunch. (Brunch, here, simply denotes the fact that the meal hovers nearer to the midday mark than the breaking of the fast – the menu is strictly breakfast only. The rest of the day is for ordinary food.) Everyone gets a bit of a lie-in after the night before, before a low-key, relaxed kind of socializing where most of the chat revolves around the newspapers spread over the table, crowned with coffee cups and crumbs, and the odd bit of gossip from Saturday's shenanigans. It's nicer than fighting for a table in a buggy-crammed café, and there's no danger of soggy toast.

The first meal of the day is a great indicator of personality, and quite mild-mannered sorts often have surprisingly strong opinions about what constitutes a good breakfast. Some of us like to sugar-coat the bitter pill of another day – figs and honey; chocolate and churros; coconut milk congee – whereas for others, the very idea of anything sweet before lunch is abhorrent. I must admit to tending, in true British style, towards the second camp – in fact, for me, the more savoury and spicy the better. Great dollops of English mustard, rather than sweet brown sauce, with my bacon; chorizo picante, not Cumberland sausages, with my fried eggs; I'd rather have masala dosa than blueberry muffins any day. But ripe fruit and thick yoghurt, or good, homemade jam can sometimes sway me.

This early-morning sensitivity can often lead to quite surprising preferences, as one Major L, author of *Breakfasts, Luncheons and Ball Suppers* (1887), observes when recounting 'the late Sir Tatton Sykes'' taste for starting the day with apple tart and home-brewed ale – '*chacun à son goût*', he notes wryly, before continuing, disapprovingly, that although he 'feels the greatest respect for the memory of this most worthy and excellent of baronets …

Any one caring to try such a breakfast must cater for himself.' And this from a man who opines that a country house kitchen should provide 'a variety to suit all tastes, viz: fish, poultry, or game if in season; sausages, and one meat of some sort, such as mutton cutlets, or fillets of beef; omelets, and eggs served in various ways; bread of both kinds, white and brown, and fancy bread of as many kinds as can be conveniently served; two or three kinds of jam, orange marmalade and fruits when in season; and on the side table, cold meats, such as ham, tongue, cold game, or game pie, galantines, and in the winter a round of spiced beef'. Roll on lunch.

Despite the best efforts of the croissant-crunching chattering classes, breakfast is perhaps the one meal where we continue to display a distinct national independence – not only would most of Britain be puzzled by the fruit pudding that often puts in an appearance on Scotland's breakfast table, or the Welsh taste for laverbread, but I suspect all of us would shy away from a Sicilian granita or grits and gravy, let alone Turkish sheep's head soup (one to file away for a hangover). One of the great benefits of a later breakfast, however, is that such things, brain broth aside, start to tempt the appetite – what might be repulsive at 7 a.m. becomes intriguing at 11.30, after a lie-in and a few preparatory cups of tea.

Practicalities

If you have house guests, of course, breakfast time will be dependent on their habits, and any plans they might have for the day (although I'd always suggest establishing a rough window the evening before – otherwise I wake up absurdly early, and lie awake worrying that they might be dying of hunger along the corridor, only to be found tetchy and exhausted by the time my guests finally surface). When inviting people, I usually suggest about 11 a.m. – late enough for all but the most determined party-goers to have had sufficient sleep, but sufficiently early that the day still stretches ahead invitingly, ready for a walk or some other wholesome weekend activity. Do bear in mind that most people will be at least twenty minutes late to a breakfast invitation. We all just move slower in the mornings.

The keyword at breakfast time should be relaxed: this isn't the moment for witty conversation or elaborate menus. Choose one or two dishes, ask someone to bring the newspapers with them, stick the radio on (no shouty talk radio here – the gentle murmuring of *The Archers* omnibus or some soothing monkish chanting usually does the trick), and ensure you have a cup of tea handy throughout the proceedings.

I have a horror of the idea of shopping before breakfast, so, with the exception of any fresh bread (which I often request from one of my guests), I make sure I have everything ready to go, and a clean and tidy table at which to seat people. Breakfast should be informal, of course, but, as the first meal of a new day, I also feel strongly that it ought not to be slovenly, with people pushing aside wine glasses and post to make space for their orange juice. Sweep everything into another room the night before, get some flowers on the table if at all possible, and make the effort to decant the milk into a jug (one of my mum's greatest bugbears, which, unwittingly, I seem to have inherited – those ugly plastic bottles, so reminiscent of rushed weekday breakfasts, entirely spoil the illusion of leisured elegance that a breakfast party depends upon), and you've got instant atmosphere. All you need now is the food to match.

Breakfast in bed

This, like impossibly high heels, or coalition government, is one of those ideas which is more seductive in theory than in practice, when it generally ranges from uncomfortable to downright messy (although there are virtues to the latter, if you wholeheartedly embrace it). A few suggestions:

* Find a tray or, if not a tray, something that will serve as a reasonable substitute – a (clean) chopping board or even a very large and solid book of arty photographs.

* Take as few things up as possible – you don't want to be balancing bottles of ketchup or jugs of milk on your laps, and an empty banana skin or browning apple core is, as an emblem of ageing and decay, definitely one of the least sexy things I can think of.

* Choose your menu carefully if you hope your efforts will reap romantic rewards – fruit compote or honey-soaked muffins (oo-er) are, for most people, more likely to lead to tender feelings than anything involving egg (my sheets!) or smoked fish. Sausages, however, can go either way. Finger food is definitely the way forward if possible, supplied with a clean napkin.

* Always, always, take your apron off before bringing the tray upstairs. Unless you happen to know the intended recipient particularly likes it.

Drinks

A nice cup of tea

First things first: what your guests need as soon as they come through the door is a drink. For me, that means tea. And, I must admit, although I know that using cheap teabags is the culinary equivalent of getting all your news from the *Daily Mail* – you get what you pay for – I have a weakness for mouth-puckeringly tannic, slightly stewed stuff during the week. It's quick, it's tidy, and it leaves you in no danger of hitting the snooze button. At weekends, however, I push the boat out; after all, if you're clearing up after guests anyway, a few tea leaves make next to no difference. Think of it as the equivalent of offering a cafetière instead of instant – these days, most of us would rather pretend we had no coffee in the house than admit to a Nescafé habit.

A few good teas to offer at the breakfast table (you will note they are all black – delicate green and white versions have no place this early in my day):

English breakfast
A robust blended tea, this is the classic choice over breakfast, hence the name. Queen Victoria allegedly liked it.

Assam
The main constituent of most English breakfast blends, this has a similarly rich, malty character.

Earl Grey
The eponymous nineteenth-century prime minister was apparently sent a freebie of zesty, citric black tea by a Chinese mandarin, and liked it so much he asked Twinings to recreate it for him. Infused with the rind of the bergamot orange, native to southern Italy, it has a delicate, fresh flavour which, in my opinion, is best enjoyed without milk.

Lapsang souchong
This Chinese tea is dried over wood fires, which explains the distinctive, smoky bacon smell. Not for everyone, but I think it's the perfect complement to a fry-up.

See page 164 for advice on brewing.

Coffee

We're much more willing, as a nation, to make a fuss over coffee – perhaps the problem with tea is over-familiarity? – and consequently, you're far less likely these days to accept the offer with alacrity, only to find yourself staring down the barrel of a cup of musty-tasting instant. Whether you own a bells and whistles, full-steam-ahead bean-to-cup espresso machine, or a cafetière, making a decent coffee isn't difficult.

First of all, decide what you like to drink in the mornings: rich Javanese, fresh and zingy Kenyan, smooth, chocolatey Brazilian…and make sure it's fresh. Ideally you'd grind your own, freshly roasted beans, but if you have neither the room nor a particular yen for a coffee grinder, you can at least make the effort to check your supplies before you go shopping, and chuck out any coffee that's over a fortnight or so old. There's no easier way to make a mediocre cup than to use stale grounds. Keep any open bags in an airtight container somewhere with a cool, but stable temperature.

Play around with how much to use to get the flavour you like (I personally think coffee should be served punchy and strong enough that you can only handle one cup without getting the shakes), and always use freshly boiled water, although coffee is less sensitive than tea over the exact temperature. Serve with warm, but not hot milk.

Juices and smoothies

I'm not a big fan of fruit juice over breakfast – I find the acidity slightly offensive so early in the morning. However, I accept I'm in the minority camp here, and when I do indulge (often in the somewhat spurious hope of cancelling out the negative effects of what's to come), I think it's worth putting in a little effort and making one's own. Freshly squeezed orange juice, for example, is so much nicer than anything I've ever found in even the matiest of chilled cartons that it's worth putting in the time with the citrus juicer just before your guests arrive so everyone can have a small glassful, rather than the pints of pasteurized stuff they'd ordinarily glug down.

If you have a hand blender (or even the jug sort), smoothies are also much more cost-effective to make at home – they're a cunning way of using up elderly fruit which is bringing the tone of the fruit bowl down, and you can play around with the flavours. All you need to do is remove any pips, stones or other inedible bits (I generally leave the peel on for extra fibre, except in obvious cases like bananas; use your common sense here), then purée, loosen with citrus or apple juice, and add any other flavours you might fancy, such as fresh herbs, yoghurt, oats or even, if you happen to be into such things, and have more money than sense, spirulina or blue-green algae.

Smoothie classics

*   Pear, white peach and mint

*   Strawberry, banana and yoghurt

*   Mixed berries (buy frozen if out of season, or if you fancy a teeth-tinglingly slushy sort of experience) with a little peeled root ginger and some honey

*   Mango, chilli flakes (easy on these) and lime juice

Breakfast cocktails

It's funny how drinking at breakfast time is utterly unacceptable when it involves a modest 7 a.m. lager at the airport, yet somehow manages to become sophisticated where hard spirits are concerned. That being said, it can't be denied that a drink before noon feels gorgeously decadent on an occasional basis. It simply reinforces the feeling that, like lingering for two hours over the papers, or scoffing the entire day's calories before lunch, this isn't something one can do every day.

Of course, you can drink anything you like at breakfast time, including whatever's left from the night before, but there are some obvious classics of the genre which will probably leave your guests less worried about you in the long term.

Mimosa

The outrageously retro Buck's Fizz died a death in respectable circles years ago (the cocktail, not the pop group. I'm sure lots of people still enjoy the upbeat message of our 1981 Eurovision victors) and is now found only at particularly depressing weddings and corporate breakfast parties. However, done with care, it can still charm – especially when renamed with something more reminiscent of the French Riviera than the Tory party conference.

In fact, the Buck's Fizz, invented at London's Buck's Club (said to be the inspiration for P. G. Wodehouse's bun-throwing Drones), is actually a variant on the traditional Mimosa, as it replaces some of the orange juice with sugar syrup. By leaving the sweet stuff out, you get a classier drink, and neatly sidestep the naff name.

Although traditionally made with champagne, I think the more acidic, but lighter character of cava works better here, as well as being far better value for money – as always, don't try to make a cocktail with anything you wouldn't drink neat.

PER PERSON
25ML FRESHLY SQUEEZED ORANGE JUICE
110ML CHILLED CAVA

ORANGE SLICE, TO GARNISH
(ENTIRELY OPTIONAL)

1. Pour the orange juice into a champagne flute. Top with fizz. Add an orange slice garnish, if you're feeling fancy, and serve.

The Bloody Mary

MAKES 1 JUG, TO SERVE 8

The undisputed king of early-morning drinks, apparently on the spurious basis that, being largely tomato juice, and often garnished with a stick of celery, it's almost a smoothie, without the irksomely infantile associations of the 'alcoholic smoothie' genre. Alcohol deserves to be treated with respect. One of the beauties of this particular drink is that, like breakfast itself, it positively encourages customization – as American cocktail guru Dale DeGroff puts it in his masterwork, *The Craft of the Cocktail*, 'the Bloody Mary is like the backyard barbecue: everyone thinks theirs is the best'. And, like the cremations of which he speaks, Bloody Marys are very easy to make, but rather more difficult to perfect – fortunately, refining your own particular recipe is a lot more fun than biting into a half-cooked sausage.

A bit of history. DeGroff claims the Bloody Mary was invented in Paris just after the First World War, inspired by the newly available tinned tomato juice imported from the States, and named after a regular at Harry's American Bar, who was frequently left nursing one of these cocktails as she waited for her heinously unreliable boyfriend. 'A comparison was made between the imprisonment of Mary, Queen of Scots, and young Mary's long, solitary hours at the bar.' Hardly a very apt comparison in my view, given that the former was locked up for eighteen years and then had her head cut off with an axe, but the fact remains that, whoever invented the drink, it's a corker. Soothing, slightly savoury tomato juice, spicy Tabasco and salty sweet Worcestershire sauce, with a subtle undercurrent of alcoholic heat, means it almost qualifies as an entire meal in a glass.

I've had some truly inspired Bloody Marys in my time, flavoured with horseradish, wasabi, Bristol cream sherry and the occasional oyster, but below is the simple recipe which always hits the spot at home. Feel free to tweak to your own taste.

300ML VODKA (YOU CAN SUBSTITUTE GIN, IN WHICH CASE IT'S KNOWN, BY PEDANTS AT LEAST, AS A RED SNAPPER)
1 LITRE TOMATO JUICE
1 LEMON, CUT INTO 6 WEDGES
4 TEASPOONS WORCESTERSHIRE SAUCE
2 TEASPOONS TABASCO SAUCE
CELERY SALT
BLACK PEPPER
8 CELERY STICKS, WASHED AND TRIMMED

1. Pour the vodka into a large jug and top up with the tomato juice. Squeeze the lemon wedges briefly into the mixture (rather than wringing every last bit of juice out of them), then add to the jug.

2. Stir in the Worcestershire sauce, Tabasco, a little celery salt and a good grinding of black pepper (never shake a Bloody Mary, it makes it oddly fluffy). Taste and adjust the seasoning if necessary.

3. Pour into glasses and garnish each with a celery stick – I always put the Worcestershire and Tabasco sauces on the table as well, so people can add more if they secretly think my drinks are insipid.

Breakfast martini

I don't know many people, outside my *Mad Men* box-set, who can stomach a martini before 6 p.m., but I live in hope that they still exist. This drink was created at the bar of the Lanesborough Hotel in London, but a similar concoction, known as the Marmalade Cocktail, was created by Harry Craddock at the Savoy in the 1920s. Traditionally garnished with a triangle of toast, I think the peel from the marmalade decoration enough for this time of day, but you could also add a twist of orange peel if you're feeling fancy.

PER PERSON

1 TEASPOON THIN-CUT MARMALADE,
   PEEL REMOVED AND RESERVED
50ML GIN
20ML FRESH LEMON JUICE
20ML COINTREAU
ICE, TO SHAKE
TRIANGLE OF TOAST OR TWIST
   OF ORANGE PEEL, TO GARNISH

1. Stir together the marmalade and gin in a cocktail shaker until the marmalade has dissolved.

2. Add the lemon juice, Cointreau and a generous amount of ice and shake hard, then pour into a chilled martini glass. Stir in the reserved peel and garnish with a thin and elegant triangle of plain toast or a twist of orange peel balanced on the rim.

The classics
Proper porridge

The first porridge of the autumn is as welcome as an early strawberry in May, heralding, as it does, the kind of cold weather that gives one a licence for gluttony. In theory, of course, porridge is an indulgence of the chastest kind: made with water, as is traditional north of the border, and scattered with a very untraditional mix of nutritious seeds and berries, it's the kind of slow-release energy bomb you'd expect to find on offer at the gym. Unless you've seriously over-indulged the night before, however, this is not the kind of porridge you ought to serve your guests for breakfast.

Real porridge cannot be microwaved. Setting aside my own utter inability to do so without coating the machine with a slurry of glutinous grain matter, it's a question of texture – as with a risotto, oats need to be stirred for maximum creaminess.

Getting down to the nitty-gritty of oats, I like steel-cut, rather than the more common rolled sort – they take longer to cook, but I think flavour- and texture-wise, it's worth it, particularly at the weekend when you've got twenty minutes to stand peaceably over the stove.

Sybil Kapoor recommends matching porridge with a smoky Islay whisky such as a Lagavulin sixteen-year-old, and if the weather's bitter enough, I think you might just get away with it.

PER PERSON
¼ MUG OF STEEL-CUT OATS
½ MUG OF WATER
½ MUG OF MILK
A PINCH OF SALT

TO SERVE
WHOLE MILK OR SINGLE CREAM
DEMERARA SUGAR, HONEY OR
   GOLDEN SYRUP

1. Put the oats, water and milk into a pan and bring to the boil. Stir well, then turn down the heat and allow to simmer for about 25–30 minutes, stirring regularly. Add a pinch of salt about a quarter of an hour into cooking.

2. When the porridge is creamy and thick, take it off the heat and serve in a cold bowl with milk or cream to pour around the edge (I like to create a moat for this purpose) and something sweet, and preferably crunchy, to sprinkle over the top.

Winter fruit compote

It's easy enough to give the impression of a healthy lifestyle in summer, with a big bowl of fuzzily ripe peaches and apricots as your centrepiece – just help yourself to fruit, you cry merrily, knowing there's no way, as a host, you could be expected to improve upon perfection. As the weather turns colder, however, fruit needs a bit more of a helping hand. There's stewed apple of course, which always has the whiff of the school dining-room about it, and those packets of frozen berries can work well with a bowl of thick Greek yoghurt, but this gently spiced compote is so warming that you wouldn't want to eat it at any other time of year. It also has the benefit of needing to be made in advance, so you can nonchalantly whip it out of the fridge on the morning concerned, for all the world as if you started every day like this.

4 RIPE PEARS, PEELED, CORED AND QUARTERED	5 TABLESPOONS CLEAR HONEY
1 CINNAMON STICK	100G CASTER SUGAR
½ A VANILLA POD, SPLIT AND SEEDS SCRAPED	75G DRIED APRICOTS
	75G DRIED PRUNES
	75G DRIED FIGS
1 UNWAXED LEMON	THICK NATURAL YOGHURT, TO SERVE

1. Arrange the pears in a pan just big enough to hold them in a single layer and cover with about a litre of cold water. Add the cinnamon stick, vanilla seeds and pod, grated lemon zest and the juice of half the lemon. Bring to a gentle simmer, stir in the honey and sugar, then cover with a lid and leave for 10 minutes, until the pears are soft, but not disintegrating. Remove the pears and set aside.

2. Bring the syrup to the boil and bubble until it's reduced to about 400ml, which will take about 20 minutes. While it's reducing, put the pears and dried fruit into a shallow dish. Pour the hot syrup over the top, leave to cool, then cover and chill overnight in the fridge. The dried fruit will absorb the syrup and become plump and juicy. Remove from the fridge, take out the cinnamon stick and vanilla pod, and bring to room temperature before serving with thick creamy yoghurt.

Eggs Benedict, Royale and Florentine (also known as poached eggs with muffins, hollandaise, and ham, smoked salmon or spinach)

I almost always order eggs Florentine when I go out for breakfast, on the basis that, although by no means a difficult dish, it has a sufficient number of different stages to be slightly fiddly to do at home. (Saying that, I have a friend who makes it, or some variation on it, just about every weekend – but then she has sufficient willpower to dispose of any leftover hollandaise, rather than eating it straight from the pan – and to those saying, what leftover hollandaise, I agree with you in spirit, but in reality, it's damned hard to make the stuff in small quantities, and even I suffer after eating enough for seven.) On special occasions, however, it's well worth pushing the boat out, even if you buy in the muffins.

Numerous historical Benedicts have attempted to claim the inspired combination of poached eggs, hollandaise, ham and muffins as their own, as well they might – but whether it's the Wall Street stockbroker's favourite hangover cure or the invention of a bored retired naval officer, it's almost certainly America's greatest contribution to the breakfast table.

Note that the following recipes are presented in the order you should prepare them if attempting the whole shooting match. To assemble your eggs Benedict, Royale or Florentine, toast the split muffins under a hot grill and butter them generously, then divide between plates and add a portion of ham, smoked salmon or spinach to each half muffin. Lift the eggs out of the pan with a slotted spoon, pat dry with kitchen paper, put them on top of the ham, smoked salmon or spinach, then top with a generous spoonful of hollandaise and a little black pepper. Serve immediately.

English muffins

MAKES 12

Much as I'd love to indulge my latent jingoistic side and simply label these good plain muffins, I fear the creeping encroachment of the cakey American sort makes it incumbent upon me to be clearer on the subject. For the avoidance of doubt, these are the fluffy-centred, flat cakes which can be split in the middle (cutting such a muffin is popularly supposed to instantly render it unpalatably heavy) to make two excellent vehicles for large amounts of melted butter. They can be made a few days in advance – they keep well.

The disparaging verdict of the girlish American heroine of *What Katy Did*, in the third volume of her pious Victorian adventures, has always endeared English muffins to me: 'How queer and disagreeable they are!' said Katy. 'I feel as if I were eating rounds cut from an old ironing-blanket and buttered! Dear me! What did Dickens mean by making such a fuss about them, I wonder?'

230ML MILK
2 TEASPOONS FAST-ACTION DRIED YEAST
1 TEASPOON CASTER SUGAR
450G STRONG WHITE BREAD FLOUR

1 TEASPOON SALT
FINE POLENTA, FOR DUSTING
BUTTER, TO COOK

1. Heat the milk and 50ml of water in a small pan until warm, but not simmering. Empty it into a bowl, add the yeast and the sugar and mix briefly. Leave in a warm place for about 15 minutes, until it's got a good froth to it.

2. Put the flour into a large mixing bowl and add the salt. Whisk briefly to get rid of any lumps, then make a well in the middle, pour in the yeast and milk mixture and mix the whole lot into a soft dough that comes out of the bowl cleanly – if it's too sticky, add a touch more flour (a very little at a time), and if it's too dry, do the same with water.

3. Put the dough on a flat, lightly floured surface and knead for 10 minutes, until smooth and elastic, then return it to the bowl, cover and leave in a warm place until doubled in size (this should take about 45 minutes).

4. Roll out the dough on the same surface until about 1cm thick, then cut out twelve 7.5cm rounds, re-rolling it as necessary. Lightly dust a baking sheet with polenta and space the muffins out well on it.

5. Dust with more polenta, then leave to rest for 30 minutes in a warm place.

6. Lightly grease a large, wide, heavy-based frying pan with butter and set over a medium heat. Cook the muffins, in batches, for 15–20 minutes on each side until lightly golden and cooked through, turning the heat down to low once they're in the pan. Allow to cool.

7. When you're ready to eat, break them open in the middle, then toast and serve.

Hollandaise sauce

MAKES 300ML

I am happy to boast that, following the publication of my super-easy hollandaise sauce recipe in *Perfect*, more than one person has contacted me to say it has changed their life. And yes, that's how seriously some of us take the alchemy of butter and egg yolk. If you don't understand why, you've never had a good hollandaise.

There's no need to be scared of hollandaise, just because it contains egg yolks and has a reputation for meanness. You can even make it an hour or so in advance and keep it warm by pouring it straight into a Thermos, or keeping it over a pan of lukewarm water – don't try to reheat it, though, or you'll get a taste of its infamously temperamental side.

4 LARGE EGG YOLKS
1 TABLESPOON WHITE WINE VINEGAR
250G COLD UNSALTED BUTTER, DICED

¼ OF A LEMON
SALT AND PEPPER

1. Put the yolks, vinegar, butter and 2 tablespoons of water into a pan and heat very gently, whisking all the time. As the butter melts, the sauce will begin to thicken – don't be tempted to hurry things along by turning the heat up, the sides of the saucepan should be cool enough to touch at all points. Do not leave your station at the pan under any circumstances, imminent danger excepted.

2. Once the butter has melted, turn up the heat to medium-low and whisk vigorously until the sauce thickens – if it begins to steam, take it off the heat, but do not stop whisking.

3. When the sauce is thickened to your taste, stir in 1 tablespoon of lemon juice and some seasoning. Taste and adjust if necessary. Serve immediately, or store in a warm place or even a Thermos flask until needed – hollandaise does not reheat very well.

Sautéd spinach (for the eggs Florentine)

SERVES 4

I am absolutely obsessed, Popeye-like, with spinach: if it's on the menu, I have to have it. The mature, big-leafed sort seems to have fallen out of fashion in recent years, but I prefer it to the aggressively irony baby stuff, which is better kept for salads. Although it's rarely found in supermarkets, most greengrocers and markets will carry it, sold in big dirty bunches, so if you can find it, give it a try – it's far better value too.

Obviously I believe that sautéd spinach goes excellently with just about everything, including both smoked salmon and ham, so, for a splash of green, you could also add it to the other (savoury!) dishes in this section.

A SPLASH OF OLIVE OIL	20G BUTTER
IKG SPINACH, WASHED AND LARGE STEMS REMOVED	FRESHLY GRATED NUTMEG, TO TASTE
	SALT AND PEPPER

1. Put a large frying pan on a high heat and add a splash of olive oil. When it's hot, add the spinach, in batches if necessary, and cook for a couple of minutes until wilted, moving it around regularly.

2. Decant into a colander and squeeze out any excess water. Return to the pan, add the butter, season to taste with nutmeg, salt and pepper and keep warm until you're ready to serve.

Poached egg

Egg-poaching gadgets are the single biggest swindle since onion goggles and spaghetti forks. They save no time, are fiddly to use, and give your egg a tell-tale conical shape which will instantly betray your cack-handedness in the kitchen. Do them the traditional way instead – it's really only a matter of confidence.

Although poaching them to order will always give the best results, if you're catering for a crowd, and want everyone to eat at the same time, it's probably preferable to cook the eggs in advance and store them in iced water until you're ready. They can be warmed through in a pan of simmering water just before serving.

PER PERSON

I LARGE FRESH EGG	A DROP OF MALT OR WHITE WINE VINEGAR

1. Half fill a medium saucepan with water and bring to the boil. Meanwhile, crack the egg into a small jug or bowl and add a drop of vinegar.

2. Stir the boiling water vigorously with a balloon whisk until you have a whirlpool, then immediately slip the egg into the centre, lowering the jug a couple of centimetres into the water.

3. Turn the heat down low and cook for 3 minutes – use a timer to prevent overcooking.

4. Drain the egg on kitchen paper and serve immediately. If you're poaching it in advance, drop it straight into a bowl of iced water instead, or it will carry on cooking; to reheat, simply warm the egg through in a pan of gently simmering water.

Omelette Arnold Bennett (breakfast for 2, very generously, or 4 more moderate appetites)

SERVES 2–4

This is a dish close to my poor put-upon heart, first because it is quite inordinately rich, but more because it was created by the kitchens of the Savoy to honour the Edwardian novelist who is one of my favourite writers. He returned the favour in somewhat dubious fashion by basing the hotel in his last novel, *The Imperial Palace*, upon the Savoy, where he lived for three months with the excuse of 'research', an idea which I've always found very inspirational.

The two sauces involved means that this is something to make for someone you like very, very much, because it's a lot of effort to go to for a maybe, or even a perhaps. Bear in mind, though, that, after poaching smoked haddock, you probably won't smell terribly saucy, so however keen you are on them, it's definitely not first date material. Also, you'll be so full afterwards that all you'll be able to do is roll around the sofa clutching your stomach and moaning softly. If you can't face making the hollandaise, it's pretty good just with the béchamel too.

½ QUANTITY OF HOLLANDAISE SAUCE
   (SEE PAGE 38)
150–200G PIECE OF UNDYED SMOKED
   HADDOCK
200ML MILK
1 BAY LEAF
¼ OF AN ONION
2 PEPPERCORNS
FRESHLY GRATED NUTMEG, TO TASTE

30G BUTTER
1½ TABLESPOONS PLAIN FLOUR
2 TABLESPOONS DOUBLE CREAM
6 EGGS, BEATEN
SALT AND PEPPER
2 TABLESPOONS GRATED PARMESAN
A SMALL BUNCH OF FRESH CHIVES,
   SNIPPED, TO SERVE

1. Make the hollandaise and keep warm. Put the fish skin side up into a small pan and cover with the milk: you may have to cut it up to make it fit. Add the bay leaf, onion and peppercorns. Bring the milk to the boil, then turn down the heat and leave for 3–5 minutes, depending on the thickness of the fish, until just cooked. Take the fish out of the pan and set aside, then add the nutmeg to the milk in the pan and leave to infuse for at least 15 minutes.

2. To make the béchamel sauce, strain the milk into a jug, discarding the bay leaf and onion. Melt half the butter in a heavy-based pan and stir in the flour.

3. Cook for a minute or so, then start to add the milk, little by little, stirring it in well, until you have a sauce. Simmer for a couple of minutes, until thickened, then stir in the cream and set aside.

4.   Heat the grill. Pull the fish from its skin and flake the flesh. Stir half the flakes into the hollandaise sauce and the other half into the beaten eggs. Season these lightly – the fish will be quite salty.

5.   Melt the remaining butter in an ovenproof frying pan over a medium-high heat, and, when hot, add the eggs. When they begin to set, push the edges into the middle and swirl the pan so the liquid pools round the edge. Once the bottom has set, and while the top is still runny, pour over the béchamel and the hollandaise, sprinkle on the Parmesan and put under the hot grill for about 5 minutes, until golden and bubbling. Top with the chives and serve immediately.

Ridiculously easy homemade bread and jam

The idea of baking bread for breakfast may seem impossibly time-consuming – indeed, although I might like the idea of spending the occasional Saturday afternoon mixing, kneading and idling while the dough proves, sadly life rarely admits of such luxuries. One solution is to ask a guest to pick up some good fresh bread on their way – fortunately it's increasingly easy to find; even supermarkets sell decent sourdough these days, although if you do have a local bakery, please support it. I'm always astounded at how few there are left, given our vast national appetite for toast and sandwiches.

The other option is soda bread, which is ridiculously easy to make. It uses a combination of bicarbonate of soda and buttermilk (or sour milk) as a raising agent, which means there's no waiting around for yeast to get going – indeed, once the reaction between bicarb and acid has begun, it's imperative to get the bread in the oven as quickly as possible.

Particularly popular in Ireland, it was historically baked in the embers of the fire, insulated with sods of turf, but thankfully has adapted well to the modern world, although the tradition of scoring the top with a cross, 'to let the devil out', remains, probably because it also helps the bread cook through. It can be on the table in just over an hour, including cooling time, but you could also make it the night before, along with the jam – I think it's at its best toasted.

Soda bread

MAKES 1 LOAF

200G PLAIN WHOLEMEAL FLOUR
200G PLAIN WHITE FLOUR, PLUS A LITTLE
   EXTRA TO DUST
50G ROLLED OATS

2 TEASPOONS BICARBONATE OF SODA
1 TEASPOON SALT
1 TEASPOON SOFT BROWN SUGAR
400ML BUTTERMILK

1. Preheat the oven to 200°C/gas mark 6. Combine the dry ingredients in a large mixing bowl. Whisk briefly to get rid of any lumps, then make a well in the centre. Add 300ml of buttermilk and stir quickly until it comes together into a soft dough: you may well need to add more buttermilk, but be careful not to overwork the dough.

2. Tip the dough on to a lightly floured surface and, with clean hands, form it into a round loaf shape. Put it on a lightly floured baking tray and cut a deep cross in the top. Bake for 30–35 minutes, until it sounds hollow when you tap the bottom. If it isn't ready after 35 minutes, turn it over on the baking tray and cook for another 5 minutes.

3. Put on a wire rack and leave to cool – eating bread hot from the oven is very tempting, but a bad idea, digestion-wise.

Quick jam

MAKES 2 JARS

Homemade preserves are the ultimate symbol of domestic virtue, but, if you're not planning to keep them in smug splendour in your airy pantry to tide you through the winter but gobble them up in a matter of days, they're actually surprisingly quick to make. This recipe, which is a very good way of using up overripe fruit (thrifty shoppers take note), produces a jam of a loose-ish consistency that works over yoghurt as well as on thickly buttered toasted soda bread.

300G VERY RIPE SOFT FRUIT, E.G. BLACKBERRIES,   A SQUEEZE OF LEMON JUICE
    PLUMS, RASPBERRIES, STRAWBERRIES
300G CASTER SUGAR

1. Stone and hull the fruit as necessary and put into a large wide pan. Add the sugar and lemon juice and crush together with a potato masher or fork. Heat gently until it comes to the boil.

2. Boil rapidly for about 15 minutes, or until the jam thickens slightly, regularly skimming off any foam or scum from the top as this will taint the flavour.

3. Spoon the thickened jam into a clean bowl or jar and refrigerate until needed – it will keep for about a week.

Scotch pancakes and fruit compote

These used to be a favourite weekend breakfast treat during my childhood – although I must admit they came in a packet from Waitrose, rather than hot from my grandmother's ancient griddle pan. Still, we can always create our own traditions, and these are definitely better than the ready-prepared sort, even given the rose-tinted spectacles of memory.

I like them simply buttered, but they're also excellent with honey or maple syrup and crisp bacon, American-style, or with the fruit compote opposite and creamy yoghurt.

Lemon zest and buttermilk pancakes

SERVES 4

BUTTER, TO COOK
175G PLAIN FLOUR
½ TEASPOON BICARBONATE OF SODA
50G GOLDEN CASTER SUGAR
½ TEASPOON SALT

I EGG, BEATEN
ZEST OF 2 LEMONS
75ML BUTTERMILK
150ML MILK

1. Heat a heavy-based frying pan over a medium-high heat and add the butter. Meanwhile, sift the flour, bicarbonate of soda, sugar and salt into a bowl. Add the egg, lemon zest, buttermilk and half the milk and stir together, then add enough extra milk to make a thick batter.

2. When the butter sizzles, drop a couple of tablespoons of batter into the pan for each pancake, cooking only as many at once as you can fit comfortably into the pan. Flip them over after 1–2 minutes, when the bubbles on top pop, and cook them on the other side. Lift out and store wrapped in a tea towel while you cook the remaining batter. Serve with the compote spooned over the top.

Fruit compote

SERVES 4

500G FROZEN MIXED BERRIES
OR SUMMER FRUITS

50G CASTER SUGAR OR TO TASTE
JUICE OF ½ A LEMON

1. Put the fruit and sugar into a saucepan along with a tablespoon of water. Bring to a simmer, then cook gently for about 20 minutes, until the fruit has thawed and the mixture has become syrupy.

2. Stir in the lemon juice and keep warm while you make the pancakes.

Very quick storecupboard breakfast ideas for unexpected guests

Classic omelette

Whisk together 2 eggs and season. Heat a 23cm pan over a medium-high flame, add a knob of butter, and, when foaming, add the eggs. Shake the pan so they cover the base, then leave to set for 20 seconds. Add any filling (ham, cheese, chopped herbs – or nothing at all), then use a spatula to draw in the edges of the omelette to the centre and shake the liquid centre out to the edges. The omelette is done when still slightly runny in the centre.

Spiced French toast

Mix 2 eggs with 150ml of milk, a pinch of cinnamon and a pinch of grated nutmeg. Pour over 2 slices of stale bread and leave to soak for 5 minutes. Meanwhile, melt 25g of butter in a frying pan over a high heat, and when bubbling, add the bread. Cook for 1 minute on each side. Serve with sliced banana and a drizzle of honey.

Beans on toast

Heat a tin of baked beans in a small pan with a dash of Worcestershire sauce, a glug of olive oil and a pinch of smoked paprika. Toast 2 slices of bread, drizzle with olive oil and sprinkle with salt. Top the toast with the beans and sprinkle with grated Parmesan. If you've got eggs, a poached one would also be welcome here.

Breakfast smoothie

Drain a 400g tin of fruit (prunes, pineapple, apricots, peaches) and put into a blender along with 6 tablespoons of natural yoghurt. Whiz until smooth, then add a little milk or apple juice to loosen if necessary. Add 50g of oats and divide between two glasses.

Scrambled eggs

Crack 2 eggs per person into a small frying pan and add a knob of butter and a little salt. Put on a medium-high heat and stir the eggs together with a spoon. Stir every 10 seconds, add any other ingredients (flaked smoked fish, diced tomatoes, fresh chilli, wilted spinach, shredded ham), then, just before they're done, take off the heat and stir in 1 teaspoon of crème fraîche per person if available. Serve immediately.

Exotica

Espresso, fig and walnut muffins

MAKES 12

A weekend breakfast has to include coffee in some shape or form – even if you don't drink it, the aroma is so utterly redolent of lazy mornings that you may as well prepare some as the culinary equivalent of a scented candle. Alternatively, of course, you could bake these muffins. (Strictly speaking, Americans might quibble with the name – muffins are often made with oil, rather than butter, but I prefer the flavour and texture of these, and it sounds more acceptable than cake at breakfast time.)

The Viennese, possibly the world's most enthusiastic scoffers of *Kaffee und Kuchen*, like their coffee scented with fig, a combination which I think works wonderfully well – the sweet earthiness of the fruit marrying perfectly with the rich toasty flavour of the beans to give a kind of sophisticated fig roll effect (not that I'm saying one ever grows out of a fig roll). The walnuts, as well as adding a kind of muesli-ish vibe that helps to justify piggish consumption, also give the muffins a more interesting texture.

200G SOFT DRIED FIGS, STALKS REMOVED	A PINCH OF SALT
150ML VERY HOT, STRONG COFFEE	115G BUTTER, MELTED
½ TEASPOON BICARBONATE OF SODA	2 EGGS, BEATEN
200G SOFT LIGHT BROWN SUGAR	75G WALNUTS, ROUGHLY CHOPPED
250G PLAIN FLOUR	

1. Line a 12-hole muffin tray with muffin papers, and preheat the oven to 200°C/gas mark 6.

2. Purée 150g of figs with a little of the coffee, then put into a bowl with the rest of the coffee and the bicarbonate of soda and set aside to cool slightly. Finely chop the remaining figs.

3. Put the sugar and flour into a large mixing bowl with a pinch of salt, and combine the melted butter and eggs in a jug. Pour the liquid ingredients into the dry ones, add the fig and coffee mixture, the walnuts and the chopped figs, and stir together quickly – it's important not to over-mix.

4. Spoon the batter into the prepared cases and bake for about 25–30 minutes, until well risen and golden.

Breakfast cranachan

SERVES 2

Perhaps you have to grow up in a Highland idyll to find the idea of oats outside breakfast an entirely comfortable one – I'll allow them on a crumble, but the classic combination of soft Scottish raspberries, cream and oats has always seemed a better way to start the day than to end it, in my opinion. As a concession to the time of day, I'm swapping the cream for yoghurt (the luxuriously thick sort, obviously), but, in my commitment to authenticity, I'm keeping the whisky to make it a breakfast that will put hairs on your chest.

Note that this can be prepared in advance (the night before, say) up to the end of step 2, but keep the oats and nuts separate from the yoghurt until you're ready to serve, or they'll lose their crunch.

40G OATS

15G FLAKED ALMONDS

2 TABLESPOONS CLEAR SCOTTISH HONEY,
    PLUS A LITTLE EXTRA TO SERVE

2 TABLESPOONS WHISKY
    (OPTIONAL – YOU COULD ALSO
    USE A GOOD APPLE JUICE HERE)

300ML GREEK YOGHURT

1 PUNNET OF RASPBERRIES

1. Preheat the grill to medium. Put the oats and almonds on a foil-lined baking tray and toast under the grill for about 3 minutes, stirring every 30 seconds – they burn very easily, so don't wander off at this point! Leave to cool.

2. Beat the honey and the whisky, if using, into the yoghurt.

3. Gently fold in the raspberries, then the oats and almonds, and serve immediately with an extra drizzle of honey. Alternatively, if you want to make a real impression, spoon a quarter of the raspberries into the base of two glasses and top with a layer of yoghurt, then a layer of oats. Repeat, finishing with a layer of oats, and serve immediately.

Bircher muesli

As a fully paid-up north Londoner, I love every muesli in the variety pack, but this version, which I first happened across at Raymond Blanc's Le Manoir aux Quat' Saisons (which vies with Myrtle Allen's Ballymaloe House for the title of best breakfast of my entire life), is the least preachily worthy, and thus the most suited to serving to guests who might not be as enamoured of the joys of buckwheat as I am. I suspect the version there was made with cream, which is not quite in the spirit of the dish – I like a mixture of milk and apple juice, but you can use just apple juice, which is handy if you have any lactose-intolerant guests and would prefer not to go down the rice or oat milk road.

The Oxford Companion to Food informs me that muesli is a 'Swiss-German diminutive form of mus, "pulpy food", which is particularly apt in this case, where the finished dish is a tasty halfway house between cereal proper and porridge – I find the texture incredibly comforting in the mornings. Invented by Dr Maximilian Bircher-Benner, proprietor of the Alpine 'Life Force' clinic (*On Her Majesty's Secret Service*, anyone?) and raw food fanatic, the original muesli contained far more grated apple than cereal, and was mixed with condensed milk, which, before widespread pasteurization, was considered more suitable for invalids than the fresh stuff. True muesli fanatics will be pleased to know that the recipe is widely available online – once I can face buying a tin of condensed milk for any other purpose than dulce de leche production, I might just give it a try myself. In the meantime . . .

200G ROLLED OATS
300ML MILK
200ML APPLE JUICE
150ML NATURAL YOGHURT
1 MEDIUM APPLE, GRATED, AND PIPS
  AND CORE DISCARDED

2 TABLESPOONS HONEY, PLUS MORE
  TO DRIZZLE
100G MIXED DRIED FRUIT, NUTS AND SEEDS OF
  YOUR CHOICE

1.   Mix together the oats, milk and apple juice, cover and refrigerate for at least an hour – I like to do this the night before, though.

2.   Stir in the yoghurt, then add the remaining ingredients. Drizzle with a little more honey just before serving.

Chorizo hash with fried eggs

SERVES 4

Although corned beef au naturel (if that's not a contradiction in terms) instantly transports me back to prep-school teas where, up against fish paste and luncheon meat, it was the sandwich of reluctant choice, I remain oddly fond of corned beef hash, preferably served with pickled red cabbage and plenty of mustard. Good as it is, though, this version, using the spicy, violently orange Spanish sausage that has become so happily ubiquitous in recent years, is even better. It looks prettier, it tastes punchier, and you don't even need a tin opener to make it. Bonus.

This recipe is easily doubled or even tripled, and keeps warm quite happily, so it's an ideal choice for feeding a crowd, especially a hungry and (dare I say it) male crowd who like their meat and two veg more than their muesli.

500G WAXY POTATOES

SALT AND PEPPER

2 CHORIZO SAUSAGES (ABOUT 250G IN WEIGHT – YOU NEED THE COOKING SORT, RATHER THAN THE SALAMI TYPE), CUT INTO CHUNKS

1 RED PEPPER, ROUGHLY DICED

1 RED ONION, ROUGHLY DICED

OLIVE OIL, TO COOK

4 EGGS

CHOPPED FRESH CHIVES OR CORIANDER, TO SERVE

1. Put the potatoes into a large pan and cover with cold water. Salt generously and bring to the boil, then simmer until just cooked through – if they're too tender, they'll cause you problems later when you add them to the hash. When cool enough to handle, cut into slices or chunks and set aside.

2. Heat a large frying pan and add the chorizo chunks. Fry until crisp – the sausage should have rendered out a good amount of oil. Spoon out on to kitchen paper and set aside.

3. Put the pepper and onion into the pan and cook in the chorizo oil for about 10 minutes, until soft, adding a little olive oil if necessary. Add the potatoes, turn up the heat and fry until crisp.

4. Meanwhile, heat some oil in a second frying pan, and, when hot, crack in the eggs. Cover with a lid, ideally one slightly smaller than the pan itself, so you can wedge it just above the eggs. Cook for 2½ minutes, or until the eggs are done to your liking.

5. Stir the chorizo through the potato mixture, season lightly and sprinkle with the chopped herbs. Divide between plates and top with a fried egg.

Halloumi, pea and mint fritters with spicy tomato relish

SERVES 6

Most of my local cafés are Turkish. While this means bacon sarnies are sadly in short supply, it has introduced me to the wonder that is the Turkish breakfast – slabs of chargrilled halloumi, served with warm flatbreads, honey, tomatoes, green olives and a boiled egg. Easy enough to put together at home (don't stint on the olive oil), and even better if you can lay your hands on a spicy *sucuk* sausage – but this is a slightly more complicated take, also good served with flatbreads, tomatoes and olives, as well as, less authentically, some spicy homemade salsa.

250G FROZEN PEAS	**FOR THE RELISH**
A SMALL BUNCH OF MINT, LEAVES ONLY	350G RIPE TOMATOES (4 LARGISH ONES)
125G SELF-RAISING FLOUR	2 TABLESPOONS OLIVE OIL
I TEASPOON BAKING POWDER	I RED ONION, FINELY CHOPPED
I TEASPOON CHILLI FLAKES	I RED CHILLI, FINELY CHOPPED
I EGG, PLUS I EXTRA EGG WHITE	¼ TEASPOON GROUND ALLSPICE
100ML MILK	¼ TEASPOON GROUND CINNAMON
50ML NATURAL YOGHURT	2 TABLESPOONS DARK BROWN SUGAR
250G HALLOUMI, CUT INTO SMALL DICE	I TABLESPOON CIDER OR WINE VINEGAR
½ A LEMON	SALT AND PEPPER
OLIVE OIL, TO COOK	

1. To make the relish, heat a frying pan over a very high heat, then add the tomatoes and scorch the skins, turning them as necessary. Meanwhile, heat the oil in a saucepan over a medium-low heat and soften the onion and chilli for 5 minutes without colouring.

2. Roughly chop the tomatoes and put them, skins and all, into the pan with the onion. Stir in the spices, sugar and vinegar and season. Mash the tomatoes roughly, bring to the boil, then cook until almost dry. Taste again for seasoning, then set aside while you make the fritters.

3. Cook the peas in salted boiling water for a couple of minutes, then drain and cool under running water. Tip three-quarters of the peas into a food processor, add the mint leaves and purée until smooth.

4. Sift the flour and baking powder into a large bowl and add the chilli flakes. Stir in the whole egg, milk and yoghurt to make a batter, then stir in the puréed peas and mint. Fold in the rest of the peas, the halloumi and the zest of the half lemon. Season, and add a spritz of lemon juice.

5. Put the egg white into a clean bowl and whisk to soft peak stage, then very gently fold it into the mixture.

6. Heat 2 tablespoons of olive oil in a frying pan over a medium-high heat, then spoon a tablespoon of the mixture into the pan to make each fritter – you'll have to do this in batches. Fry for about 4 minutes on each side, until crisp and golden, and keep warm until ready to serve with the relish.

Mexican baked eggs

SERVES 4–6

There's something about the idea of baked eggs that makes me feel as warm and gooey as a soft-boiled yolk – they just sound so wonderfully cosy. They come in all sorts of permutations – Yotam Ottolenghi serves a spicy, oily North African version with peppers at Nopi, and Jamie Oliver makes an unashamedly indulgent one involving cream, Parmesan and smoked haddock. Both recipes are online, and come with my hearty recommendation. This one, however, is from my own head, and inspired by the largely breakfast-based memories from the month I spent in Mexico after finishing university. I'm sure we had many great adventures after these epic breakfasts, but my abiding memory involves plastic baskets of warm corn tortillas, searingly hot salsas and so many eggs that, a fortnight in, we all realized the true meaning of the word 'eggbound'. If you prefer a bit of meat in your breakfast, add a couple of cooking chorizos, cut into chunks, along with the onion and peppers.

It's very easy to create your own baked egg recipes according to whim and the contents of the fridge – the only hard bit is working out how to get the whites cooked through without spoiling the yolk. Having suffered many disappointments (and truly, what is more tragic than an overcooked egg?), I decided the only sure way was to cheat – to which end I now separate the two and then add the yolk later. If you're not so fixated on the image of a yolk splitting into liquid gold under the pressure of your fork, you could cook them together.

2 TABLESPOONS OLIVE OIL
2 ONIONS, FINELY DICED
1 GREEN PEPPER, DESEEDED AND FINELY
    DICED
1 RED PEPPER, DESEEDED AND FINELY
    DICED
2 CHIPOTLE CHILLIES, GROUND, OR
    1 HOT RED CHILLI, DESEEDED AND FINELY
    CHOPPED, PLUS 1 TEASPOON SWEET
    SMOKED PAPRIKA
2 TEASPOONS GROUND CUMIN
2 TEASPOONS GROUND CORIANDER
2 X 400G TINS OF CHOPPED TOMATOES

1 TEASPOON SALT
2 X 400G TINS OF COOKED BLACK BEANS
(YOU COULD ALSO USE PINTO BEANS),
    DRAINED
BLACK PEPPER
4–8 EGGS (DEPENDING ON APPETITE),
    INDIVIDUALLY SEPARATED
2 RIPE AVOCADOS
JUICE OF 1 LIME
A SMALL BUNCH OF FRESH CORIANDER, FINELY
    CHOPPED
4 TORTILLAS (I LIKE THE CORN SORT)
100G CRUMBLED FETA

1. Preheat the oven to 180°C/gas mark 4. Heat the olive oil in a large ovenproof pan (if you don't have one of these, you can transfer the mixture to a baking dish later) and soften the diced onion and peppers over a medium heat for about 5 minutes, until the onions are translucent.

2. Stir in the spices and cook for 2 minutes, then add the tomatoes and salt and bring to the boil. Turn down the heat and leave to simmer for about 5 minutes, until slightly thickened. Stir in the drained beans and heat through for a couple of minutes, then check the seasoning and adjust with a little more salt and a grinding of black pepper if necessary.

3. Transfer the mixture to a baking dish if your pan is not ovenproof. Make some slight indentations in the surface and add an egg white to each one. Season lightly, then put into the oven for about 15 minutes, until the white is almost set. Meanwhile, peel the avocados, remove the stones and cut into rough chunks. Put into a serving bowl, sprinkle with lime juice and mash roughly with a fork. Stir in the coriander and season to taste.

4. Add the yolk to the top of each white and put back into the oven for about 5 minutes, until done to your liking. Toast the tortillas in a dry frying pan, then cut into triangles and wrap in a tea towel to keep warm.

5. Serve the baked eggs at the table with the tortillas, avocado and crumbled feta on the side.

Bacon and marmalade cornbread

SERVES 6

It would be remiss of me to conclude a chapter on breakfast with nary a mention of bacon, that most beloved of British breakfast stuffs. My general view is that bacon is best fried until crisp, then stuck in between two slices of soft, floury white bread with slightly more English mustard than is wise, but as everyone knows how to prepare that, I'll concede it works pretty well in this American recipe too.

Cornbread has been eaten for millennia in the Americas – the corn tortillas of central America were a key part of the Mayan and Aztec diets, and European settlers were quick to develop a taste for corn pone, johnny cakes and other such unfamiliar delicacies. (According to Wikipedia, 'the term "corn pone" is sometimes [wonderfully!] used to refer to one who possesses certain rural, unsophisticated peculiarities'.) These would traditionally have been prepared in a cast-iron skillet, which can go from stovetop to oven – if you don't have an ovenproof pan, you can bake this in a cake tin instead, although you'll miss out on some of that lovely bacon-y flavour.

Because one of my favourite foodie discoveries of the last couple of years has been the joy of bacon and marmalade sandwiches, I've added some chopped peel too, in homage to the northern American tradition of sweet cornbread, but you can leave it out if you don't fancy it.

20G LARD OR I TABLESPOON OIL	½ TEASPOON SALT
4 RASHERS OF STREAKY SMOKED BACON,	½ TEASPOON SOFT BROWN SUGAR
FINELY CHOPPED	I EGG, BEATEN
200G MEDIUM CORNMEAL	500ML BUTTERMILK
I TEASPOON BAKING POWDER	2 TABLESPOONS CHOPPED MIXED PEEL

1. Preheat the oven to 220°C/gas mark 7 before starting this dish. Heat the fat in a small, ovenproof, heavy-based frying pan (about 20cm diameter) until it sizzles, then add the bacon and cook until crisp.

2. Meanwhile, mix the cornmeal, baking powder, salt and sugar in a large mixing bowl and whisk together the egg and buttermilk in a jug. Lift the bacon pieces out of the pan with a slotted spoon and set aside, keeping the pan on the heat.

3. Pour the liquid ingredients into the dry ones and stir together, then fold through the bacon pieces and chopped peel, followed by the bacon drippings from the pan.

4. Tip the batter into the hot pan and put into the hot oven for about 25 minutes, until golden on top. Let it sit for a few minutes before turning out. Serve cut into wedges, with plenty of butter.

Food
without a fuss

'Supper' seems to have had a makeover in recent years, no longer denoting the light meal of Horlicks and biscuits our grandparents might have snacked on before bed, but a casual dinner with friends. Which, although I obviously am a massive show-off, is exactly my favourite sort: those last-minute after-work gatherings, where everyone chips in with the preparation, and a little too much wine is drunk than is strictly wise on a weekday.

But whatever time of day you're entertaining, the important word to remember here is 'casual'. This is not a time to get out the best cutlery (if, indeed, you are lucky, or married enough to possess more than one set), or worry about canapés, or seating plans. None of these things are conducive to a relaxed, friendly experience: not only do they mean more work for you, but, whatever your intentions, they will scream 'best behaviour' to your guests. And best behaviour is not always hugely fun.

There are times to impress (the next chapter should take care of that) and there are times to simply enjoy the sharing of food and conversation. You provide the food, your guests (in theory, at least) provide the gossip, and perhaps the odd drink. The menus in this chapter are designed for just such occasions. They're all either quick enough to knock up easily after work (or, indeed, the morning after a well-rounded Saturday night) or happy to be prepared in advance, leaving you time to get on with the more important business of chat.

Practicalities

Although the casualness of the occasion shouldn't put you off inviting people you know less well – the point I made in the introduction about mixing up old friends and new for optimal conversational brilliance still stands, even if you're eating off your knees – bear in mind that you'll need to put a bit more effort in with them, so if you're opting for supper because you're rushed off your feet at work, you might want to stick to people who are happy to fend for themselves in your house.

Sunday and Monday nights are sacrosanct for many people, so I usually avoid issuing invitations for either. Tuesday can be good for a quiet catch-up with old friends – the kind where people arrive claiming they're going to have a single glass of wine with dinner, and don't leave until every single mutual acquaintance has been discussed and dissected over several bottles – but Wednesdays and Thursdays are the optimal nights for supper in my experience. People are willing to stay out a bit later, and they're not yet worn out by the week: wait until Friday, and not only do you run up against prior commitments, but certain people have a tendency to arrive late, straight from work drinks, and rather the worse for wear. Suppers are also nice on Saturdays, if you've been out late the night before, as long as you don't invite people who are expecting a full-blown party.

No one minds mucking in a bit – in fact, they'll often feel much happier if they've helped out in some way before sitting down with a drink, so take advantage of their kindness and delegate tasks. Handing round nibbles, laying the table, washing the salad: all little jobs that will take the pressure off you a bit – although in this kind of situation I generally plonk the glasses and wine, gin, tonic, slices of lemon and so on on a side table and urge people to help themselves.

I quite often ask guests to bring a piece of cheese, rather than wine – perhaps I associate with people abnormally passionate about the stuff, but they get quite excited about introducing their particular cheese (saying that, a frenemy who will remain nameless once brought one so excruciatingly smelly that I had to eject it from the flat after she left, and throw it over the park railings into a public litter bin. I woke up the next morning convinced the square was going to be covered with the feathery corpses of poisoned pigeons. I have a strong feeling her choice was deliberate).

Finally, don't be afraid to chuck people out on a work night – they'll thank you for it the next morning.

Nibbles

Although none of the suggested menus include starters, three courses being rather too much work for most of us to contemplate on the average Thursday evening, I would strongly suggest investing in a little something to take the edge off the collective appetite before you sit down. This will buy you, the chef, some precious time, if things don't go quite to plan (and, in obedience to the inimitable Sod's Law, they generally won't), and should also prevent that scenario familiar to viewers of *Come Dine with Me*, where the guests wait so long for their food that they're utterly sloshed by the time they pick up knife and fork.

Olives, nuts, crisps – they'll all do the trick here, especially if you take five minutes to smarten them up a bit before letting the wolves at them. (There's no real need of course, when amongst friends, but if I do so much as add a sprinkle of smoked paprika to a bowl of crisps, I start to truly believe I've cooked the whole lot from scratch.) Always decant snacks from their original packaging: it takes a second, and makes them look far more appetizing. If you've got a bit more time, have a look at the nibbles on page 294.

Olives

Unless you're going for stuffed olives, buy fruit with the stone intact. It always has a firmer, more satisfying texture (remember to provide a bowl for pits). Tip them into a bowl, draining any brine or oil they've been sitting in, which will inevitably drip on people's dry-clean-only skirts, and add a little finely grated lemon zest, some chopped flat-leaf parsley or coriander, a very finely chopped chilli or a sprinkling of chilli flakes – or anything else you think might work as a flavour combination. Avoid anything too wet (see above), or raw garlic, which is rarely a pleasant surprise.

Nuts

Put a frying pan on a high heat and, when hot, add a packet of salted, roasted nuts and a good pinch of ground cumin, smoked paprika or cayenne pepper. Toss well, toast until you can smell the spice, then tip into a bowl.

Crisps

Choose plain or salted crisps and add a pinch of the spice of your choice. You'll need to toss them well as you add it, or it will all get stuck on the top layer, so don't go for anything too hot, or someone might get a shock.

Breadsticks

Wrap in thinly sliced cured ham, or serve with a plate of salami with cornichons and capers.

Cheese

Arrange thin slices of Parmesan, or any other good hard cheese you might have lying around (and by hard I do not mean cracked and wizened), and drizzle with a little honey.

Three quick dips
using things you might
conceivably already
have in the house

Hummous in a hurry

Stick a drained tin of chickpeas in the blender along with 2 crushed cloves of garlic, a pinch of ground cumin, 5 tablespoons of tahini and the juice of half a lemon. Whiz until smooth, then season to taste and scoop into a bowl. Drizzle some olive oil round the edge and decorate with a pinch of cayenne pepper.

Beetroot dip

Put 250g of cooked beetroot (not the pickled sort) into a blender with 50g of soured cream and a squeeze of lemon juice and pulse until you have a rough purée. Stir in horse-radish sauce, salt and pepper to taste. Good topped with chopped chives or dill.

Feta and olive

Crumble 150g of feta into a bowl and stir in 225ml of plain yoghurt and 50g of roughly chopped stoned black olives. Drizzle with olive oil and season with black pepper before serving – even better with a few torn basil leaves.

Autumn menu

SERVES 4

At the risk of displeasing our notoriously fickle weather gods, summer can sometimes drag on a little bit in this country: much as I love the sunshine, it's difficult to get excited about some of the new season's produce when it's still barbecue weather outside. If there's one thing you can rely on in Britain, however, it's that the rain will come; and when it does, it's time to tuck in with gusto. Game, wild mushrooms, nuts, berries and apples: in autumn, every meal should be like a Sunday afternoon walk, the ground crunchy with fallen leaves, the air scented with woodsmoke – and a pub with a roaring fire and some local scrumpy waiting at the end. Now there's a thought to get you through those first depressingly dark evenings, eh?

Alex's partridge on toast

SERVES 4

This recipe comes from my most proudly rural friend, who boasts a freezer full of small birds (the fruit of many Saturdays of muddy work on her dad's farm shoot) and is often to be found rustling up something like this for herself after work, when the rest of us are reaching for the pasta. It's actually remarkably quick and easy: five minutes of prep, then enough time in the oven for you to enjoy a glass of wine and a natter before – ta da! – presenting everyone with their bird and bread. Roasts always look impressive, however small the subject.

Alex advises that it's important not to make the slices of toast too thick: the idea is that they should be well greased with meat juices, rather like 'very delicious fried bread'.

4 TABLESPOONS BUTTER, AT ROOM
    TEMPERATURE
4 LARGE SPRIGS OF THYME, LEAVES ONLY
4 PARTRIDGES, ABOUT 300G EACH
    IN WEIGHT

2 SMALL ONIONS, CUT INTO WEDGES
SALT AND PEPPER
6 RASHERS OF STREAKY BACON
4 MEDIUM SLICES OF STURDY BREAD
GREEN SALAD, TO SERVE

1. Preheat the oven to 220°C/gas mark 7. Mash together the butter and thyme leaves and divide between the cavities of each partridge, along with the onions. Season well.

2. Cut each rasher of bacon in half and stretch it on a chopping board by running the back of a knife along its length. Arrange the strips to cover each bird. Put the bread into a roasting tin, and top with the partridge. Roast for 20 minutes, then remove the bacon, which should be crisp, and set aside. Return the birds to the oven for another 5–10 minutes, until the skin is golden and the juices run clear. Leave to rest for 5 minutes, then serve on the toast, with the bacon on top, alongside a green salad.

Hungarian chestnut and cherry creams

SERVES 4

We don't eat enough chestnuts in this country: even those chaps with the charcoal braziers seem to be few and far between these days (possibly because of their extortionate pricing: you have to be feeling really nostalgic to pay £2 for a bag of half-burnt nuts), which is a shame, because the smell alone is incredibly evocative. Perhaps the vendors should be subsidized by the tourist board? They're more popular on the continent, however – indeed, until the nineteenth century, they were the staple starch for many people in southern areas where wheat flour was considered a luxury – and this is an Eastern European version of the more famous French Mont Blanc, combining sweet nut purée with cream and (my own touch) some boozy fruit. Always the cherry on the cake in any situation.

3 TABLESPOONS ICING SUGAR
1 X 435G TIN OF UNSWEETENED CHESTNUT
  PURÉE
300ML WHIPPING CREAM
5 TABLESPOONS DARK RUM
5 TABLESPOONS SOFT LIGHT BROWN SUGAR

1 X 400G JAR OF CHERRIES IN BRANDY OR
  KIRSCH, DRAINED (OR FRESH CHERRIES IF
  IN SEASON)
2 SQUARES OF DARK CHOCOLATE, TO GRATE

1. Beat the icing sugar into the chestnut purée. Pass it through a potato ricer, if you have one, until fluffy – if not, beat it well with a wooden spoon to loosen it.

2. Whip the cream with the rum and sugar until it has thickened and makes soft peaks. Divide the chestnut purée between four dishes and top with the cream and cherries. Chill for a minimum of 2 hours and up to 6, and grate a little chocolate on top just before serving.

Winter menu

SERVES 4

Christmas aside, there aren't many upsides to winter in Britain, but one of them is that the reliably foul weather does give us an excuse to tuck into the kind of food more usually reserved for those who have spent the day off piste. The way I see it, skiing is (in theory) fun, while going to work in sleet is not, so actually those of us stuck at home are more in need of cheering sustenance.

Alpine macaroni cheese

SERVES 4

I'm a late convert to macaroni cheese, having been put off by the gloopy school version, but, after making six or seven different versions for the *Guardian*, I finally worked out what everyone was on about. As insurance against blandness, however, I usually add a few extra ingredients to the dish, just in case I fall out of love again: this particular spin on the traditional recipe is inspired by a wonderful warm leek and lardon tart that I enjoyed after a gruelling day falling over in the French Alps last year. It can be prepared right up until step 3 a day ahead: in that case, you'll need to chill it, without the breadcrumbs, in the buttered dish, then cover it with foil and reheat in a 180°C/gas mark 4 oven for 30 minutes before uncovering, adding the breadcrumbs, and baking for about another 10 minutes until golden and bubbling.

50G BUTTER, PLUS A LITTLE EXTRA TO GREASE	3 TABLESPOONS PLAIN FLOUR
	500ML MILK
2 LEEKS, TRIMMED AND THINLY SLICED	250G GRUYÈRE, FINELY GRATED
150G SPECK OR SMOKED BACON LARDONS	1 TABLESPOON WHOLEGRAIN MUSTARD
400G MACARONI	FINELY GRATED NUTMEG, TO TASTE
SALT AND PEPPER	50G BREADCRUMBS

1. Heat half the butter in a frying pan over a medium-low heat and gently cook the leeks for about 10 minutes, until soft. Add the speck or bacon, turn up the heat and fry until crisp.

2. Cook the macaroni in plenty of salted boiling water until al dente, according to the instructions on the packet, and drain.

3. Melt the remaining butter in a medium saucepan and stir in the flour. Cook for a couple of minutes, then whisk in the milk and cook, stirring, until the sauce has thickened. Stir in 200g of the cheese, the mustard and a grating of nutmeg. Taste and season if necessary. Add the pasta, leeks and bacon and toss together well. Heat the grill to medium.

4. Butter a baking dish and tip the pasta in. Mix the breadcrumbs with the rest of the cheese, sprinkle on top of the pasta, and grill until golden and bubbling.

Ananas au rhum

SERVES 4

One of the most valuable lessons I've learnt in recent years is that you can have too much of a good thing – in other words, don't follow something rich and unctuous with a pudding in the same mould. You may still have the appetite for it, but afterwards you, and your guests, will be consumed with queasy self-loathing. Trust me. This classic French recipe, more often made with kirsch, is more than the sum of its parts, and much simpler, and more interesting, than a boring old fruit salad.

I SMALL, RIPE PINEAPPLE
3 TABLESPOONS DARK RUM

I TABLESPOON DEMERARA SUGAR

1. Trim the top and bottom off the pineapple to give yourself a flat base, then cut down around the circumference of the fruit to slice off the peel. Use a peeler to gouge out any remaining eyes (less gruesome work than it sounds), then cut the pineapple in half vertically. Carefully cut out and discard the hard woody core, then slice the pineapple thinly into half rings.

2. Arrange the half rings on a plate and sprinkle with the rum and sugar. Refrigerate and leave to macerate for at least an hour before serving.

Spring menu

The British spring is often rather chillier than we like to admit, as we shiver over the first Pimm's of the year, but after the long winter, a change of season demands a change in diet. Out with the slow-cooked stews and bakes which have served us so well for the past six months, and in with lighter, fresher flavours and quick cooking to make the most of the ever-lengthening days.

This menu celebrates the versatility of the egg, traditional symbol of new life and Easter gluttony, in the simple richness of a well-made omelette, and the glorious, childish joy of a proper ice cream sundae – a small taste of the summer to come.

Omelette aux fines herbes

SERVES 4

Anyone who believes that omelettes are just breakfast fare has never had a good one: they're one of the simplest and most elegant suppers in my repertoire, and certainly the quickest. And should your guests need any more persuasion, tell them Elizabeth David was so enamoured of 'the almost primitive and elemental meal evoked by the words: "Let's just have an omelette and a glass of wine"' that she devoted an entire essay to this glorious egg dish. And who dares quibble with Her taste?

Be aware, however, that it is fairly pointless to try making a decent omelette for any more than one person, so you'll need to make them in pretty swift succession, just before serving. Although an omelette is nicest scoffed straight from the pan, they'll be happy enough covered in foil for ten minutes, which is all you should need to make four. Make sure you have any accompaniments (a green salad, proper bread or a bowl of warm new potatoes) ready on the table before the off: time is of the essence.

12 LARGE EGGS
SALT AND PEPPER
4 TABLESPOONS MIXED FRESH HERBS
  (I LIKE CHIVES AND TARRAGON)

4 KNOBS OF BUTTER

1. Put four plates into a low oven to warm. Whisk 3 of the eggs until just mixed, and season. Place the mixed herbs within easy reach of the hob.

2. Heat a heavy-based, approximately 23cm pan over a medium-high flame. Add a knob of butter and swirl to coat. When the foam begins to abate, pour in the whisked eggs. They should sizzle.

3. Shake the pan to distribute the eggs evenly, then leave for 20 seconds, until they begin to bubble. Add 1 tablespoon of herbs.

4. Using a spatula or fork, draw in the sides of the eggs to the centre while shaking the pan to redistribute the liquid to the edges. The omelette is done when still slightly runny in the middle.

5. Take off the heat, and fold two edges into the middle. Shake the pan so they roll together, then tilt it and turn your omelette on to a warm plate (you can tidy it up before serving if you like). Cover with foil while you make the rest.

Poires Belle Hélène

SERVES 4

This classic sundae always reminds me of childhood holidays, eating ice cream in ornate glass boats as big as our heads in provincial French squares. Although I'm no longer stuck with suspiciously yellow soft-scoop at home, it still seems like a treat all these years later. Out of pear season, or when time is short, I've discovered what most French cafés have known for ages: Escoffier's classic is pretty good with tinned fruit too (in which case, start the dish at step 3). Fresh pears look much more impressive, however.

The original crystallized violet petals are often replaced with toasted almonds these days, but, if you can find them in the baking section, I like the slightly Victorian feeling they lend to a dish created in 1864.

200G CASTER SUGAR
1 VANILLA POD, SPLIT
JUICE OF 1 LEMON
4 RIPE PEARS
8 SCOOPS OF GOOD-QUALITY
  VANILLA ICE CREAM
1 TABLESPOON CRYSTALLIZED VIOLETS OR
  TOASTED FLAKED ALMONDS (OPTIONAL)

FOR THE CHOCOLATE SAUCE
150G DARK CHOCOLATE, BROKEN INTO PIECES
50ML WHIPPING CREAM
2 TABLESPOONS GOLDEN SYRUP
A KNOB OF BUTTER
A PINCH OF SALT

1. Put the sugar and vanilla pod into a pan wide enough to hold all the fruit sitting upright, and add 1 litre of water. Bring to the boil over a medium heat, stirring to dissolve the sugar, then stir in the lemon juice.

2. Meanwhile, peel the pears, leaving the stalks intact. Slice a little off the bottom of each to make a flat base, and use a sharp-ended vegetable peeler to remove the core from the bottom. Put the pears into the saucepan and cover with a circle of greaseproof paper to keep them under water: if they're not submerged, add just enough water to cover. Simmer gently for about 20 minutes, until the fruit is tender. Take off the heat and leave to cool in the syrup: you can do this the night before, and store them in the fridge if you like.

3. To make the chocolate sauce, put the chocolate and cream into a small pan over a low heat and warm, stirring, until the chocolate has melted into the cream. Add the golden syrup, then the butter and salt, and stir until you have a glossy sauce.

4. Get the ice cream out of the freezer 10 minutes before you want to serve. To assemble the sundae, put 2 scoops of ice cream into each bowl or glass and top with some of the chocolate sauce. Dip the stalk end of each pear, drained of syrup, into the remaining chocolate sauce, and place on top of the ice cream. Sprinkle with violets or almonds, if using, and serve immediately.

Summer menu

My love affair with squid began in an unpromising shack on a Mexican beach. The Swiss owners offered no menu, just plates of smoky chargrilled peppers and meltingly tender squid, with brown rice (über Alpine). I ate a lot of good food on that trip, but I already knew I liked quesadillas – the squid was a revelation.

Since then, I've grown to love the cephalopod in all its incarnations – crisply salt-and-peppered, Cantonese style, stuffed in the Mediterranean fashion – but griddled or barbecued is still my favourite. The smoky flavour works brilliantly with the natural sweetness of the squid – although if you're not a fan, giant prawns would be an acceptable substitute. But you'd be missing out.

Note that squid benefits from freezing, which helps to tenderize the notoriously rubbery flesh, and I find oriental supermarkets can be a good source of competitively priced bags to feed my habit.

Warm Mediterranean squid salad with aioli

SERVES 4

400G BABY SQUID, CLEANED
4 TABLESPOONS OLIVE OIL
1 TABLESPOON CHILLI FLAKES
SALT AND PEPPER
2 COURGETTES, CUT INTO THIN SLICES
   LENGTHWAYS
1 RED PEPPER, DESEEDED AND CUT INTO
   THIN STRIPS
JUICE OF 1 LEMON
2 TABLESPOONS EXTRA VIRGIN OLIVE OIL
1 X 400G TIN OF CHICKPEAS, DRAINED
200G ROCKET

FOR THE AIOLI

1 EGG
1 FAT CLOVE OF GARLIC, CRUSHED
1 TABLESPOON WHITE WINE VINEGAR
250ML OLIVE OIL

1. To make the aioli, put the egg into a food processor along with the crushed garlic, vinegar and 1 tablespoon of oil. Whiz until well combined, then slowly drizzle in the rest of the oil, with the motor running, until you have a creamy mayonnaise. If it's too thick, add a little water to loosen. Chill until you're ready to use (this can be made the day before).

2. Cut the squid tubes into 2 or 3 pieces, depending on size, and score with a criss-cross pattern on both sides. Leave any tentacles intact. Toss with a little oil, the chilli flakes and salt and pepper, and set aside.

3. Heat a griddle pan until smoking. Meanwhile, brush the courgettes and red pepper with oil and season well. Griddle them in batches until cooked through and charred. Set aside, keeping them warm by covering them with foil.

4. While the vegetables are cooking, whisk together the lemon juice and extra virgin olive oil and season well to make a dressing. Put the chickpeas and rocket into a large salad bowl.

5. Griddle the squid for about a minute on each side, until cooked through and charred. Add to the salad along with the vegetables and the dressing and toss together well to combine. Serve immediately, with the aioli to spoon over the top.

Gooseberry and elderflower fool

Two of my favourite summer flavours, both quintessentially British, just like the wonderfully named fool (don't believe the theory about it coming from the French word to crush: it's clearly in the trifle school of glorious whimsy). You can make this the night before, and chill it.

400G GOOSEBERRIES, TOPPED AND TAILED	4 TABLESPOONS ELDERFLOWER CORDIAL
2 TABLESPOONS GOLDEN CASTER SUGAR	400ML DOUBLE CREAM

1. Put the fruit into a pan with the sugar and 2 tablespoons of water. Bring to the boil and cook until most of the gooseberries have burst, which should take about 10 minutes, then drain (you can save the juice and use it for cocktails – it's good with gin and soda water, or added to sparkling water). Stir the cordial into the fruit and leave to cool completely. Meanwhile, put an empty mixing bowl into the fridge.

2. Pour the cream into the cold bowl and whip until thick, then fold through the fruit and serve (or chill until ready to eat – it'll keep in the fridge for about 4 hours).

Vegetarian menu

SERVES 4

I eat quite a lot of vegetarian food, more, if I'm honest, because I really, really like vegetables than because I'm consciously trying to cut down on the amount of meat I eat, despite being fully behind the idea that we should all eat less, and better. I'll leave the campaigning to the McCartney family, but please don't always think that you have to cook meat if you're having people round. In my experience, only boys occasionally mind, and if it's that big a deal, they can stop for a kebab on the way home.

Courgette carbonara

SERVES 4

This is one of my favourite things to eat when I'm on my own, and no one can judge me for being a glutton for pasta. It's sort of inspired by my friend Ali, who likes to throw together unlikely things and see how they turn out, and also by a wonderful Rome-based food blog by the name of Rachel Eats, which finally taught me how to make a proper carbonara, rather than pasta and scrambled egg. The lemon zest is, I think, entirely my own – it adds a pleasing freshness, which might well fool you into eating more of this than is strictly wise. Which is the idea.

Note that if you're cooking for strict vegetarians, you'll need to replace the two cheeses with a vegetarian-friendly alternative, often billed simply as 'Italian hard cheese'.

400G DRIED SPAGHETTI OR LINGUINE
3 TABLESPOONS OLIVE OIL
I SMALL RED ONION, THINLY SLICED
2 COURGETTES, THINLY SLICED
    LENGTHWAYS (A FLAT PEELER IS THE
    EASIEST WAY TO DO THIS, I FIND)
4 EGGS
50G PECORINO CHEESE, GRATED
    (OR VEGETARIAN ALTERNATIVE)

50G PARMESAN, GRATED (OR VEGETARIAN
    ALTERNATIVE)
ZEST OF I LEMON, FINELY GRATED
BLACK PEPPER
A SMALL HANDFUL OF FRESH MINT OR
    BASIL, TORN

1. Put a large pan of salted water on to boil, and when boiling, add the pasta and cook for about 8–10 minutes, until al dente.

2. Meanwhile, put the oil into a frying pan over a medium-high heat and cook the onion until softened. Add the courgettes and cook for a couple of minutes to wilt.

3. Beat together the eggs with most of the cheese, the lemon zest and a generous amount of black pepper, reserving a little pecorino to garnish.

4. Drain the cooked pasta, but not too thoroughly, then tip into the frying pan and toss with the courgettes and onions until well coated. Tongs are handy here to pick it up and throw it back down.

5. Take the pan off the heat, add the egg and most of the mint or basil and stir together until the sauce thickens. Garnish with the remaining herbs and cheese, and serve immediately.

Rhubarb and almond crumble
with spiced crème fraîche

SERVES 4

From a bastardized Italian favourite to a bona fide British classic: it wouldn't be a decent recipe book without a crumble. This makes quite a saucy version, which frankly doesn't look too elegant, but then it's not really that kind of a dish.

There's no need to stew the rhubarb first, as many recipes do — it will cook in its own juices. Nice additions, should you wish to ring the changes, include finely grated fresh ginger, orange zest — or even some brandy. You can make the topping and the crème fraîche the day before, and refrigerate, then simply bung it all together and into the oven just before you make the carbonara.

150G PLAIN FLOUR
50G GROUND ALMONDS
150G CHILLED, UNSALTED BUTTER,
   CUT INTO CUBES
45G DEMERARA SUGAR
145G CASTER SUGAR
A PINCH OF SALT
900G RHUBARB, TRIMMED
2 TABLESPOONS FLAKED ALMONDS

FOR THE SPICED CRÈME FRAÎCHE
300G CRÈME FRAÎCHE
½ TEASPOON GROUND CINNAMON
½ TEASPOON GROUND STAR ANISE
ZEST OF 1 ORANGE

1. To make the crumble topping, combine the flour, almonds and butter in a food processor and pulse briefly, or rub the butter into the dry ingredients with your fingertips. Add the demerara sugar, 45g of caster sugar and a pinch of salt, then sprinkle over enough cold water to bring the mixture together in large lumps. Place in a bag or small bowl and put into the freezer for about 10 minutes, or, if making ahead, refrigerate until ready to use.

2. Preheat the oven to 200°C/gas mark 6. Cut the rhubarb into batons about 2cm long and toss with the remaining sugar. Put into a baking dish about 24cm square and top with the crumble and the flaked almonds. Bake for about 35 minutes, until golden.

3. Meanwhile, mix the ingredients for the spiced crème fraîche together and chill. Serve the two together.

Gluten and dairy free menu

I feel a bit wary of labelling this menu as such, because I know that, if I saw it in a cookbook, I'd immediately flick on by with the assumption that whatever it was was just going to be a disappointing substitute for the real thing. So, to be clear, these are dishes which, fortuitously, never contained any of the offending ingredients in the first place: they're just naturally gluten and dairy free, and you won't miss a thing. And your coeliac or lactose-intolerant guest can breathe easy knowing you haven't attempted anything too crazy.

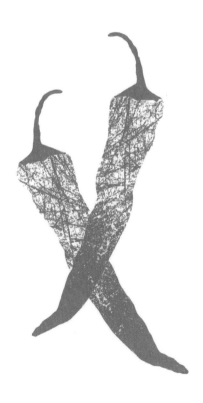

Tomato and spinach dal

Dal, the soupy, spicy comfort food of the Indian subcontinent, is one of those dishes, like mashed potato, that I could eat for breakfast, lunch and dinner all year round. I know this because I did just that in Nepal a few years ago, and came away more in love with the lentil than ever.

This version is full of flavour, and defiantly wholesome: the kind of dish that might make you feel better if you've been a bit under the weather, but don't feel quite bad enough to cancel an invitation. You can make it in advance, then reheat it while the rice cooks. (It's also good with flatbreads, if gluten isn't an issue.)

500G RED LENTILS, WASHED
3 TABLESPOONS GROUNDNUT OIL
5 CLOVES OF GARLIC, FINELY CHOPPED
2–4 SMALL GREEN CHILLIES, DESEEDED AND
   FINELY CHOPPED
2 TEASPOONS CUMIN SEEDS
1 TEASPOON GROUND CORIANDER
1 TEASPOON BROWN OR YELLOW
   MUSTARD SEEDS

½ TEASPOON TURMERIC
2 X 400G TINS OF CHOPPED TOMATOES
1½ TEASPOONS SALT
200G SPINACH, WASHED
SQUEEZE OF LEMON JUICE
STEAMED RICE, TO SERVE

1. Put the lentils into a large pan with 1 litre of water and bring to the boil, then partially cover and simmer for 10 or so minutes, skimming when necessary, until they are soft.

2. Meanwhile, heat the oil in a medium saucepan on a medium-high heat and gently fry the garlic and chillies for a couple of minutes. Add the spices and cook, stirring, for another minute or so.

3. Tip in the tomatoes and salt, bring to the boil, simmer until the oil begins to separate from the sauce, then stir in the spinach. Turn the heat down slightly, then cover and cook until the spinach has wilted.

4. Once the lentils are cooked, drain if necessary, then return them to the pan and stir in the tomato and spinach mixture. Squeeze in a little lemon juice, taste for seasoning, and keep warm until ready to serve, with rice.

Fancy fruit salad

You can use any exotic fruits you like for this salad, which has the benefit of bringing a little ray of sunshine to times of the year when homegrown fruit is thin on the ground. It's important that the mangoes are really juicy and ripe (they should dimple when discreetly prodded) to counteract the sourness of the lime and passion fruit dressing, so if you don't have a good source of on-the-turn fruit (i.e. a market) near you, make sure you buy them a few days in advance and ripen them at home.

It's gorgeously zingy as it is, but, as with so many things in life, is improved with a dollop of yoghurt or a scoop of ice cream (I like coconut, which always puts me in mind of frozen piña coladas – a treat sadly only really acceptable on holiday).

2 LARGE RIPE MANGOES
JUICE OF 1 LIME
2 PASSION FRUIT
200G LYCHEES, PEELED AND STONED
   (TINNED ARE FINE)

A SMALL BUNCH OF FRESH MINT, LEAVES FINELY
   CHOPPED, TO SERVE

1. Peel the mangoes and cut into chunks, discarding the stones. Purée a quarter of the fruit with the lime juice to make the dressing. Cut the passion fruit in half, scoop out the seeds and add to the dressing.

2. Put the remaining mango chunks into a serving bowl along with the lychees. Pour over the dressing and refrigerate for at least an hour.

3. Garnish with the chopped mint leaves just before serving.

Thrifty menu

SERVES 4

Thrifty sounds about as appetizing as gluten and dairy free to most people, I know, but the fact remains that sometimes you've got less left over once the rent is paid, or you've shelled out for a new laptop, than you might wish. But that should be no reason to make a hermit of yourself: having people over for dinner can easily work out cheaper than an evening in the pub – especially as they generally bring the drinks – and I'd tuck into these two dishes even if I won the lottery. Although probably from gold plates, rather than Ikea's finest.

Savoy cabbage and bacon gratin

SERVES 4

This was one of my staples at university, sometimes with stock and Cheddar replacing the more luxurious ingredients, and it's one of my favourite recipes in this entire book: so very much more than the bare, depressing idea of a cabbage bake suggests. If you make it for fewer people, please cover it before you sit down, or you will not be able to resist picking at it long after you've eaten more than is entirely healthy. It really is that good.

SALT AND PEPPER
1 LARGE SAVOY CABBAGE, SHREDDED
A KNOB OF BUTTER, PLUS A LITTLE EXTRA
   TO GREASE
1 ONION, FINELY SLICED
6 RASHERS OF STREAKY SMOKED BACON,
   CHOPPED

300ML DOUBLE CREAM
1 TABLESPOON WHOLEGRAIN MUSTARD
50G BREADCRUMBS
15G PARMESAN, GRATED (OPTIONAL)

1. Preheat the oven to 180°C/gas mark 4. Heat a large pan of salted water until boiling and add the cabbage. Blanch briefly, until just wilted, then drain and set aside.

2. Melt the butter in a large frying pan over a medium heat and cook the onion until softened and golden. Add the bacon, and turn up the heat to crisp.

3. Turn down the heat again, then mix together the cream and mustard and add to the pan, followed by the cabbage. Season and toss everything together well.

4. Grease a large baking dish with a little butter, then tip in the cabbage mixture, cover with foil and bake for about half an hour.

5. Heat the grill. Mix together the breadcrumbs and cheese. Remove the foil, sprinkle the crumbs and cheese over the cabbage, and grill until golden.

Baked apples

SERVES 4

A mum special, which can be cooked at the same time as the cabbage and left in the oven while you eat that noble dish, thus cleverly making the most of the pricey heat. Nothing groundbreaking here, but I've never met anyone who doesn't like a baked apple.

4 MEDIUM COOKING APPLES OR LARGE
   DESSERT APPLES
8 TABLESPOONS MIXED DRIED FRUIT AND
   NUTS OF YOUR CHOICE (I LIKE CURRANTS,
   FLAKED ALMONDS AND MIXED PEEL)

2 TABLESPOONS DEMERARA SUGAR
1 TEASPOON MIXED SPICE
A KNOB OF BUTTER

1. Preheat the oven to 180°C/gas mark 4. Wash and partially core the apples, making sure you don't go right through, otherwise the filling will come out. Score them horizontally around the middle to prevent the skins bursting during cooking, then put them into a baking dish.

2. Mix together the dried fruit and nuts with the sugar and spice, and divide between the apples, stuffing well into each. Top with a little butter and pour 3 tablespoons of water into the dish.

3. Bake for about 40 minutes, until the top of the stuffing has caramelized, but not burnt. Serve with crème fraîche, ice cream, yoghurt or – and ideally – Bird's custard.

Box-set menu

Obviously you can serve this up any time you're feeding a crowd, but the vaguely American theme puts me in mind of a film night – my former flatmate Anna, who is an excellent cook, used to make something quite similar when we all sat down to gorge on the box set de jour, laying everything out on the table and letting people help themselves as and when they could bear to leave the sofa, rather than offering silver service.

Pulled pork and black bean chilli

SERVES 6–8

This might seem a lot of effort, but actually, it's one of those nice recipes where you get to take a few hours off in the middle while heat and time work their magic, and anyway, it's completely worth it. I seem to remember Jamie Oliver explaining that coffee found its way into chilli as one of the few ingredients in the cowboy's travelling pantry; whatever the truth of it, it adds a rich, earthy, almost smoky flavour which more than justifies its inclusion, even if its only connection to the Wild West is a natural affinity with John Wayne movies. As well as the coleslaw opposite, this is very good served with guacamole (see page 298) and crumbled feta.

2 TABLESPOONS DARK BROWN SUGAR
2 TEASPOONS GROUND CUMIN
2 TEASPOONS SMOKED SWEET PAPRIKA
1 TEASPOON SALT
2KG PIECE OF BONELESS PORK SHOULDER, SKIN SCORED
2 TABLESPOONS VEGETABLE OIL
2 ONIONS, CUT INTO THIN WEDGES
6 CLOVES OF GARLIC, PEELED

2–3 RED CHILLIES, FINELY SLICED
1 GREEN PEPPER, DESEEDED AND SLICED
1 TABLESPOON CIDER VINEGAR
1 X 400G TIN OF CHOPPED TOMATOES
200ML STRONG BLACK COFFEE
2 X 400G TINS OF BLACK BEANS, DRAINED
A DASH OF BOURBON
TORTILLAS (PREFERABLY MAIZE, THEY'RE MUCH NICER), WARMED IN A DRY PAN, TO SERVE

1. Combine the sugar, cumin, smoked paprika and salt and rub all over the pork, working it into the scored skin. Leave at room temperature for half an hour, or in the fridge overnight.

2. Preheat the oven to 160°C/gas mark 3. Heat the oil in a large lidded casserole pan over a medium-high heat, and brown the pork on all sides. Remove the meat from the pan and add the onions, garlic, chillies and green pepper. Sauté until beginning to char, then add the vinegar and tomatoes and scrape any bits from the bottom of the pan.

3. Pour in the coffee and bring to a simmer, then put the meat back into the pan, cover and put into the oven for about 4 hours, checking occasionally, until the meat is tender.

4. Leave the meat to cool slightly, then remove from the pan and, using two forks, shred, discarding any large chunks of fat and cutting any crackling into strips. Spoon off the excess fat that will have risen to the top of the sauce, then return the pork to the pan, along with the beans and the bourbon. Reheat, and check the seasoning before serving with tortillas.

Tex Mex slaw

Crunchy, zingy and fresh, this is the ideal foil to the rich and smoky pork. It can be made in advance, then refrigerated until you're about to press play.

JUICE OF 2 LIMES
75ML AVOCADO OR EXTRA VIRGIN OLIVE
   OIL
A PINCH OF SUGAR
A PINCH OF SALT
1 SMALL WHITE CABBAGE, CORE REMOVED,
   FINELY SHREDDED

3 CARROTS, GRATED
A SMALL BUNCH OF SPRING ONIONS, FINELY
   SLICED
½ A SMALL RED CABBAGE, CORE REMOVED, FINELY
   SHREDDED
A SMALL BUNCH OF FRESH MINT, CHOPPED

1. Whisk together the lime juice, oil and sugar with a pinch of salt to make a dressing.

2. Pour half the dressing into a large serving bowl and add the white cabbage, carrots and onions. Toss well, then pour over the rest of the dressing and toss again. Just before serving, stir in the red cabbage and mint.

Rocky road

SERVES 6–8

Not one of those stodgy packed-lunch bars, but a magnificent tablet studded with so many good things that you might be hard pushed to spot the chocolate holding it all together. If you don't like, or can't find, any of the ingredients, just leave them out, or make your own substitutes: it's so simple even a child could make it, if you happen to have one on hand.

500G DARK CHOCOLATE
100G HONEY-ROASTED PEANUTS
100G SALTED ALMONDS
2 CRUNCHIE BARS, BROKEN INTO CHUNKS

5 DIGESTIVE BISCUITS, BROKEN INTO CHUNKS
100G SOUR CHERRIES
100G MARSHMALLOWS
SEA SALT FLAKES

1. Melt the chocolate in a heatproof bowl set over a pan of boiling water – make sure the bowl doesn't touch the water.

2. Line a baking tray with baking parchment. Stir most of the other ingredients into the chocolate, except for the salt, keeping a little of each back, then pour on to the parchment and leave to set.

3. After 15 minutes, sprinkle with the remaining ingredients and a little sea salt, and leave to set completely at (cool-ish) room temperature. Serve whole, for people to break off bits as the greed takes them.

Menu for two which doesn't look like you've tried too hard

SERVES 2

In my very limited experience, the first time you invite someone over for dinner, rather than meeting them for a drink, or going out to eat, is usually quite a significant moment. It suggests that they're in it for the lounging around watching bad telly together, and the companionable Sunday morning paper reading, as well as the more glamorous aspects of romance.

But, early on, you really don't want to look like you're trying too hard – you're just a naturally great cook, right?

Lamb, harissa and courgette kebabs with jewelled couscous

SERVES 2

You can't accuse kebabs of pretensions – no one can carry on looking effortlessly glamorous while eating griddled meat off a skewer, which is the whole idea. Not only is this utterly delicious, but it exudes casual competence in the kitchen, and can be cooked in less than ten minutes: you can talk up the effort that went into marinating the lamb if you feel you're looking a bit lazy. The garlic is optional: it does taste good, but some people wrongly believe it's a passion-killer. Perhaps it's best to be cautious at this early stage.

300G BONELESS LEG OF LAMB
2 TABLESPOONS ROSE HARISSA
1 TEASPOON CORIANDER SEEDS
1 TEASPOON CUMIN SEEDS
JUICE OF ½ A LEMON
2 CLOVES OF GARLIC, CRUSHED
   (OPTIONAL)
SALT AND PEPPER
1 LARGE COURGETTE
1 TABLESPOON OLIVE OIL

100G COUSCOUS
1 TABLESPOON EXTRA VIRGIN OLIVE OIL
½ A POMEGRANATE
50G FLAKED ALMONDS, TOASTED IN A
   DRY PAN
A SMALL BUNCH OF FRESH CORIANDER,
   CHOPPED
200ML GREEK YOGHURT, MIXED WITH A LITTLE
   EXTRA VIRGIN OLIVE OIL AND SALT

1. Cut the lamb into roughly 2cm chunks. In a bowl, mix together the harissa, coriander and cumin seeds, lemon juice and garlic, if using, along with a good pinch of salt. Add the lamb, stir and leave to marinate for at least 45 minutes – you can do it the night before, or that morning, and leave it in the fridge.

2. If you're using wooden skewers, soak them in water for 20 minutes before use. Cut the courgette into thin strips lengthways using a peeler, then brush with a little olive oil and season. Thread the lamb and courgette strips on to the skewers, concertina-ing the courgette to fit it on.

3. When you're ready to cook, heat a griddle pan until smoking hot. Cook the couscous according to packet instructions, then stir in the extra virgin olive oil, pomegranate seeds, flaked almonds and fresh coriander and season generously.

4. Cook the kebabs for about 4 minutes each side, until charred on the outside but still pink in the middle. Serve on top of a mound of couscous, with the yoghurt on the side.

Whisky chocolate pots

SERVES 2

These might seem rather parsimonious in size, but trust me, a little goes a long way – and queasiness has never been conducive to romance. If you, or your special guest, have a sweet tooth, you could swap the dark chocolate for milk, or half and half – and needless to say, the recipe also works with dark rum, amaretto, and, I imagine, many other spirits and liqueurs that marry well with chocolate.

Depending on how the evening is going, you could serve a little well-chilled glass of whatever you've used along with it, although I'll leave you to make that particular judgement call.

140ML DOUBLE CREAM
60G DARK CHOCOLATE
A PINCH OF SALT

3 TABLESPOONS WHISKY
ZEST OF 1 ORANGE

1.   Pour the cream into a small pan and heat gently. Meanwhile, break the chocolate into pieces (whacking it, still tightly wrapped, against the kitchen counter generally does the trick).

2.   When the cream begins to simmer, remove it from the heat, add the chocolate, and stir until melted. When the mixture is smooth, stir in a pinch of salt and the whisky.

3.   Divide the mixture between two ramekins, and chill for at least 2 hours, until set. Top with orange zest.

Cooking
to impress

This chapter is designed for those times when you'd like to make a bit more effort: it could be for a special occasion – meeting your partner's parents for the first time, celebrating a housemate's birthday – or it could just be because you fancy spending Saturday afternoon fiddling around in the kitchen, cooking for your friends. That said, there's nothing particularly complicated – a few of the recipes need long, slow cooking, or some other advance preparation that renders them unsuitable for knocking up after work, but we're not talking bacon candy floss or tequila foams here.

If I've got the time, I love this kind of entertaining – planning the crowd and the menu, decorating the table, dressing up for dinner – but there's nothing more guaranteed to put me in a grump than if I have to end up rushing. (You know you've been too laid back on the preparation front when the first thing a guest says when you open the door is, 'Oh God, are you all right?') There's no big secret to success: just plan ahead, and you'll be fine. Boring but true.

Timing and numbers

You can always take a chance and invite people last minute for an impromptu feast, but, to get the guest list you want, it's wise to think about a month ahead, especially as these menus work best on weekend lunchtimes or Saturday evenings, which tend to get cluttered up with birthday bashes, hen and stag nights, weddings and the like, depending on your age. If you are hosting such a meal on a weeknight, try to set aside the evening before to prepare as much as possible: there's usually at least one course you can tick off, as well as getting little things like laying the table and cleaning the bathroom out of the way.

Decide what works for you, but at lunchtime I invite people for 1.15 p.m., to sit down at 2 p.m., and at dinner, 7.30 p.m. for 8.15 p.m. A cushion of extra time is useful, not only to give you the chance to have a few drinks and nibbles with your guests before the meal, but also because some people will inevitably be late – occasionally even through no fault of their own – and this way, they'll miss out on the cheese straws rather than the starter.

These menus serve from two to six people, but can often easily be halved or multiplied – use your common sense, and always err on the side of generosity. Much better to have leftovers to gorge upon for lunch the next day than to realize belatedly, as you all sit down, that there's not enough chicken to go round. Assess how many people you can seat before issuing invitations, but unless it's a really posh affair, no one will mind sitting on bathroom stools and garden chairs, as long as they're clean and comfy.

Invitations

Realistically, these days we do most of our inviting by text message, email, or even Facebook, but if it's a really special occasion, nothing beats an invitation by post. It also has the great benefit of encouraging a speedy RSVP: the ephemeral nature of electronic communication seems to prompt a certain disregard for good old-fashioned manners, whereas something sitting solid and accusing on the mantelpiece has a tendency to jog the memory. I like the packets of plain postcards you can buy at any Post Office or stationer's for this purpose – you can do a silly little sketch on the blank side if you're feeling particularly creative.

Virtual or not, it's surprisingly easy to send an invitation minus a detail such as the address, so double-check you've included all the vital information.

* Date and time – specify a time about forty-five minutes before you actually want to sit down and eat, for drinks and to allow for traffic, public transport, and general tardiness.

* Occasion (even if it's just 'for dinner').

* Address (postcodes are good in this age of smartphone maps, but if it's at all difficult to find, provide helpful directions, such as 'entrance round the side' or 'above The Codfather'. If you live in a city, the nearest bus, tram or tube stop is also handy).

* Dress code – this may sound very stuffy, but if you're secretly hoping for stylish sophistication, then a simple 'smart' might be kind so that the friend who lives in tracksuit bottoms doesn't feel silly.

* RSVP, with any dietary requirements/violent dislikes.

Even those four magic letters don't guarantee a response, however, so some gentle prodding might be necessary. At the risk of sounding like a stalker, start with an email or text, and then, if that doesn't work, use the phone to demand a yes or no on the spot. (If they don't answer, or ring you back, you should probably assume that they're not coming – and also that you might have offended them in some way.) Some people, however lovely, are just habitually and unthinkingly disorganized, so invite someone else instead, rather than waiting too long for a response, and risking a gap at the feast.

Setting the scene

First thing, arrange all your chosen chairs, stools, occasional tables, and anything else being pressed into use as a seat, around the table, and sit down at each in turn to check there's enough room, and no one's pressed up against a leg. In theory, the host should sit at the end of the table, but it's nicer to take the least comfortable place for yourself, as long as it's easily accessible. You'll be up and down anyway, and no doubt you'll get your reward in heaven.

Unless you have a particularly lovely table, a tablecloth is a cunning, and quick, way to transform it from the everyday, and covers a multitude of sins. New ones can be expensive, so measure up your table, then have a hunt around charity shops and jumble sales for one that fits: ideally you'll need an extra 20cm on each side as an overhang (so if your table measures a neat 2m x 1m, you'll need a cloth 240cm long and 140cm wide). Another option, which is generally even cheaper, is to keep an eye out for bedcovers and flat sheets that you like (avoid the fitted ones, they look very bizarre at dinnertime). Iron them before use, and align any folding creases parallel to the edges of the table.

As long as you're not frantically trying to conjure them up at the last minute, table decorations can be fun to put together. It's difficult to beat flowers, but make sure they aren't very fragrant (apt to spoil the flavour of your food) or blocking the view across the table: however beautiful the bunch, people tend to like to make eye contact with whoever they're talking to. Little posies of unassuming wild or garden flowers, stuck into clean jam jars, look sweet, and will save you a lot of dosh. (Soak the jars in water overnight to make removing the labels easier.)

If it's autumn or winter, and flowers are thin on the ground, try sprigs of holly or seasonal ingredients instead. A big glass bowl crammed full of bright clementines, pears or chestnuts can look surprisingly effective as a centrepiece.

Candles are a quick way to create atmosphere when the light starts to fade: we may have invented electricity, but we're not duty bound to use it at every opportunity. If you have a large table, tea lights, scattered haphazardly down the middle, look particularly lovely – avoid anything scented unless you're eating outside, at the mercy of mosquitoes or midges.

You don't need to have enough cutlery for everyone to have a new set for every course: as long as you're not forced to crack your crème brûlée with the same spoon you used for the soup, no one will mind keeping hold of it. The same goes for plates, if you're making life easier for yourself by putting food on the table for people to serve themselves, but consider giving them a quick wash between if the starter involved something very pungent which could spoil the main course.

Don't forget napkins: I'm not a fan of the disposable sort – they look sordid after one crumple, and tend to waft on to the floor after about five minutes. Charity shops are full of decent old-fashioned napkins which just need a wash and an iron: dark colours and patterns hide a multitude of Chianti-coloured sins.

Music, at a civilized volume, can be a good way of making the first guests feel less self-conscious, but I'd turn it off when you sit down to eat.

Practicalities

Think of somewhere you can hang coats and leave bags: clear your own pegs if you have them, or designate a clear bed for them if not. I'm happy to sling most of my things anywhere, but other people are rightly more fastidious.

You don't need to tidy the personality out of your home: if you usually live amongst tottering piles of books and a clutter of knick-knacks, your guests may be somewhat unnerved to find themselves in a minimalist paradise. There's a fine line between personality and slatternliness, though: tidy away that rack of drying socks into the bedroom, and move the final demand for the phone bill to underneath a pile of more edifying reading matter. When I've got people over, I think of my flat as representing my vision of myself as I'd like to be, rather than the reality, which means putting the foot scrub out of sight, and replacing it with those posh body lotions I got for Christmas and am too mean to use.

While we're in the bathroom, put out a new hand towel, make sure there's enough soap and give at least the sink and the loo a good clean; unless it's a really good dinner party, people will be unlikely to require the shower. Put a spare loo roll somewhere obvious, and, if you're still looking for somewhere to stick that scented candle …

Seating

The very idea of telling people where to sit seems bossy and old-fashioned, but it does have its merits, especially for the host with a casual interest in social engineering. At a big dinner, a plan allows you to split up little knots of old friends and really get the conversation flowing: having invited Richard from work because you think he'll really get on with your schoolfriend Dudley, it would be a shame if they never got the chance to discover their shared love of fly fishing because Dudley is stuck reminiscing with Rosie at the other end of the table. If you're actually attempting to set up two friends, such a plan becomes absolutely imperative, although you may wish to do it more subtly by tipping off other people to steer them into sitting together, rather than presenting a formal blueprint for 'seduction'.

Think about the shape of your table: if it's round or very wide, people are more likely to talk to the person next to them, rather than across, whereas if you're all crowded on benches, you're often too close to your neighbour to be able to comfortably look them in the eye. Beware of leaving people marooned: if you're secretly hoping that Lucinda and Lars are going to fall in love over pudding, put one of them on the end, so the person to their other side isn't playing gooseberry (or, and worse, distracting one of your intended from their romantic destiny).

Traditionally, things went 'boy/girl/boy/girl', but there's no need to do that now if that doesn't fit your plans: unless they're very new, or one party is extremely shy, however, I never seat couples together, on the basis that they probably see enough of each other anyway. (Seat new couples apart and you may well find them snogging outside the loo between courses. I speak from experience.) And do make sure you're sitting next to someone interesting – host's privilege.

Work out who might get on with who, and draw out the plan in advance, then make some obvious place markers, so people don't sit down willy-nilly and spoil things. Old-fashioned luggage labels, tied loosely around the base of a wine or water glass, look nice, but you can fashion markers from whatever you want: badges, pieces of fruit, biscuits (labelled with writing icing): as long as it's obvious, it'll do the job. One friend did the place markers for her wedding using pebbles from her favourite beach: gathering them was apparently an awful task, but I've still got mine, which acts as a handy paperweight as well as a very happy memory.

Planning

Once you've established who's coming, and what they do and don't eat, you can plan the menu, and accompanying drinks, check your equipment and cupboards, and make a shopping list. I find the internet invaluable for a big shop, although it can backfire if you're the victim of a substitution, and find yourself with Wispas instead of the dark chocolate that you ordered. If possible, have it delivered the day before, so you can deal with just such a misfortune (by scoffing the Wispas on the way to the shops).

Make a time plan. This can just be as simple as working backwards from when you want to sit down, to ensure you give yourself enough time to get ready; I try to fool myself into believing that I've invited people half an hour before I actually have, because that way, even if I'm running late, there's room to rush off and sling on a dress.

Logistics

Let's assume we're in an ideal world for a moment. All the advance preparation is done, the kitchen is tidy, if bursting at the seams, you've laid the table, chilled the wine and aperitifs, and put out the nibbles (see pages 60–61 for some ideas). The music's playing, and you've poured yourself a very cold, very stiff drink. Just as you finish your toilette, the doorbell rings, and, voilà! you have your first guest.

Once you've taken their coat, offer them a drink, and, even if you've just remembered something that remains undone, take five minutes to catch up: making people feel welcome is far more important than cutting those lemons (disregard this advice if the thing you remembered is threatening to set off the smoke alarm at any moment). As other guests arrive, you can repeat this process and then leave them to it if necessary, always introducing each to the assembled company and waiting until the conversation begins flowing before departing – providing all's gone to plan, however, you should simply need to return to the kitchen to serve the starter shortly before sitting down. Ask a good friend to look after drinks if you're on your own: other guests might not feel confident enough to fetch another bottle from your fridge, and an empty glass reflects very badly on your hosting skills.

Always move guests to the table before you're quite ready: relaxed people move slowly, and there'll be a bit of discussion over the seating, plan or no plan, while your soup gently cools. Remember to heat the plates if appropriate, and leave a gap of about fifteen minutes between courses, to give people a chance to work up a bit of an appetite – as well as go to the loo, have a smoke, or whatever else they might wish to do. Otherwise, encourage them to stay at the table: however well-meaning, help with clearing is often more stressful than doing it yourself, and breaks up the conversation.

I like to linger at the table at the end of the meal, over either pudding or cheese, and bring out the spirits for those who want them. This is when all the best conversation happens, and transplanting the action to more comfortable surrounds sometimes ruins everything, as everyone suddenly starts to realize how sleepy all that good food and wine has made them. Whichever you go for, offer coffee or tea at the end of the evening – a good way of signalling to people it might be time to think about ordering that taxi . . .

A note on cheese

I don't understand the concept of pudding *or* cheese – of course it's nice to have something sweet at the end of the meal, but you need something else to sustain you if you're going to chat well into the night. A good cheeseboard that you can happily pick at for hours is perfect. This is where the French go wrong with all that cheese before pudding nonsense – no one's going to sit around nibbling at a Charlotte Russe until four in the morning.

Our Victorian and Edwardian forebears had it right with the savoury course – but there's no way I'm popping back into the kitchen to knock up some Scotch woodcock or Welsh rarebit at this point in the evening. A cheeseboard, however, can, and indeed should, be laid out well before dinner, so it has a chance to come to room temperature: all you'll need to do to serve is tip some biscuits into a dish and pass round the plates.

I'd prefer one big chunk of really good cheese to lots of mean pieces for the sake of variety, but, to cater for fussy appetites, I usually aim for three when doing a big dinner party: one soft Brie-style cheese, which will have spread itself generously over the board by the time we come to eat it, one pungent goat's or blue cheese, and one Cheddar, Gruyère or other hard cheese of the kind favoured by fussy eaters and the pregnant and fragile.

Something sweet, like chutney, quince jelly, dried fruit, grapes, apples or pears (celery on a cheeseboard frankly puzzles me, as does salad – no one wants anything so worthy at this point in proceedings), and a selection of biscuits are essential accompaniments. If you're feeling French, serve hunks of bread instead, but I find them too filling: some water biscuits and a nice wheaty cracker are far nicer to nibble on. That said, you'll be surprised at how much cheese people can put away, even as they moan they'll never eat again. Salad, like baguette, is another example of the French completely misunderstanding the idea of the cheese course . . .

Two good aperitifs
A really great gin and tonic

You may well think you know how to make a great G&T – but if it's so easy, why do I find myself drinking so many mediocre ones? Sometimes it's worth going back to basics. The choice of gin is yours: personally, I favour Tanqueray, Beefeater or Plymouth for a gin and tonic (Hendricks, although delicious, is a whole other kettle of fish).

PER PERSON

2 FRESHLY CUT WEDGES OF LIME

60ML GIN, CHILLED (PREFERABLY KEPT
   IN THE FREEZER)

ICE CUBES

90ML INDIAN TONIC WATER, CHILLED
   (NOT THE DIET SORT, IT'S ALWAYS TOO
   SWEET – PREFERABLY FEVER TREE IF YOU CAN
   RUN TO IT – BUT ALWAYS NICE AND FIZZY)

1. Put a tumbler in the freezer for 20 minutes. When you're ready to make your drink, rub the inside of the glass, up to the rim, with a wedge of lime, squeezing it gently, then add the gin, a scoop of ice and a spritz of lime juice from the other wedge, chucking this into the glass as you go.

2. Top up with tonic water: you may like more or less than this, but play around with the ratios. I also sometimes like a dash of bitters in my G&T, particularly if it's hot and stuffy outside.

The Bellini

MAKES 6

More of a festive drink, this – invented by Harry's Bar in Venice, which, as anyone who's ever visited and tried to order anything else will know, has been trading off the fact ever since, it's popularly supposed to have been named after the Renaissance painter whose peachy skin tones the drink is said to emulate, a story as charming as the cocktail itself. This is a frivolous drink in the very best sense of the word.

2 WHITE PEACHES (YOU CAN USE YELLOW,
   BUT THEY'RE MORE ACIDIC, SO DO HAVE A
   GOOD HUNT BEFORE YOU SETTLE FOR THEM)

750ML PROSECCO, CHILLED

1. Peel the peaches (they will be quite juicy, so this is best done over a bowl) and chop, removing the stone. Use a hand blender, or a fork and some determination, to purée them until smooth, adding any extra juice from the chopping board or bowl.

2. Line up 6 flutes and pour a tiny amount of prosecco into each, then add a teaspoon of purée. Top with fizz, allowing the foam to die down before adding more, stir gently and serve.

Spring menu

Spring's a funny time of year for food. Those tentative early rays of sunshine, the first day you dare to venture out without gloves – they all seem so joyously incredible after the dark damp of winter that the temptation is to rush into the kitchen and knock up a celebratory feast, yet instead of the asparagus and strawberries which spring boldly to mind, the shops are still full of the same old winter veg. This is what's known to gardeners as the 'hungry gap', as stocks of last year's crops dwindle, but we're still a couple of months away from the new season's bounty.

This menu is designed to make the most of what we do have at this time of year: root vegetables, smoked foods, and, of course, the magnificent citrus fruits of the Mediterranean, at their best in cold weather. From bitter experience, I'd advise against the temptation to wipe down the garden furniture, however bright it might be outside – enjoy this in the warmth of the kitchen, then follow it up with a brisk walk to check on spring's progress instead.

This menu is easily made gluten free by serving the mackerel pâté with gluten free bread or crackers, and serving the chicken with potatoes or rice, rather than baguette.

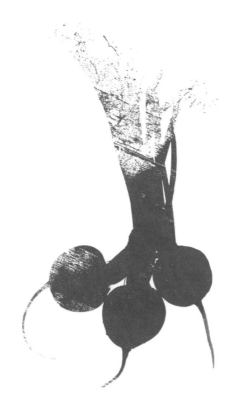

Smoked mackerel pâté with quick pickled beetroot

SERVES 4

I love smoky flavours: Islay whisky, Black Forest ham, those amazing American smoked almonds sold in dangerously large tubs – the merest puff and I'm sold. (My newest discovery is smoked salt, to add a lick of fire to everything from scrambled eggs to caramel.) Mackerel, meanwhile, is my favourite fish, so this recipe, which always seems to be on the menu at my parents' house, is a combination made in heaven – particularly as it takes less than five minutes to make, and is amenable to advance preparation.

The beetroot is my own addition: my dad loves pickles, which means that I assumed beetroot came out of the ground tasting of vinegar until embarrassingly recently. The acid cuts through the richness of the oily fish and creamy cheese, while the crunch provides a nice contrast of textures. I'd serve this with dark rye bread, because I'm completely obsessed with it, but my mum would go for wholemeal toast, and salad.

FOR THE MACKEREL PÂTÉ
320G SMOKED MACKEREL
200G CREAM CHEESE
50G CRÈME FRAÎCHE
2CM FRESH HORSERADISH, FINELY
    GRATED (OR JARRED, TO TASTE)
JUICE OF 1 LEMON
BLACK PEPPER

FOR THE BEETROOT
2 MEDIUM RAW BEETROOT
1 SHALLOT, THINLY SLICED
1 SMALL CRUNCHY GREEN APPLE,
    CORED AND FINELY SLICED
300ML CIDER VINEGAR
½ TEASPOON SALT
2 TEASPOONS CASTER SUGAR
½ TEASPOON JUNIPER BERRIES

TO SERVE
RYE BREAD
A SMALL BUNCH OF FRESH DILL, CHOPPED

1.   Peel the beetroot and cut into thin slices. Put it into a bowl. Mix together the rest of the beetroot ingredients and pour over the top. Leave to marinate for at least an hour.

2.   Meanwhile, pull the skin off the fish if necessary, and flake it into a food processor. Add the cream cheese, crème fraîche and horseradish and whiz until smooth. Add lemon juice and black pepper (and more horseradish if you like) to taste, then refrigerate for up to a day, until ready to use.

3.   Cut the rye bread into triangles. Arrange a dollop of mackerel pâté in the centre of each plate, and circle with rounds of drained beetroot. Sprinkle with dill, and serve with the bread.

Spring chicken

SERVES 4

I still remember (this is a bit tragic) the transgressive thrill of my first cooked lettuce. Previously it had been a tedious vehicle for vinaigrette, something eaten more for health than enjoyment, but suddenly, it could rise above all that, and become a vegetable in its own right. As someone forced to eat an awful lot of lettuce in her formative years, I still haven't got over the excitement, which is why there are two recipes using it in here (see also the chilled salad soup on page 118). This dish is based on the bistro classic *petits pois à la française*, and uses ingredients available all year round. It looks after itself for a good half an hour in the middle, so you can sit down and have a drink: stir in a little crème fraîche at the end if the weather's particularly chilly.

I SMALL CHICKEN, JOINTED, OR 8 PIECES OF CHICKEN, ON THE BONE (ABOUT 1.2KG)	150ML BOILING WATER
	100G SMOKED BACON LARDONS
	4 SHALLOTS, CHOPPED
2 TABLESPOONS OLIVE OIL	4 LITTLE GEM HEARTS, QUARTERED
SALT AND PEPPER	400G FROZEN PETITS POIS
50G BUTTER	2 TABLESPOONS CRÈME FRAÎCHE (OPTIONAL)
300ML WHITE WINE	I BAGUETTE, SLICED, TO SERVE

1. Rub the chicken with a little olive oil and season well. Heat half the butter and 1 tablespoon of oil in a large, heavy-based casserole pan over a medium-high heat until foaming, then add the chicken pieces. Cook, turning, until golden on all sides.

2. Turn down the heat to medium-low and cover the casserole. Cook for 30–40 minutes, until the chicken is cooked through, turning occasionally. Remove from the pan with a slotted spoon and keep warm.

3. Turn the heat up and pour the wine into the pan. Scrape the bottom of the pan to deglaze, then pour the wine and chicken juices into a jug. Add the boiling water and set aside.

4. Put the rest of the butter into the pan and, when melted, add the lardons. Cook for a couple of minutes, then add the shallots and cook until soft.

5. Add the lettuce quarters and fry for a couple of minutes on each side, then pour in the wine mixture, add the peas and season well. Bring to the boil and simmer for about 5 minutes, until the peas and lettuce are cooked. Stir in the crème fraîche if using, and taste for seasoning. Serve the chicken on a base of lettuce and peas, with hunks of French bread to mop up any remaining juices.

Orange, polenta and almond cake

SERVES 4

The citrus and almond flavours here suggest, to me at least, the warmth of a Mediterranean climate. It's inspired by my friend Marie's unbelievably delicious Tunisian orange cake – she once very kindly gave me the recipe, and I promptly lost it. In trying to recreate it, I decided to make it both gluten and dairy free (although it is even better served with a dollop of sharp crème fraîche). Don't be put off by its resolutely flat appearance – it's not supposed to rise. This is the kind of cake that gets stickier and more delicious the longer you leave it, so try to make it a day ahead if you can.

2 ORANGES
4 EGGS
50ML EXTRA VIRGIN OLIVE OIL, PLUS EXTRA
   FOR GREASING
300G CASTER SUGAR
150G GROUND ALMONDS
100G POLENTA
A PINCH OF SALT

FOR THE SYRUP
1 LEMON
1 ORANGE
4 TABLESPOONS CLEAR HONEY

CRÈME FRAÎCHE OR GREEK YOGHURT,
   TO SERVE (OPTIONAL)

1. Put the 2 oranges into a pan and cover with cold water. Bring to the boil, then turn down the heat, cover and simmer gently for an hour, until soft. Drain and allow to cool. Preheat the oven to 180°C/gas mark 4, and grease and line a 20cm cake tin.

2. Cut the oranges in half and remove the pips, then put, skin and all, into a food processor and purée.

3. Meanwhile, beat together the eggs and the oil in a jug, and combine the caster sugar, almonds and polenta in a mixing bowl with a pinch of salt. Beat the eggs and oil into the dry ingredients, followed by the orange purée.

4. Spoon the mixture into the prepared tin and bake for about an hour, until a skewer inserted into the top comes out clean. Keep an eye on it: you may need to cover it with foil towards the end if it begins to brown too much on top.

5. Leave the cake in its tin to cool slightly while you make the syrup. Zest the lemon, and cut 5 thin strips of peel from the orange. Add these to the pan, then squeeze in the juice from the fruit and warm over a low heat. Stir in the honey until dissolved, then bring to the boil and boil until it becomes syrupy: this should take about 8 minutes.

6. Use a skewer to poke holes across the top of the warm cake, then carefully transfer to a serving platter with a lip to catch the juices, and pour the syrup and peel on top. Leave the cake to cool before serving, preferably with crème fraîche or Greek yoghurt.

Summer menu

Probably the best time of year as far as ingredients are concerned: fingernail-sized broad beans, as much asparagus as you can stuff in your gaping maw, soft berries and ice creams all make entertaining a doddle. If you feel moved to make a bit more of an effort, however, this menu pays homage to a few of my favourite places to spend a summer's afternoon: a British garden, the French Riviera (with someone else's credit card) – and anywhere serving ice cream. Everything, save cooking the fish, can be prepared in advance, leaving you more time to waft about serving Pimm's, lounging in a deckchair or doing whatever floats your nautically striped boat.

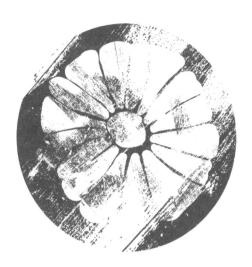

Chilled salad soup

I like a marinated artichoke heart as much as the next foodie, but I do mourn the passing of our native salads: a mild, soft lettuce rather than spiky southern rocket, a fine cucumber in British racing green, perhaps a peppery pink radish by way of exotica. This chilled soup celebrates the delicately fresh flavours of an English summer – no strident Mediterranean interlopers here, just a simple dish the colour of a Cornish meadow in June, made tangy with buttermilk. Make sure you give it enough time to chill before serving, because lukewarm soup is surprisingly unpleasant – if it's a really hot day (or you haven't quite left enough time for it to cool) you can serve the soup garnished with a couple of ice cubes for extra refreshment. And should summer let you down, it's pretty good hot too.

25G BUTTER
6 SPRING ONIONS, CHOPPED
500G CUCUMBER (ABOUT 1½ CUCUMBERS),
    PEELED, DESEEDED AND CHOPPED
1 ROUND LETTUCE, SHREDDED

150G WATERCRESS, CHOPPED
1 LITRE CHICKEN OR VEGETABLE STOCK
SALT AND PEPPER
3 RADISHES, THINLY SLICED, TO GARNISH
2 TABLESPOONS BUTTERMILK, TO GARNISH

1. Melt the butter in a large pan on a medium heat and add the spring onions. Cook gently for about 3 minutes, and then add the cucumber and cook for about another 3 minutes.

2. Add the lettuce and watercress and stir well. Cook for about 7 minutes, until wilted, then pour in the stock. Bring to a gentle simmer and cook for 10 minutes.

3. Use a blender or stick blender to liquidize the soup to a fine purée, then season to taste, cool and chill.

4. To serve, pour into bowls, put 3 overlapping slices of radish in the middle of each, and pour a ring of buttermilk around them.

Provençale fish stew

My parents had a house in deepest, darkest Provence for many years (not, they would always stress, anywhere remotely fashionable or Peter Mayle-esque), where we'd all repair for several baking weeks each summer. Being, as they were, an hour or so from the coast, the locals weren't big fish eaters (a travelling fish van visited the village once a week), but on the occasion anyone could rouse any energy to spring from the loungers and drive to the beach, the seafood was magnificent.

Like the classic bouillabaisse, everything came with a full complement of untranslatable, tiny, spiny Mediterranean species, but you can use just about any combination that's available to you (although salmon or trout would seem, well, like fish out of water here to me). You can make this ahead up to the end of step 2, then reheat it to cook the fish just before serving.

2 TABLESPOONS OLIVE OIL

4 CLOVES OF GARLIC, THINLY SLICED

4 ANCHOVIES, FINELY CHOPPED

1 LARGE BULB OF FENNEL, TRIMMED AND
  CUT INTO 3–4CM PIECES

½ TEASPOON DRIED THYME

3 STRIPS OF DRIED ORANGE PEEL (USE A
  PEELER TO REMOVE THIN STRIPS OF PEEL
  AND LEAVE TO AIR-DRY FOR 2–3 DAYS,
  PREFERABLY SOMEWHERE SUNNY, OR
  DRY IN THE OVEN AT 110°C/GAS MARK ¼
  UNTIL CRISP – OR FIND READY-DRIED
  IN ASIAN SUPERMARKETS)

150ML NOILLY PRAT VERMOUTH OR
  WHITE WINE

2 X 400G TINS OF CHOPPED TOMATOES

500ML FISH STOCK

A PINCH OF SUGAR

50G BLACK OLIVES

SALT AND PEPPER

360G BASMATI RICE OR 500G NEW POTATOES,
  TO SERVE

500G CLAMS OR MUSSELS, SCRUBBED

500G FIRM WHITE FISH FILLETS, E.G. POLLACK,
  COLEY, POUTING, SKINNED AND CUT INTO
  2CM CHUNKS

400G SQUID, CLEANED AND CUT INTO
  CHUNKY RINGS

1. Heat the oil in a large, heavy-based pan over a medium-low heat and soften the garlic and anchovies for a couple of minutes, then add the fennel and cook for another couple of minutes. Stir in the thyme and orange peel and cook for 5 or so minutes, until you can smell the herbs. Pour in the vermouth and bubble for 3 more minutes to reduce slightly.

2. Add the tomatoes and stock, along with a generous pinch of sugar and the olives. Season well and bring to the boil, then turn down the heat and simmer for about 30 minutes, until the fennel is soft and the sauce slightly reduced and well flavoured.

3. Meanwhile, prepare the rice or potato accompaniment. Put the rice, if using, in a pan with 460ml of water and a teaspoon of salt, bring to the boil, stir, cover the pan and leave to simmer for 25 minutes. Leave for 5 minutes, then fluff up with a fork. Cook the potatoes, if using, in salted boiling water for 20–25 minutes, until tender.

4. Bring the broth back to the boil, tip in the shellfish, cover and simmer for about 3 minutes, then add the white fish and squid. Cover and simmer until the fish is cooked through and the shellfish have opened – this will probably take about 5 minutes.

5. Remove the orange peel and serve in bowls with the rice or potatoes, with an extra bowl in the middle of the table for the clam or mussel shells.

Campari and pink grapefruit granita

SERVES 6

I'd like to say I drank Campari before it started popping up in every pop-up bar and magazine, but actually, I didn't. I do love it, though – save for tonic water, bitter flavours don't really seem to appeal to the British as much as to our continental neighbours, which is a shame, because they make the most brilliantly refreshing aperitifs. Here, the same quality is deployed as a palate cleanser – people are always inordinately impressed when you make your own ices, and the great thing about a granita is that all you need to make it is a freezer and a fork. No churning required.

125G CASTER SUGAR
2 PINK GRAPEFRUIT

4 TABLESPOONS CAMPARI
A SMALL BUNCH OF FRESH MINT, TO SERVE

1. Bring 125ml of water to the boil in a small pan. Mix together the sugar and the finely grated zest of 1 grapefruit, and stir into the water until the sugar has dissolved. Set aside.

2. Juice both grapefruit, then pour the juice through a sieve to remove any pips – you should have about 300ml. Add the syrup, 200ml of water and the Campari and mix well. Pour into a shallow dish – it should be about 2cm deep – then cover and put into the freezer.

3. After an hour or two, when the mixture has started to freeze on the bottom and around the edges, use a fork to scrape away the solidified ice into the middle and stir the whole thing well. Repeat at half-hourly intervals, until the granita has an even, granular consistency. This takes about 4 hours.

4. Serve, preferably in glasses, each garnished with a small mint leaf.

Autumn menu

SERVES 4

Keats hit the nail on the head with his 'season of mists and mellow fruitfulness' line – its creeping soft dampness is a welcome relief after the bleaching heat of summer, heralding as it does all sorts of foresty goodness: mushrooms, berries, game and the like. This menu celebrates some of those ingredients, and feels like the kind of thing one might enjoy on a cold, wet October evening, when diners linger long over the cheese, perhaps with a glass of tawny port or two, and you realize with relief that you don't have to clean the barbecue again for another year.

Pear and black pudding salad

SERVES 4

I adore black pudding in all its guises, from sweetly spicy Spanish morcilla to chunky Bury blood sausage, but my favourite is the Irish variety, studded with enough barley to crisp up very satisfyingly on contact with the frying pan. It's a far cry from the days when, following my mum round the supermarket, I used to make a special pilgrimage to the deli counter in order to gaze at the stuff in horrified fascination. The rich, earthy flavour works wonderfully with autumn pears, although if you're not a fan, you could replace it with blue cheese instead.

3 TABLESPOONS BUTTER
1 LARGE PEAR, CORE REMOVED, SLICED
    INTO 8 WEDGES
1 TEASPOON SOFT BROWN SUGAR
4 TABLESPOONS WALNUTS
8 SLICES OF BLACK PUDDING, CUT INTO
    CHUNKS, SKIN PEELED IF NECESSARY
150G SALAD LEAVES (WATERCRESS WOULD
    BE GOOD, BUT IF YOU CAN GET MUSTARD
    GREENS, EVEN BETTER)

FOR THE DRESSING
2 TEASPOONS DIJON MUSTARD
1 TABLESPOON CIDER VINEGAR
1 TABLESPOON WALNUT OIL
2 TABLESPOONS RAPESEED OR OLIVE OIL
SALT AND PEPPER

1. Heat 2 tablespoons of butter in a frying pan over a medium-high heat. Sprinkle the pear slices with the sugar and add to the pan. Cook for a couple of minutes on each side, without stirring, until golden and caramelized. Remove from the pan and set aside. Add the walnuts to the pan and cook for a minute or so, then remove from the pan and set aside with the pears.

2. Add the rest of the butter to the pan and, when bubbling, cook the black pudding for about 3 minutes, until crisp.

3. Meanwhile, mix together the mustard and vinegar, then whisk in the oils to make a vinaigrette. Season well, and pour some into the base of your salad bowl. Add the leaves and toss to coat with vinaigrette. Add the rest of the dressing, and toss again.

4. Divide the salad between plates and top with the black pudding, pears and walnuts. Serve immediately.

Rabbit stuffed with prunes and Armagnac, with nutty Brussels sprouts

SERVES 4

I like rabbit, first because of its rich flavour, and second because, as long as you can find the wild version, it's great value for money (the plump and pricey farmed ones are, in my opinion, bland in comparison). This recipe is inspired by one of Katie Caldesi's, which appeared in the *Observer*'s food supplement some years ago. Hers is Italian in spirit, all Parmesan and garlic, but I've looked to south-west France, arguably the epicentre of Gallic gastronomy, for my prune and brandy stuffing.

It looks very impressive but the pancetta hides a multitude of sins – and as long as you can get your butcher to bone the rabbit for you, which is a fiddly old job (although certainly not impossible, even with my basic knife skills), it's a cinch to prepare. If not, it's still pretty easy: you just might like the rabbit a little less at the end of it. (I'd strongly advise consulting one of the instructive videos online for tips before getting to work with your knife.)

You can also get all the hard work done up to a day before, so all you have to do on the day is pop it into the oven and prepare the sprouts. If you don't like sprouts (why?), this would also be good with a small Savoy cabbage, or kale or similar. And it goes without saying that this, as with so many things, can be accessorized with mash or roast potatoes if you're particularly hungry.

100G PITTED SOFT DRIED PRUNES
50ML ARMAGNAC OR OTHER BRANDY
200G PORK MINCE
2 TABLESPOONS DRIED THYME
FINELY GRATED NUTMEG, TO TASTE
SALT AND PEPPER
12 SLICES OF PANCETTA OR THIN-CUT
    STREAKY BACON, STRETCHED WITH
    A KNIFE

1 WILD RABBIT, BONED
A LITTLE OLIVE OIL, TO GREASE
100ML MADEIRA

FOR THE SPROUTS
500G BRUSSELS SPROUTS
2 TABLESPOONS BUTTER
25G HAZELNUTS, ROUGHLY CHOPPED
ZEST OF 1 LEMON

1.   At least 2 hours before you're ready to assemble the dish, put the prunes into a dish with the brandy. Cover and leave them to steep. Put the mince into a bowl, add the thyme and a grating of nutmeg and season well. Roughly chop the prunes and add, along with any remaining brandy, to the bowl, then use your hands to mix it all together.

2.   Lay a large rectangle of clingfilm on a work surface and arrange the slices of pancetta in a rectangle towards one edge, with each slice slightly overlapping the one beneath. Lay the boned rabbit on top, and spoon the stuffing mixture in a line down the centre. Use the clingfilm to roll it up into a tight sausage shape. Refrigerate until ready to cook.

3. Preheat the oven to 180°C/gas mark 4 and lightly grease a roasting tin with olive oil. Put the rabbit into the tin, and carefully remove the clingfilm. Roast for 30 minutes, then pour the Madeira into the tin and cook for another 20 minutes, until the pancetta is crisp.

4. Meanwhile, trim the sprouts and cut each one in half. Bring a large pan of well-salted water to the boil and cook the sprouts for about 5 minutes, until tender. While they're cooking, heat the butter in a large pan over a medium-high heat, then add the nuts and toast until golden. Drain the sprouts well, add to the pan of nuts along with the lemon zest, and toss to coat with butter. Take off the heat and keep warm.

5. Remove the rabbit to a serving platter, and put the roasting tin on the hob. Add about 50ml of boiling water and simmer until you have a well-flavoured gravy. Season it to taste and strain into a jug.

6. Cut the rabbit into slices at the table, and serve with the sprouts and gravy.

Cheese and salted caramelized nuts

SERVES 4

Much as I love puddings, if I have to choose one or the other in a restaurant, I usually go for cheese (especially if I've clocked that glorious thing, a proper, old-fashioned cheese trolley awaiting my greedy inspection). Of course, at home it's perfectly acceptable to serve up both, but, with some fresh fruit (a few gently glowing russet apples or late grapes), these crisp, sweet nuts should hit both spots with a satisfying thwack.

I always think it's nicer to get one generous wedge of really good cheese than a few sad scraps to suit all tastes, and these go particularly well with Stilton or Gorgonzola – or, for those still not persuaded of the undoubted virtues of blue cheese, a nutty, really mature Cheddar. They can, indeed should, be made in advance: and please, don't forget to bring the cheese to room temperature before serving (unless you live in a sauna).

100G WALNUTS OR PECANS, OR	½ TEASPOON SALT
A MIXTURE	4 TABLESPOONS WATER
100G CASTER SUGAR	

1. Toast the nuts in a dry non-stick pan until fragrant, then set aside. Prepare a baking tray with baking parchment and place near the hob.

2. Put the sugar and salt into a heavy-based saucepan along with the water and heat, swirling the pan to dissolve them – don't stir. Heat until the mixture begins to colour, then stir in the nuts and cook until the sugar turns golden, but no darker, or they'll taste all bitter and treacly. Do not, please, leave the pan at this point – that way disaster lies.

3. Spoon the nuts on to the baking tray, breaking up any clumps with a spoon (they'll be hot, so this is quite fiddly). Allow to cool (meanwhile, I'd pour some boiling water into the saucepan to make life a bit easier for yourself when it comes to washing up), and serve with ripe blue cheese and some sort of wholesome wheaty biscuits (see page 187).

Winter menu

SERVES 6

At its best, the British winter is crisp and clear: all frost and tingling fingers, accessorized with oversized woolly hats and jolly newspaper pictures of children sledging instead of learning to read. The reality, however, is generally greyer, damper, and infinitely more depressing. Cheer yourself up with the thought that at least there's a good excuse to stay indoors and cook – I can never help feeling a bit regretful about being stuck in the kitchen when the sun's out, but it's lovely being all toasty and warm and gainfully employed when it's hardly worth opening the curtains in the morning. That's not to say this menu will have you chained to the stove – there should easily be enough time to see if there's an old war film on …

Cauliflower and saffron soup with almonds

SERVES 6

Until relatively recently, I thought I didn't like cauliflower – boiled, it's one of those ingredients so bland that it's as if it's actually sucking all the taste out of your tongue. Baking, however, transforms this creamy cloud of a vegetable into something worth eating without a blanket of gloopy cheese – you just need to caramelize those sugars. Its subtle flavour works well with mild, milky almonds and the sweetness of roasted garlic, but the dominant note here should be saffron. Most recipes seem to call meanly for 'a pinch', presumably in deference to the price of these crimson crocus stigmas, but it's not a spice you use that often, so you may as well make sure you can taste it when you do. They don't put pockets in shrouds, you know.

3 TABLESPOONS OLIVE OIL
1 LARGE CAULIFLOWER, DIVIDED INTO
   FLORETS
3 CLOVES OF GARLIC, LEFT WHOLE AND
   UNPEELED
50G FLAKED ALMONDS

1 ONION, FINELY CHOPPED
1.2 LITRES CHICKEN OR VEGETABLE STOCK
¼ TEASPOON SAFFRON
50ML SINGLE CREAM (OPTIONAL), PLUS A
   LITTLE EXTRA TO GARNISH
SALT AND PEPPER

1. Preheat the oven to 180°C/gas mark 4. Pour 2 tablespoons of olive oil into a roasting tin and add the cauliflower florets and unpeeled garlic cloves, tossing well to coat with oil. Bake for 20 minutes, until the florets are beginning to colour. Add the almonds, keeping a few back to use as garnish, mix well and bake for another 10 minutes.

2. Meanwhile, heat the remaining oil in a large pan over a medium heat and soften the onion. When the cauliflower is cooked, remove the garlic to a plate and tip the cauliflower into the pan with the onion. Squeeze the garlic out of its skin and add to the pan, along with the stock and the saffron. Bring to the boil, then turn down the heat and simmer, partially covered, for about 20–30 minutes, until the cauliflower is soft.

3. Use a mixer or stick blender to blend the soup to silky smoothness, then stir in the cream. Season to taste, divide between small bowls, and serve with a few of the reserved almonds in the middle, surrounded by a little cream.

Venison and stout stew with anchovy dumplings

SERVES 6

A couple of years ago, I spent a magical morning stalking deer on the lightly frosted South Downs. (Well, I wasn't really stalking, I was shadowing a gamekeeper, and trying desperately not to sniff, or step on any twigs.) We didn't manage to bag anything, but just the sound of the rutting stags, croaking away somewhere deep in the forest, for all the world like some enormous, ladykilling toads, was enough to make it worth the 4 a.m. start and the three hours of fiercely studied silence.

Fortunately, you don't have to get up that early to make this dish, although, because venison is quite lean, it does need long, slow cooking. However, you can prepare it up until the end of step 3 in advance – in which case, bring the casserole to a simmer on the hob while you make the dumplings as in step 4, then add the dumplings, re-cover, and cook for 25 minutes. Like most stews, it actually seems to taste better the next day. Good with kale or red cabbage.

3 TABLESPOONS VEGETABLE OIL
600G DICED VENISON
1 TABLESPOON FLOUR
SALT AND PEPPER
1 LARGE CARROT, DICED
1 ONION, FINELY SLICED
6 BABY TURNIPS, TRIMMED, OR 3 SMALL
   ONES, TRIMMED, PEELED AND CUT
   INTO WEDGES
1 TEASPOON JUNIPER BERRIES, CRUSHED
200ML CREAM/SWEET STOUT (MACKESON'S
   IS THE MOST WIDELY AVAILABLE NEAR ME)

2 TABLESPOONS REDCURRANT JELLY
1 TABLESPOON CIDER VINEGAR
500ML BEEF STOCK

FOR THE DUMPLINGS
100G PLAIN FLOUR
1 TEASPOON BAKING POWDER
50G SUET
A SMALL BUNCH OF FRESH HERBS
   (PARSLEY, CHIVES, TARRAGON WORK WELL –
   OR A MIX), CHOPPED
4 ANCHOVY FILLETS, FINELY CHOPPED

1. Preheat the oven to 150°C/gas mark 2. Heat 2 tablespoons of oil in a large lidded casserole pan over a medium-high heat, and, while it's warming up, toss the meat in the flour and season well. Brown it in batches, being careful not to overcrowd the pan, then remove and set aside.

2. Add the remaining oil to the pan and add the carrot, onion and turnips. Fry, stirring, until softened and beginning to turn golden, then stir in the juniper berries and cook for another couple of minutes.

3. Pour in a little stout and scrape the bottom of the pan to dislodge any flavourful crusted bits left by the meat, then add the rest, followed by the redcurrant jelly, vinegar and stock. Return the meat to the pan and season, then bring to a simmer, cover and put into the oven for about 3 hours, until the meat is tender.

4. Make the dumplings by putting all the ingredients into a bowl and stirring in enough cold water to just bring them together into a dough (about 80ml should be sufficient). Shape into 6 dumplings and place them on top of the stew. Put back into the oven, without the lid this time, and cook for another 25 minutes.

Almond and salted caramel chocolate terrine

SERVES 6

Perfectly amenable to being made a couple of days ahead, this solid block of chocolatey joy is so decadently rich that it's best served in thin slices – you'll certainly have some left over, as a reward the next day. And if you don't, you should take a long, hard look at yourselves.

A LITTLE VEGETABLE OIL, TO GREASE
400G DARK CHOCOLATE, BROKEN INTO
    PIECES
250G SALTED BUTTER, DICED
125G GOLDEN SYRUP
2 EGGS
100G SALTED ALMONDS
100G SHORTBREAD BISCUITS, BROKEN INTO
    PIECES
CRÈME FRAÎCHE, TO SERVE

FOR THE CARAMEL
250G CASTER SUGAR
125G SALTED BUTTER, DICED
100ML SINGLE CREAM
1 TEASPOON SEA SALT FLAKES

1. Line a 21cm loaf tin with lightly greased clingfilm. To make the caramel, put the sugar into a large pan with 75ml of water over a medium-high heat and stir until dissolved. Add the butter, stir to melt and simmer until it turns a toffee colour – this should take about 30 minutes.

2. Take the pan off the heat and stir in half the cream (be careful, it will spit), then cool slightly before stirring in the rest, along with the salt flakes. Taste, and add a little more salt if necessary (bear in mind the chocolate layer will be quite sweet). Pour into the prepared tin and chill until set.

3. Once the caramel's set, put the chocolate into a heatproof bowl set over a pan of simmering water, making sure it doesn't touch the water, and allow to melt, stirring occasionally to help it along. Meanwhile, melt the butter in a small saucepan and stir in the golden syrup.

4. Stir together the chocolate and the butter/syrup mixture, then beat in the eggs. Allow to cool to warm, then fold in the almonds and shortbread and pour on top of the caramel. Allow to cool to room temperature, then pop into the fridge to set.

5. Loosen the terrine all round with a knife and invert on a suitable plate. Carefully remove the clingfilm – the caramel should trickle down the sides of the terrine as you cut it, so don't worry if some sticks to the clingfilm.

6. Cut into slices with a sharp knife, and serve with a dollop of crème fraîche.

Astonishingly cheap menu

SERVES 4

A thrifty menu without a pulse or a piece of pasta in sight: what a relief. Don't feel you need to be feeling impecunious to indulge, however: this feast will hit the spot even on payday. It works all year round too, although you'd probably want to make a green salad to go with the main in warmer months, and perhaps serve it with pasta instead.

The ragù happily goes very well with the kind of wines generally described as 'rustic' or 'gutsy' – a Montepulciano d'Abruzzo, say, or a New World Shiraz.

Pea, feta and mint toasts

SERVES 4

A classic combination of summery flavours which is easily produced all year round, thanks to the wonder that is the frozen pea. (Because peas convert their sugars to starch so quickly after picking, they're one of those things which are often actually better frozen. Although you do miss out on the joy of podding them into your lap and pretending you're Catherine Zeta-Jones in *The Darling Buds of May*, for those of you who remember our Cath before she went off to Hollywood.)

If you're not so worried about money, then ciabatta is even better here – treat it in the same way but serve it up as bruschetta instead (for extra fancy points, make sure you pronounce it bruSKetta. They'll be so impressed they won't notice you're serving them peas on toast).

300G FROZEN PEAS	A SMALL BUNCH OF FRESH MINT, FINELY
3 TABLESPOONS EXTRA VIRGIN OLIVE OIL	CHOPPED
100G FETA, CRUMBLED	BLACK PEPPER
½ A LEMON	1 BAGUETTE

1.   Bring a pan of water to the boil, and tip in the peas. Allow them to sit and defrost for a couple of minutes, then drain.

2.   Put the peas, reserving a teaspoonful as a garnish, into a food processor with 1 tablespoon of oil, and pulse until you have a chunky purée – it shouldn't be smooth. Add the crumbled cheese and the zest of the lemon and pulse briefly to combine.

3.   Squeeze in lemon juice to taste, and stir in the chopped mint, reserving a teaspoonful as a garnish. Add a little black pepper, and refrigerate until you're ready to serve.

4.   Heat the grill and cut the baguette into slices. Arrange on a grill pan and drizzle with 1 tablespoon of oil. Season and grill until golden, then turn over and grill the other side.

5.   Garnish the dip with the reserved peas and mint, then spoon on to the toasts and drizzle the remaining oil on top before serving.

Ox cheek ragù with gremolata

SERVES 4

It seems, unfathomably, that some people are squeamish about ox cheek – whether this stems from the cheek's proximity to those big liquid brown eyes, I'm not sure, but I'm fairly certain they can't have actually tried it, because when slow cooked, ox cheek melts into the most deliciously tender, flavourful stew that ever graced the bargain bin. Of course, their weirdness is our gain, and it's still a pretty cheap option (if not quite as much of a steal as it was before we all started going on about it in print). If you can't face, or find, ox cheek, use shin of beef or another stewing cut instead. I'd serve this with mash or polenta (which, despite its fancy associations, is pretty cheap, as it ought to be, given it's only cornmeal. It's often particularly good value in the Caribbean section of the supermarket).

3 TABLESPOONS VEGETABLE OIL
800G OX CHEEK, CUT INTO LARGE CHUNKS
1 ONION, SLICED
1 LARGE CARROT, FINELY DICED
2 CLOVES OF GARLIC, SLICED
1 BAY LEAF
500ML BEEF STOCK
1 X 400G TIN OF CHOPPED TOMATOES
2 TABLESPOONS CORNFLOUR
SALT AND PEPPER

FOR THE GREMOLATA
ZEST OF 1 LEMON
4 TABLESPOONS CHOPPED FRESH FLAT-LEAF
 PARSLEY
1 CLOVE OF GARLIC, FINELY CHOPPED

1. Heat a third of the oil in a large casserole pan over a medium-high heat and brown the meat on all sides – you'll probably need to do this in three batches, adding a little more oil as you go. Scoop out and set aside.

2. Add the onion and the remaining oil, then turn the heat down slightly, add the carrot, and gently fry until both are soft. Add the garlic and bay leaf and fry for another couple of minutes.

3. Pour in the stock and scrape the bottom of the pan to dislodge any meaty bits. Add the tomatoes and the browned meat, stir well, bring to the boil, then turn down the heat, cover and simmer for about 3 hours, until the meat is tender enough to be cut with a spoon.

4. About 15 minutes before the end of cooking, put the cornflour into a mug, whisk in a couple of spoonfuls of sauce to make a smooth paste, and stir this into the pan. Simmer, uncovered, for the remaining cooking time until thickened. Season to taste.

5. To make the gremolata, mix together all the ingredients. Put the casserole on the table for people to help themselves, along with the gremolata and any mash or polenta.

Moroccan orange salad

SERVES 4

Some light relief after that gloriously rich and savoury meat. Like much fruit and veg, oranges are almost always cheaper in markets or small shops than they are in supermarkets, if you're lucky enough to have any left in your local area. This simple salad works well with natural yoghurt, but is pretty delicious on its own too, if you're feeling virtuous. You can make this a good few hours in advance, or even the day before, but don't add the mint until the last minute.

4 LARGE ORANGES
1 TEASPOON ICING SUGAR, SIFTED

½ TEASPOON GROUND MIXED SPICE
A HANDFUL OF FRESH MINT LEAVES

1. Cut the top and bottom off each orange, then use a knife to cut down around the circumference to remove the peel and pith. Cut into rings, and push out any pith from the middle of each. Arrange in an overlapping pattern on a platter and pour any juices from the chopping board on top.

2. Sprinkle over the icing sugar and mixed spice, then cover and refrigerate for at least an hour.

3. Just before serving, finely chop the mint and sprinkle over the top.

Vegetarian menu

SERVES 6

This menu could just as easily be titled 'a whistlestop tour of the Greater Middle East', taking in, as it does, Georgia, Iran and Turkey – with an even briefer detour up to Russia. Broadly speaking, these are not cuisines most of us tend to be terribly familiar with, Turkish kebabs aside, but this makes them ideal for impressing guests. After all, anyone can make a curry, or a moussaka, but only those with their finger on the cutting edge of culinary fashion (us foodies must suffer for our art) would cook up an Iranian rice dish, or some Georgian spinach. Make sure you get that in somewhere.

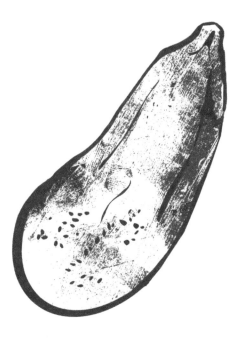

Moscow zakuski

Strictly speaking, neither of the following two little dishes is exclusively Russian: fresh cream cheese is made like this throughout Eastern Europe, and the spinach salad is actually from Georgia – but, although diplomatic relations between the two countries might not always be happy, Muscovites love their neighbour's food. I do too – happily there are no fewer than three Georgian restaurants within a twenty-minute cycle of my house, and I'm still trying to decide which does the best cheesebread: a fluffy round of oozy heaven that's the acceptable face of a stuffed-crust pizza round these parts. Such is my devotion to this dish that I seriously considered including it here, but then I realized that, realistically, just one slice will ruin you for any other food – and no one's ever stopped at a single slice.

The spinach salad I went for instead, intriguingly flavoured with fenugreek, coriander, saffron and dill, and studded with bright pomegranate seeds, is almost as good – and, with a homemade cheese (always one to wow the guests), perhaps even better. Certainly classier. Serve with warm flatbreads, cut into triangles.

Russian farmhouse cheese

SERVES 4

A small miracle, homemade cheese – but if you don't have time (really, there's only five minutes of work involved, mostly it does its own thing), Diana Henry gives an interesting recipe for Russian 'pot cheese' in *Roast Figs Sugar Snow*, which mashes together feta and soured cream to give a slightly similar result. It won't get you quite the same applause, though.

I LITRE WHOLE MILK	SALT
200ML BUTTERMILK	

1. Combine the milk and buttermilk in a large bowl, cover, and put somewhere warm for about 12 hours, until it develops the consistency of thick yoghurt. (Magic!)

2. Pour the mixture into a large saucepan and heat very gently for about 45 minutes, until the curds begin to separate from the whey – you'll see a large iceberg of curd, floating in a watery greenish sea of whey. Take off the heat and leave to cool until lukewarm.

3. Set a sieve over a large bowl and line it with cheesecloth or muslin. Pour the contents of the pan into it and leave it to drain for a few hours, squeezing any remaining liquid out of the bundle at the end. Add a generous pinch of salt and beat it into the cheese, then season to taste, decant into a bowl and refrigerate.

Georgian spinach and walnut salad

SERVES 6

In my limited, but greedy experience, Georgian cooks love their walnuts — and this salad, which includes both ground and whole examples, made me see them in an entirely different light. Turns out they're not just for brownies. I love the distinctive spicing too, quite different from anything you might come across further north or west — it's a country that's definitely on my to-do list.

IKG FRESH MATURE SPINACH

4 CLOVES OF GARLIC, CRUSHED

½ TEASPOON GROUND CORIANDER

½ TEASPOON GROUND FENUGREEK

A PINCH OF SAFFRON

SALT

200G WALNUTS, GROUND, PLUS A FEW EXTRA TO GARNISH

2 TABLESPOONS WHITE WINE VINEGAR

A SMALL BUNCH OF FRESH CORIANDER, FINELY CHOPPED

A SMALL BUNCH OF FRESH TARRAGON, FINELY CHOPPED

SEEDS FROM ½ A POMEGRANATE

WARM FLATBREADS, TO SERVE

1. Wash the spinach well and put it into a very large pan (I use a stock pot) with 2 tablespoons of water over a low heat. Cover and leave to wilt, shaking occasionally.

2. Tip the wilted spinach into a colander and use a wooden spoon to squeeze well until quite dry. When cool enough to handle, finely chop, or use a food processor to do the hard work.

3. Mix together the garlic, dried spices and a pinch of salt to make a paste, then add a quarter of the ground walnuts and mix together well. Tip in the rest of the nuts along with the vinegar and mix, then add enough water to make a thin paste.

4. Tip this into the spinach, add the fresh herbs, and mix well. Check the seasoning, then leave to sit at room temperature for at least a couple of hours — you can easily keep it overnight, but refrigerate if so.

5. When ready to serve, garnish with pomegranate seeds and a few extra walnuts. Serve with the cheese and some warm flatbreads, and try not to think of the cheesebread.

Roasted aubergines with jewelled pilaff and yoghurt

SERVES 6

I love the rich silkiness of the aubergines with this fabulously flamboyant rice dish, but meat-eaters might want to try it with simply grilled lamb or chicken instead (I have a vision of it with a sandalwood-smoky chicken kebab). Known as *jahaver polow* in its homeland of Iran, it's traditionally served heaped on enormous platters at weddings and other celebratory banquets, so, frankly, it can't fail to impress at a mere dinner party, however august the guests.

If you can't find tart red barberries (available dried online, or in Middle Eastern grocers', should you have one nearby), you can use dried sour cherries, cranberries or goji berries instead – the sourness is the important thing. Black onion seeds, otherwise known as nigella or kalonji, are commonly used in Indian cuisine, so if you can't find them, try an Indian grocer's – they're not essential, but they do look striking, and with this dish, that's the whole point.

FOR THE PILAFF

600G BASMATI RICE

SALT AND PEPPER

I CINNAMON STICK

4 TABLESPOONS BUTTER

2 LARGE CARROTS, GRATED

ZEST OF I ORANGE

100G SULTANAS, SOAKED IN
    BOILING WATER FOR 15
    MINUTES AND DRAINED

I RED ONION, FINELY SLICED

50G BARBERRIES OR DRIED
    CRANBERRIES, SOAKED IN BOILING
    WATER FOR 15 MINUTES AND
    DRAINED (OPTIONAL)

50G FLAKED ALMONDS

A LARGE PINCH OF SAFFRON, SOAKED
    IN 2 TABLESPOONS BOILING WATER FOR
    15 MINUTES

5 CARDAMOM PODS, CRUSHED

FINELY GRATED NUTMEG, TO TASTE

500G SHELLED PISTACHIO NUTS

2 TABLESPOONS BLACK ONION
    (AKA NIGELLA OR KALONJI) SEEDS

FOR THE AUBERGINES

12 FINGER AUBERGINES, OR 3 LARGE ONES

OLIVE OIL

I TABLESPOON CHILLI FLAKES

SALT AND PEPPER

500ML THICK NATURAL YOGHURT

JUICE OF ½ A LEMON

I CLOVE OF GARLIC, CRUSHED

A SMALL BUNCH OF FRESH MINT,
    ROUGHLY CHOPPED

1. Soak the rice in cold water for half an hour. Preheat the oven to 200°C/gas mark 6.

2. Trim the tops off the aubergines and, if using large ones, cut in half. Toss with a little olive oil and the chilli flakes and season well. Grease a roasting tin with olive oil and arrange the aubergines (cut side down if large) in one layer. Bake for about 25–40 minutes, depending on size, until tender: keep an eye on them in case they start to burn.

3. Meanwhile put the drained rice into a large pan with 550ml of cold water, a pinch of salt, the cinnamon stick and 1 tablespoon of butter. Bring to the boil and stir, then cover tightly and turn the heat right down. Simmer for 25 minutes, then turn off the heat.

4. As the rice is cooking, heat 1 tablespoon of butter in a frying pan over a medium heat and add the carrots and orange zest. Fry until soft, then remove from the pan and set aside. Add another tablespoon of butter to the pan and fry the sultanas and red onion until soft. Take out of the pan and repeat with the barberries and almonds in separate batches, using the remaining tablespoon of butter.

5. Mix together the yoghurt, lemon juice, crushed garlic and mint, and season well.

6. When the rice is done, stir in the saffron water, cardamom and a grating of nutmeg and season.

7. Decant the rice on to a serving platter and stripe with the pistachios, black onion seeds, carrot, sultana and red onion, barberries and almonds. Serve immediately, with the aubergines and yoghurt sauce.

Earl Grey apricots with orange blossom cream

SERVES 6

This dish is loosely inspired by a Turkish dessert in Claudia Roden's excellent book *Arabesque* – as usual I couldn't resist fiddling about with it, and adding my favourite Earl Grey tea. Orange flower water varies greatly in strength, so use it with caution or you may end up with something more like shower gel than pudding.

300G DRIED APRICOTS
1 EARL GREY TEABAG
2 TABLESPOONS CASTER SUGAR
1 TABLESPOON LEMON JUICE

100G SHELLED PISTACHIO NUTS
ZEST OF 1 ORANGE
ORANGE FLOWER WATER, TO TASTE
225G CRÈME FRAÎCHE

1. Put the apricots into a bowl and cover with boiling water. Add the teabag and leave to soak for at least 4 hours, or overnight.

2. Drain the apricots, and pour 100ml of the soaking water into a small saucepan over a medium heat. Add the sugar, stir until dissolved, then simmer until thick and syrupy. Stir in the lemon juice.

3. Meanwhile, stuff each apricot with 2 or 3 pistachios. Stir the orange zest and a little orange flower water into the crème fraîche, adding the latter drop by drop to taste.

4. Serve the apricots with the syrup poured over them, and the orange cream on the side.

Full-throttle seduction dinner

SERVES 2

Cooking is popularly supposed to be a great way to someone's heart – personally, given a choice, I prefer to leave the garlic chopping and fish scaling to the professionals for the first few dates, but once you're sure things are going well, it's a cunning way to show off your skills, and get a bit tipsy together within easy reach of a comfortable sofa.

This menu is designed to be mainly made in advance, with just enough cooking à la minute to dispel any suspicion that you've delegated the task to Mr Marks and Ms Spencer. It's also fairly light – so if they fall asleep before you've offered them coffee, you've only your own conversation to blame.

Asparagus or purple sprouting broccoli with Parmesan butter

SERVES 2

Asparagus is popularly supposed to be seductive because of its vaguely phallic, if rather spindly shape. Pure of mind, however, I like it because it's the kind of food best enjoyed with your fingers – getting any potential awkwardness out of the way with the first course. (Who can remain aloof when they're licking hot butter from their fingertips?) Also, of course, asparagus is one of the few vegetables to remain resolutely seasonal, so it's always a treat – for the rest of the year, use sprouting broccoli, which is almost as delicious, and even less priapic.

25G UNSALTED BUTTER, AT ROOM
TEMPERATURE
10G PARMESAN, GRATED
BLACK PEPPER
¼ OF A LEMON

8 SLIM ASPARAGUS STALKS (OR PURPLE OR
WHITE SPROUTING OR TENDERSTEM
BROCCOLI STALKS, IF OUTSIDE ASPARAGUS
SEASON)

1. Put the butter into a bowl with the grated cheese and mash with a good grinding of black pepper until well mixed. Add the zest of the lemon and a squeeze of juice and mash again, then refrigerate until ready to cook.

2. Bring a saucepan of salted water to the boil. Meanwhile, trim the woody ends off the asparagus: you may be loath to waste any, but trust me, picking fibrous bits out of your teeth is never a good look.

3. Put the asparagus, stems down, into the boiling water, resting the heads against the side of the saucepan if possible, so they slowly slip down into the water (this helps prevent them overcooking). Cook for 4–6 minutes, until tender but not mushy (this will depend on the thickness of the stalks), then drain well on kitchen paper.

4. Put the hot asparagus on to a warm serving plate and rub the Parmesan butter on top so it begins to melt and coat the spears. Serve immediately, and eat with fingers, and visible relish.

Pollack en papillote with basil and tomatoes, and crushed potatoes

SERVES 2

The idea here is that you open the little parcels of fish with a flourish at the table, releasing a cloud of lemon-scented, herbal steam (ladies, remember the waterproof mascara), so it's important that you seal them tightly with staples or a paperclip.

I LEMON

8 TABLESPOONS OLIVE OIL, PLUS EXTRA
    TO BRUSH

SALT AND PEPPER

2 FILLETS OF POLLACK, OR OTHER FIRM
    WHITE FISH

10 SEMI-DRIED TOMATOES

A SMALL HANDFUL OF FRESH BASIL LEAVES

I TABLESPOON CAPERS OR STONED BLACK
    OLIVES

2 TABLESPOONS WHITE WINE

400G WAXY POTATOES, SCRUBBED AND
    CUT IN HALF

1. Mix together the zest of the lemon and half the olive oil in a bowl and season. Add the fish and leave to marinate in the fridge for a couple of hours.

2. Preheat the oven to 180°C/gas mark 4 and put a large pan of salted water on to boil for the potatoes. Make a parcel by cutting two squares of parchment paper about 30cm across, and brushing with olive oil. Divide the tomatoes between the two, and top with the basil and the capers or olives. Arrange the fish on top, drizzling over the marinade, and sprinkle over the juice of half the lemon and the wine. Bring the edges of the paper together and secure with a paperclip or staples to make an airtight parcel (if you don't have these to hand, you could wrap them in foil). Place the parcels on a baking tray and put into the oven for about 15 minutes, until cooked through.

3. Meanwhile, cook the potatoes in the boiling water for about 12 minutes, until tender. Drain well, return them to the pan, put back on the heat for 30 seconds to dry, then add the rest of the olive oil, season, and mash roughly with a fork or potato masher so they're crushed but not smooth. Scoop into a bowl and put on the table.

4. Put the papillote parcels on plates and take to the table to be opened there – hopefully in a cloud of scented steam.

My last Rolo

SERVES 2

I'd apologize for giving a second chocolate and caramel recipe in this chapter, but I'm not in the least sorry: it's a glorious combination. And, strictly speaking, this is toffee anyway. The recipe makes a lot more of that confection than you'll need, but it's hard to make in very small quantities, and anyway, who doesn't want a freezer full of toffee?

The entire recipe can be made in advance: you can do it weeks ahead if you happen to be incredibly well prepared (in fact, if you're a habitual lothario or -ess, having a supply on tap might not be a bad thing). You'll need microwaveable clingfilm, sturdy ice cube trays, and, preferably, a sugar thermometer (which makes it sound more complicated than it is).

FOR THE TOFFEE	FOR THE FONDANTS
VEGETABLE OIL, TO GREASE	60G UNSALTED BUTTER, PLUS A LITTLE EXTRA
300G CASTER SUGAR	TO GREASE
75G UNSALTED BUTTER	60G DARK CHOCOLATE
200ML DOUBLE CREAM	1 EGG PLUS 1 YOLK
75ML GOLDEN SYRUP	45G CASTER SUGAR
¼ TEASPOON SEA SALT FLAKES	A PINCH OF SALT
	1 TABLESPOON PLAIN FLOUR

1. Start by making the toffee. Grease two pieces of microwaveable clingfilm with vegetable oil and use to line two heatproof ice cube trays, pressing it down into the holes. Place near the hob.

2. Put the sugar into a large pan over a low heat with 35ml of water and heat until it dissolves and turns golden. Take off the heat and add the butter, cream, golden syrup and salt. Put back on the heat and bring to the boil.

3. Reduce the heat and allow to bubble gently until it reaches about 120°C on your sugar thermometer, by which point it will be the same colour as the inside of a Rolo. Take off the heat immediately and carefully spoon into the ice cube trays, bearing in mind it will be incredibly hot (no tasting). Cool to room temperature, then freeze until solid. To remove the cubes, leave the tray out of the freezer for 15 minutes and then use a knife to gently ease out each cube and peel off the clingfilm. The toffee cubes store well for a week in a plastic bag, either in the freezer or in the fridge.

4. To make the fondants, grease two deep ovenproof ramekins generously with butter, then put the 60g each of butter and chocolate into a heatproof bowl set over, but not touching, a pan of simmering water and stir occasionally until melted. Allow to cool slightly.

5. Vigorously whisk together the egg, yolk, sugar and a pinch of salt until pale and fluffy. Gently fold in the melted chocolate and butter, and then the flour. Spoon into the prepared moulds, stopping just shy of the top – at this point the mixture can be refrigerated until needed, or even frozen, as the puddings will not wait around once cooked. If you're going to freeze them, push a piece of toffee into the middle when they're cool, but before you put them into the freezer. Otherwise allow them to cool.

6. When you're ready to cook, preheat the oven to 200°C/gas mark 6. Push a piece of toffee into the middle of each pudding and bake for 14 minutes (18 from frozen). Because of the stickiness of the toffee, these don't turn out very gracefully, so serve them in the ramekins as soon as they come out of the oven, while the outside is still molten.

Child-friendly menu

Although all non-parents like me fondly imagine our own offspring will be different, children can be fussy little customers, often viewing new foodstuffs with suspicion rather than the appropriate excitement. It's probably not your job, as host to your delightful nieces and nephews, or your friend's four-year-old, to force-feed them anchovies, or give them a practical education on the Scoville chilli heat scale, but that doesn't mean you have to cook them baked beans on toast either – unless their parents specifically request it. I was brought up to believe that children and adults should eat together, and this menu, with its dips and its meatballs and its frosty chocolate, should hopefully please both.

Traffic light dips

SERVES ABOUT 6

Finger food isn't just good for clumsy seduction – the potential for mess means that children love it too, so watch your soft furnishings. The smooth tomato salsa below is the kind of thing you often find on the table at Mexican restaurants, but, if your children aren't spice lovers, you can easily omit the chilli and it will still be pretty delicious – and ditto the cumin seeds in the carrot hummous. Serve the dips with crudités.

Smooth tomato salsa

4 TOMATOES, CORED AND ROUGHLY
   CHOPPED
½ A GREEN CHILLI (OPTIONAL)
3 CLOVES OF GARLIC, PEELED AND
   ROUGHLY CHOPPED

¼ TEASPOON SALT
1 TABLESPOON OLIVE OIL
½ TEASPOON GROUND CORIANDER
½ TEASPOON GROUND CUMIN
A PINCH OF SUGAR

1. Put the tomatoes, chilli, if using, garlic and salt into a food processor or blender and purée.

2. Heat the oil in a frying pan and add the coriander and cumin. Fry for a minute, then add the tomato mixture and a pinch of sugar. Simmer for about 20 minutes, until it has turned a dark red colour and thickened, then check the seasoning and allow to cool before serving.

Roasted carrot hummous

4 MEDIUM CARROTS, PEELED AND CHOPPED
4 CLOVES OF GARLIC, WHOLE AND UNPEELED
2 TABLESPOONS OLIVE OIL
½ TEASPOON CUMIN SEEDS (OPTIONAL)

50G COOKED CHICKPEAS
3 TABLESPOONS TAHINI
JUICE OF 1 LEMON
SALT AND PEPPER

1. Preheat the oven to 200°C/gas mark 6 and put the carrots into a roasting tin with the garlic, 1 tablespoon of oil and the cumin seeds, if using. Toss well to coat, then roast for 30 minutes, until starting to caramelize.

2. Allow to cool slightly, then put into a food processor with the remaining ingredients and whiz to a smooth purée. Adjust the seasoning before serving.

Pea pesto dip

400G FROZEN PEAS
SALT AND PEPPER
3 TABLESPOONS PINE NUTS

2 TABLESPOONS EXTRA VIRGIN OLIVE OIL
5 TABLESPOONS GRATED PARMESAN
3 STEMS OF FRESH BASIL, LEAVES ONLY

1. Cook the peas in boiling, salted water until tender (this should only take a couple of minutes), then drain, reserving a little of the cooking water. Heat a dry frying pan and add the pine nuts. Toast until aromatic and beginning to colour.

2. Put the peas and pine nuts, plus a little of the pea cooking water, into a food processor along with the other ingredients and whiz to a purée. Adjust the seasoning before serving.

Hungarian meatballs

SERVES ABOUT 6

Meatballs have somehow overcome the impediment of a distinctly unpromising, if helpfully descriptive name to become rather trendy in recent years – in fact, an entire restaurant devoted to them opened near me quite recently. Children, being the future, and as such at the cutting edge of such trends, have cottoned on to this and, in my experience, like them more than big chunks of solid meat. Although this is spicy, it's not hot – the sweet paprika and soured cream see to that, so it's suitable for even the most delicate of palates.

100ML MILK

2 THICK SLICES OF BREAD

400G MINCED BEEF

400G MINCED PORK

4 TEASPOONS CARAWAY SEEDS

1 RED CHILLI, DESEEDED AND FINELY
   CHOPPED

SALT AND PEPPER

3 TABLESPOONS OLIVE OIL

2 ONIONS, THINLY SLICED

1 LARGE RED PEPPER, DESEEDED AND SLICED

1 TABLESPOON SMOKED SWEET PAPRIKA

A PINCH OF SOFT BROWN SUGAR

1 X 400G TIN OF TOMATOES

150ML BEEF STOCK

2 TABLESPOONS SOURED CREAM

500G FRESH TAGLIATELLE

A SMALL KNOB OF BUTTER

A SMALL BUNCH OF FRESH CHIVES,
   CHOPPED, TO SERVE

1. Pour the milk into a shallow bowl, add the bread and leave to soak for 10 minutes. Put the meat into a large bowl with the caraway seeds and chopped chilli, then wring out the bread, mash it into a pulp and add to the bowl. Season and mix well. Form into balls about the size of a ping-pong ball (or smaller, depending on the size of the children you're feeding), put on a plate, cover and chill while you make the sauce.

2. Heat 2 tablespoons of olive oil in a large deep frying pan and add the onions and pepper. Cook over a medium-high heat until softened, then stir in the paprika and sugar and cook for another minute. Add the tomatoes and stock, season and bring to the boil. Simmer for about 25 minutes, until reduced. Taste and adjust the seasoning if necessary.

3. Heat 1 tablespoon of olive oil in a frying pan on a medium-high heat and fry the meatballs in batches, until caramelized all over. Once they're caramelized, put them all back into the pan, turn the heat down to medium-low and leave, stirring occasionally, until they're all cooked through.

4. Meanwhile, reheat the sauce if necessary and stir in the soured cream. Put a large pan of salted water on to boil and cook the pasta according to the packet instructions. Drain, then toss with the butter.

5. Add the pasta to the sauce, toss well to coat, and serve with the meatballs and a sprinkling of chives.

Iced berries with white chocolate and cardamom sauce

SERVES ABOUT 6

I discovered this dessert in a cookbook published by London's The Ivy in its celeb-studded 1990s heyday, and which somehow found its way on to my un-celeb-like parents' coffee table at around the same time. Greedy and impressionable teenager that I was, I pored over it, hoping recipes like salmon fishcakes and bang-bang chicken would bring me closer to regulars like Brad Pitt and Kate Moss – but the only one I ever actually made was their Scandinavian iced berries. Although the stars may have moved on, I still think this dish is cool: I suspect that the pleasure lies, for me, in its resemblance to that wonderfully gloopy chocolate sauce from the 1980s, which solidified when it hit ice cream – a rare childhood treat. Hopefully today's more sophisticated small people will be just as impressed.

250ML DOUBLE CREAM
3 CARDAMOM PODS, CRUSHED
500G FROZEN BERRIES
A HANDFUL OF FLAKED ALMONDS

250G WHITE CHOCOLATE (I STILL LIKE
   MILKYBAR), BROKEN INTO CHUNKS
A PINCH OF SEA SALT

1. Put the cream and cardamom pods into a small pan and heat gently until just simmering. Take off the heat and leave to infuse for at least 20 minutes.

2. Get the fruit out of the freezer about 15 minutes before you're planning to serve, and divide between plates or bowls.

3. Toast the flaked almonds in a dry frying pan until golden.

4. Reheat the cream, remove the cardamom pods and add the chocolate. Stir until melted, then add a pinch of sea salt.

5. Drizzle the hot chocolate sauce over the frozen berries and scatter a few almonds over the top. Serve immediately.

Teatime

Afternoon tea remains a peculiarly British practice and, these days, an increasingly rare one – sadly, the tiresome burden of earning an honest crust tends to eat into this thoroughly civilized institution. As Constance Spry wistfully observes in her inimitable cookbook, 'the very word tea-time has a nostalgic ring for those of us who remember the past with delight. In those days the dispositions of a woman's time made tea-time possible, and the taste for, shall I say, the cosier figure gave no cause for misapprehension.'

Although Charles II's Queen, the Portuguese Catherine of Braganza, is widely credited with having introduced tea to Britain in the seventeenth century (an occasion I feel surely deserves an extra bank holiday at the very least), tea didn't really take off for another hundred years or so, until the government relaxed the taxes on its import and sale, and it came within the reach of the middle classes.

Initially tea was taxed in liquid form, which meant that tea houses would brew an enormous barrel in the morning, which, once it had been inspected by the excise officer, would then be served, nicely stewed, throughout the day. So punitive were these taxes that by the latter half of the eighteenth century it was estimated that more tea was being smuggled into Britain than was imported legally – who would think that the humble cup of cha (food nerd fact: from the Chinese) was once so sought after?

The new drink wasn't universally embraced, however; John Wesley, the founder of the Methodist movement, preached complete abstinence, on the basis that excessive consumption had given him a 'Paralytick disorder' (although, later in life, he fell off the wagon), and the eighteenth-century philanthropist Jonas Hanway claimed that, thanks to the shocking tea-drinking habits of British women, 'there is not quite so much beauty in this land as there was'.

Old Samuel Johnson, who sounds like he was rather more fun than either, described himself proudly as 'a hardened and shameless tea drinker' – and indeed, I can imagine compiling the first proper dictionary of the English language was a task that called for many, many a strong cup of builder's.

Despite the best efforts of these well-meaning sorts, as soon as tea became more affordable it became a national obsession – and, in fact, a key weapon of the temperance movement, which, far from believing tea was a gateway drug to harder drinks, as Hanway claimed, saw it as a respectable substitute for alcohol: people were often encouraged to sign the pledge with the offer of a free cup of tea. Not much of a bargain as far as I'm concerned.

The notion of afternoon tea as a meal is generally credited to the seventh Duchess of Bedford, who famously instituted the custom in the 1840s to combat that 'sinking feeling' around five o'clock, but while Anna Maria may have popularized the idea of serving food with the tea which was already a key part of the fashionable social routine, she certainly didn't invent it. The 1821 Scottish novel *The Ayrshire Legatees* gives an approving description of the economical teas that were the norm in London at the time – 'only plain flimsy loaf and butter is served – no such thing as short-bread, seed-cake, bun, marmlet, or jeelly to be seen' – while the Edinburgh novelist Henry MacKenzie claimed that 'tea was the meal of ceremony' in his eighteenth-century childhood, boasting that 'we had fifty odd kinds of teabread'. Perhaps the Scots should take the glory for afternoon tea, then, rather than this aristocrat whose only other achievement was being named chief mourner at Princess Augusta's funeral.

Whoever we have to thank for it, afternoon tea remained a rarefied pleasure until the last half of the Victorian era. It wasn't until commuting became a way of life that the middle-class British dinner was pushed back to as late as seven o'clock (in 1798 Jane Austen's household dined at half-past three!), allowing for another meal between it and lunch. As the historian Arnold Palmer notes, 'English internal engines, designed for refuelling every four and a half hours, begin to labour when asked to run for six hours at a stretch.'

Afternoon tea was also a social occasion: a rare opportunity for informality – by Victorian standards at least. You may have just been able to drop in, but etiquette manuals suggested serving biscuits, so ladies didn't have to remove their kid leather gloves to eat. For the working classes, however, tea meant something quite different – as Mrs Beeton observes, there's 'Tea and Tea', and for most people, tea meant High Tea, or the one hot meal of the day, eaten after work, followed, perhaps, by supper just before bed.

Flora Thompson's *Lark Rise to Candleford* describes a rural tea thus: 'bacon from the flitch, vegetables from the garden, and … a roly-poly', or, at a bigger farm, 'fried ham and eggs, cakes and scones and stewed plums and cream, jam and jelly and junket'. It would have been the 'one hot meal a day … taken in the evening, when the men were home from the fields and the children from school, for neither could get home at midday'.

An afternoon tea, by contrast, according to Mrs Beeton, 'signifies little more than tea and bread-and-butter, and a few elegant trifles in the way of cake and fruit. The meal is simply to enable a few friends to meet and talk comfortably and quietly.' Which is exactly what we're after here. Afternoon tea is all the more of a treat for being a rare pleasure these days: an excuse to have people round for a natter one weekend afternoon, when you might have rolled out of bed at lunchtime, and ideal for visiting parents, or simply to stave off hunger pangs after a brisk walk, when it seems a long time until dinner.

Setting the scene

Arabella Boxer wisely observes in her classic *Book of English Food* that, in the glory days of afternoon tea, 'the keynote was simplicity, and lack of ostentation'. In other words, don't make things too hectic: this isn't the WI cake competition. One or two savoury things, depending on numbers, and a cake are quite sufficient for most teas. Instead, expend your creative energies on the atmosphere: the pleasure of afternoon tea comes as much from playing the languid Edwardian hostess as it does from the dainties themselves, so a bit of effort will pay rich dividends.

Ideally, a summer tea will take place underneath the spreading branches of a shady tree, but if you, like me, are not lucky enough to have one of these in your possession at this stage in life, you might have to improvise. You can of course turn it into a picnic tea, as long as you're close enough to the house to provide fresh boiling water for tea when required (this, after all, is the excuse upon which the whole idea of cake in the afternoon hangs), but I think that even if you don't have enough chairs to seat everyone, a small table for the food and tea things is essential. Not only is balancing pots of hot water on bumpy rugs a perilous exercise, but a table, particularly a well-laid one, lends a certain elegance to the occasion.

If you don't have any outside space, throw open as many windows and doors as possible, and fake a garden with a bunch of flowers, preferably something suitably artless and cottage garden-esque, rather than exotic hothouse blooms. (Our local farmers' market is a good source of stocks, sweet williams and the like.)

The wintry equivalent of that graceful tree is a cheerful fire – even if you've learnt the hard way that toasters were invented for a reason, it's still nice to munch hot buttered crumpets in its flickering glow on a cold, dark afternoon. Failing this, however, a judicious use of lamps and candles should create an appropriately cosy atmosphere (the Danish concept of *hygge*, or welcoming warmth, should be your inspiration here). Think cushions, tartan rugs and soft lighting.

Laying the table

Wherever you are, the aforementioned table will be the focus of your tea, whether you're all arranged loosely around it, or simply help yourself from it before going to sit elsewhere, so make sure you make it look good. As previously mentioned, I'm a sucker for a tablecloth – although, to be honest, I often press a flowery duvet cover into service instead, because I have a large table, and a small budget, and they come in prettier patterns – but if your table is presentable enough, you can go for a farmhouse-as-imagined-by-Hollywood look, and put the dishes straight on there.

The very ceremony of throwing an afternoon tea is romantic enough for you not to need to do too much other work in the way of table decorations, but if you do have some pretty china, now's the time to use it. Whatever your mum might say, it doesn't matter if it's all different – a quick flick through any food magazine should be enough to reassure you that matching sets are about as fashionable as fish in aspic – as long as it suggests a break from the sturdy, plain Ikea-type stuff you use on a day-to-day basis.

I find charity shops and tatty markets are a good source of comically clashing crockery, as are grandparents' cupboards (make sure it's a voluntary downsizing though, you don't want to make off with the cake plate they were clutching when they first saw your granddad at the church dance).

Ideally, use classic teacups and saucers, rather than the enormous mugs we all glug from the rest of the time. Yes, they hold pitifully little, but the very act of holding them delicately with your fingertips will make society ladies (or gentlemen) of you all, and people are more likely to really savour your carefully made tea if it's on the ration. The saucers can also act as plates, which is particularly handy if you're not sitting at the table.

If you're serving cake, it's probably best to put out some forks (one day I hope to acquire a set of dainty little forks for this specific purpose), but otherwise, most other things can be eaten with fingers – which demand napkins. As I may have mentioned, I'm a firm believer in the cloth variety, but as few people under fifty seem to recognize their charms, I'll reluctantly allow a paper napkin: anything as long as it's not a sheet of kitchen paper.

Before your guests arrive, lay out the food, preferably on pleasing plates and dishes (in my experience, a cake-stand makes even the wonkiest sponge look more impressive), along with the plates and cutlery and teacups or mugs, each with its own teaspoon if possible. You'll also need a pot of sugar with its own spoon, and a jug of milk: Mrs Spry notes that it is 'permissible to leave jam in its pot set on a plate unless you possess a nice, plain glass jar', but I really don't think the same rules apply to ugly plastic bottles of milk, or butter packets. Milk jugs aren't expensive (you can use a sauceboat in extremity) and, given you probably won't use it terribly often, you'll never need to buy another, and butter lives happily on a plate.

In fact, ban all packaging, save for the unusually charming, from your table: should you supplement your homemade baking with a sneaky party ring or two, decant them on to plates. There's nothing Edwardian about cellophane. Depending on your level of sophistication, you may also wish to offer slices of lemon to put in tea.

If you're inside, and dealing in crumpets or similar, putting the toaster on the table, as Yotam Ottolenghi's cafés do at breakfast time, is an excellent idea: I get very twitchy if the toasted goods are allowed to cool for a single minute before I attack them with a butter-laden knife. (From experience, I'd strongly advise emptying the crumb tray, if it has one, before moving it.)

Food

Mrs Spry is also reassuring on the vulgarity of excess at teatime: 'it was not then considered good taste to have too many small things', she writes. 'One good plum cake, one light cake, perhaps of the sponge or sponge-sandwich variety, or an orange cake, iced, might appear, and a hot dish of crumpets or buttered toast, anchovy toast or hot tea cakes…' Unless you're feeding the five thousand, I think it's quite proper to confine yourself to just the one cake, perhaps some biscuits, and a single savoury or toasted item. People can always be prevailed upon to lend a hand by bringing a contribution: baked goods don't cost much, and if you give them a theme, it can turn quite weird and wonderful (for sheer nostalgia value, I usually suggest 'children's party'. Bring on the Tunnocks tea cakes).

Drinks

Tea is the obvious thing here, but leaving that aside for a minute, if it's a hot day you might also like to offer lemonade or iced tea, recipes for which appear below. A jug of cold water, with a few lemon slices and mint leaves, is a less labour-intensive substitute. For a particularly festive tea – as part of a hen party, for example – chilled fizz is always appropriate. I'd probably be minded to go for prosecco here, either plain or as part of a Bellini (page 110), to suit the sweeter flavours of the cake.

Which brings us to the ostensible point of the whole exercise: the tea. Unless you really couldn't give a fig for the stuff, which doesn't mean you're barred from munching on cake mid-afternoon, please give some more thought to it than simply making some murky mugs of the corner shop's cheapest. Or at least try some others before you buy it – sticking with PG Tips without sampling any other kind of tea is a little bit like deciding you like Jacobs Creek Chardonnay and sticking with it for life. There are other things out there. Here's a brief guide to the possibilities awaiting you:

Black tea The most common kind in this country, black tea is made from leaves which are crushed and then left out to oxidize, giving them a dark colour and a robust flavour. English breakfast is a typical example, but you might also wish to try Darjeeling, which has a slightly astringent, refreshing flavour (ideal for an afternoon pick-me-up, in my opinion), Assam, which is stronger and maltier, and Ceylon, from Sri Lanka, which is crisp tasting and rather pale in colour.

Scented black teas are also popular in the afternoon. The classic Earl Grey is my favourite: the citrus peel flavour is particularly lovely in the summer, while smoky Chinese Lapsang Souchong, dried over fires, is more of a winter choice. Jasmine tea, meanwhile, is flavoured with flower blossoms.

Victoria Moore describes Oolong as 'the rosé wine of tea' in her excellent book *How to Drink* because the leaves are only allowed to oxidize slightly, giving it a more delicate flavour.

Green tea Instead of being rolled and left out to dry like black tea, the leaves for green tea are steamed so they retain their natural colour, hence the name. According to the UK Tea Council, both have similar levels of antioxidants and minerals – although in my experience, green tea drinkers tend to have higher levels of smugness all the same. Neither it, nor white tea, are drunk with milk. Ever.

White tea White tea is lucky enough not to be subjected to any form of violence: instead, the leaves are simply dried, giving them a subtle, delicate flavour and colour.

I won't deny that the larger part of my tea consumption comes from a bag, so, although I am trying hard to wean myself off this habit – tea leaves are only slightly more fiddly than coffee grounds, after all – I'm not really in a position to issue any lectures on the subject, except to say that most of the best teas are only available in loose form. All you need to brew them is a teapot (a Briton's birthright), and a strainer, for which I use a miniature sieve I picked up in the local pound-shop. George Orwell claimed that 'if the tea is not loose in the pot it never infuses properly' and who am I to argue with him?

Brewing up

Never do this in advance:

Tea should be made fresh, so wait until your guests have sat down, and stopped fussing about coats, or hand-washing, or all the other little pleasantries that accompany a polite arrival.

As touched upon above, a teapot is non-negotiable. Teabags infused directly in a mug, however capacious, will always be too strong, unless you whip it out immediately, in which case you'll miss out on much of the flavour.

1. Warm the pot

The jury's out on this time-honoured custom, which is said to date from the times when a pot of tea would be brought up to the drawing-room by servants, and then decanted into a smarter vessel for serving. I like to do it because, as I don't allow detergent near my teapot, it gives it another swill out, but it's not strictly necessary.

2. Add the tea to the pot

One teaspoon, or teabag, per person plus one 'for the pot' will usually do it, but obviously teas differ, so experiment to suit your taste. Do this while the kettle's boiling, so the pot is ready and waiting.

3. Boil the kettle

As a general rule, tea should be made with freshly boiled water (green and white teas should be made with slightly cooler water, around 60–80°C if possible) from a newly filled kettle; water that's already been boiled once will lack oxygen, and this will affect the flavour of the tea. As soon as it boils (if you're using a stovetop kettle, or pan of water, don't let it keep boiling, as it will lose oxygen), pour it into the prepared pot and leave it to infuse. How long depends on the tea, but 3 minutes is generally a safe bet.

4. Pour the tea

Traditionally, it's the host's job to 'be mother' and pour the tea for everyone at the party because, even at the grandest houses, it was a servantless meal (what japes!). Arabella Boxer claims that 'even when there were fifty people staying … the hostess was still expected to pour out the tea herself, and the guests would pass it from hand to hand until everyone had been served'. As you're unlikely to be serving so many, I think it's a nice custom to keep – it'll make people feel special.

5. Relax, your work is done

Leave them to add milk, if required, and sugar themselves. I prefer semi-skimmed in tea (and English breakfast and Assam only): full-fat tends to leave a greasy residue on the surface, and the depressingly insipid skimmed has no place in any respectable kitchen. Sugar-wise, white is fine: unrefined sorts have too strong a caramel flavour. I am firmly in the milk second camp, even when I'm just making tea for myself – me and G. Orwell are agreed that this allows one to 'exactly regulate the amount of milk whereas one is liable to put in too much milk if one does it the other way round'.

6. Well, not quite

If you've got a bigger pot than party, remember that tea will quickly progress from brewed to stewed. If you're using bags, you can whip them out at this point (discreetly, they always have a slightly seedy look about them), but otherwise, you'll need to make a fresh pot once cups need refilling.

Iced tea

MAKES 1 JUG

I only really get on with iced tea when it tastes like tea – all those strangely flavoured variations, so popular in the States, charm me about as much as your average fruit tea. This one is extremely refreshing: rumour has it it works well with a dash of gin, but I couldn't possibly comment.

6 HEAPED TEASPOONS EARL GREY TEA
(OR 6 TEABAGS, IF YOU MUST)
1.2 LITRES BOILING WATER
1–3 TABLESPOONS CASTER SUGAR,
ACCORDING TO TASTE

A SMALL BUNCH OF FRESH MINT
1 ORANGE OR LEMON, THINLY SLICED
ICE CUBES, TO TOP

1. Put the tea into a jug and pour on the water. Leave to steep for 15 minutes, then strain and discard the leaves. Stir in the sugar to taste, and chill.

2. When you're ready to serve, add the mint, slices of citrus and a copious number of ice cubes.

Elderflower lemonade

Make lemonade as on page 293, but, instead of adding gin, add 150ml of elderflower cordial.

Savoury

Sandwiches

I have a photograph somewhere of the instructions, on display at the National Railway Museum in York (a surprisingly good day out – the silverware from the old dining-cars is quite something to behold), for making an authentic British Rail sandwich. Younger readers will not remember this sad affair, the butt of every joke, but suffice to say the recipe was principally concerned with economy, rather than gastronomy, and involved margarine (it didn't, however, mention that the bread had to be at least three days old to qualify as suitable).

You might think you need no such instruction, but there are some aspects of sandwich preparation which bear repetition.

First of all, don't skimp on the bread: it's the public face of the entire dish, and there's no point shelling out on decent Cheddar and then shrouding it in squidgy cotton wool. Some sandwiches, like the cucumber ones on page 171, work with softer breads than others.

Second, butter is your friend. No one wants big wodges of the stuff (well, it's quite a niche taste anyway) but a thin layer on BOTH sides will act as a sealant, preventing the filling from making the bread soggy. This is particularly important when damp ingredients like tomatoes or chutneys are involved: there's not a war on.

Third, although you shouldn't skimp on filling, afternoon tea is not the time or the place for American diner-sized affairs, overflowing with meat and cheese. You should be able to eat them with your hands, without the need for a bib.

Fourth, don't forget that sandwiches need seasoning, just like everything else. The simpler the sandwich, the more important this is.

I doubt you need any help with the usual sandwich suspects – ham and mustard, cheese and pickle, egg mayonnaise and so on – but here are a few more exciting ideas, should you tire of the classics.

Egg and cress

MAKES 8 SMALL SANDWICHES

'Watercress for tea is essentially English. You get it in the most unexpected places!
I have had it in country cottages, in cathedral city tea-rooms, and the British Museum.'
– Dorothy Hartley, *Food in England* (1954)

Not quite what it says on the tin – inspired by the evocative description above, I've used robustly peppery watercress instead of the more delicate salad cress, and rich Finnish-style egg butter instead of gloopy mayonnaise. This makes the sandwiches much easier to eat without recourse to a napkin, and, if you're transporting them anywhere, should stop the bread going soggy.

I EGG	4 SLICES OF WHOLEMEAL BREAD
40G UNSALTED BUTTER, AT ROOM TEMPERATURE	35G WATERCRESS, WASHED, DRIED AND ROUGHLY CHOPPED
SALT AND BLACK PEPPER	

1. Put the egg into a small pan and cover with cold water. Bring to the boil, then turn down the heat and simmer for 7 minutes. Drain, and dunk straight into iced water to cool down.

2. Peel the egg and chop finely. Put the butter into a bowl and mash with a fork to soften. Add the egg and mash together to combine, then season well with salt and black pepper.

3. Lay the bread out on a board and divide the butter between the slices. Put half the watercress on to one slice, and half on to another, then top with the remaining bread.

4. Push down on the slices firmly to keep the watercress in, and cut each sandwich into four; please note, Dorothy Hartley firmly insists you should not 'trim the characteristic little frill of green leaflets that escape beyond the brown edge of the sandwich; their stiff green border proves the freshness of the sandwich, and adds to its enjoyment'.

Cucumber

MAKES 8 SMALL SANDWICHES

'Hallo! Why all these cups? Why cucumber sandwiches? Why such reckless extravagance in one so young?'
– Oscar Wilde, *The Importance of Being Earnest*

It might sound like the clue's in the name, but there's no room for mistakes with such a simple recipe, and the delicate art involved in the perfect cucumber sandwich is sadly one in decline.

½ A CUCUMBER, PEELED
SALT AND PEPPER
4 THIN SLICES OF GOOD, SOFT WHITE BREAD

UNSALTED BUTTER, AT ROOM TEMPERATURE,
TO SPREAD

1. Cut the cucumber into thin slices and arrange on a couple of sheets of kitchen paper. Sprinkle lightly with salt and leave for 20 minutes, then pat dry with more kitchen paper.

2. Lay the bread out on a board and butter lightly but thoroughly. Cover half the bread slices with overlapping slices of cucumber and season delicately with pepper. Top with the remaining bread slices and cut off the crusts. Cut each sandwich into quarters; I think fancy triangles are best here.

Devilled crab

MAKES 8 SMALL SANDWICHES

Strictly speaking, these aren't quite devilled crab, which is a dish made with cream or béchamel sauce, and served hot, rather than between two slices of bread, but the flavours are much the same, and I like the way it sounds. As with devilled kidneys and devilled eggs, the name refers simply to the use of hot spices, 'presumably because of the connection between the devil and the excessive heat in Hell', as *The Oxford Companion to Food* perspicaciously remarks.

200G MIXED DARK AND WHITE CRABMEAT
1 TEASPOON WORCESTERSHIRE SAUCE
A FEW DASHES OF TABASCO SAUCE
1 TABLESPOON GRAIN MUSTARD
JUICE OF ¼ OF A LEMON
1 TABLESPOON MAYONNAISE (OPTIONAL)

SALT AND PEPPER
4 SLICES OF BROWN BREAD
UNSALTED BUTTER, AT ROOM TEMPERATURE,
  TO SPREAD
A SMALL BUNCH OF FRESH CHIVES, FINELY
  CHOPPED

1.   Mix together the crabmeat, Worcestershire and Tabasco sauces, mustard and lemon juice. You should have quite a loose mixture, but, depending on the ratio of white to brown meat, it may need a little mayonnaise to bring it together, so stir it in if necessary. Season to taste.

2.   Lay the bread out on a board and butter each slice lightly (this will help stop it going soggy). Spread two of the slices with crabmeat and top with chives and the remaining bread. Cut each sandwich into four.

Roast beef, quick-pickled red onion and Stilton

MAKES 8 SMALL SANDWICHES

Inspired by a Gary Rhodes recipe for leftover roast beef, these are extremely satisfying, full-flavoured things, particularly suited to a cold-weather picnic. Don't be put off by the onion: the pickling process robs it of its bite, I promise.

½ A SMALL RED ONION
1 TABLESPOON OLIVE OIL
2 TABLESPOONS BALSAMIC VINEGAR
A SQUEEZE OF LEMON JUICE
SALT AND PEPPER
4 SLICES OF THICK WHITE BREAD

UNSALTED BUTTER, AT ROOM TEMPERATURE,
   TO SPREAD
75G COLD ROAST BEEF, SLICED
40G STILTON, CRUMBLED
A HANDFUL OF WATERCRESS

1. Cut the red onion into two wedges, keeping the root on so they stay together. Bring a small pan of water to the boil and add the onion. Simmer for 2 minutes, then drain.

2. Whisk together the oil, vinegar and lemon juice and season well, then heat to warm through (you can do this in the same pan to save on washing-up). Pour into a bowl and add the onion. Toss well to coat, then leave to soak for at least 2 hours.

3. When you're ready to make the sandwiches, spread the bread thinly with butter. Divide the beef between two of the slices, and top with leaves of onion (they should come apart easily in your fingers), crumbled Stilton and watercress.

4. Put the remaining bread on top, and cut into halves or quarters.

Quick Coronation chicken

MAKES 8 SMALL SANDWICHES

The glut of royal events over the last few years has led to a welcome revival of this long-neglected dish, created for Elizabeth II in 1953. If you want to do it properly, you'll need to poach your own chicken – but this version is infinitely quicker, and very good for leftover roast poultry of all stripes.

UNSALTED BUTTER, AT ROOM
  TEMPERATURE, TO SPREAD
4 SLICES OF THICK WHITE BREAD
BLACK PEPPER
1 TABLESPOON MAYONNAISE
1 TABLESPOON CRÈME FRAÎCHE OR GREEK
  YOGHURT
2 TABLESPOONS GOOD MANGO CHUTNEY
  (I HIGHLY RECOMMEND GEETA'S,
  IT'S AMAZING)

1 TEASPOON MILD OR MEDIUM CURRY
  POWDER
A SQUEEZE OF LEMON JUICE
100G ROAST CHICKEN, SHREDDED
1 TABLESPOON FLAKED ALMONDS, TOASTED
1 TABLESPOON CHOPPED FRESH CORIANDER

1. Butter the bread lightly and season with black pepper. Put the mayonnaise, crème fraîche or yoghurt, chutney, curry powder and lemon juice into a bowl and stir together. Sample and season, adding a little more chutney, curry powder or lemon juice to suit your taste.

2. Stir in the chicken, almonds and coriander and divide between two slices of bread. Top with the rest of the bread and cut into halves or quarters.

Cheese and Marmite scones

MAKES ABOUT 8

It's no exaggeration to say this combines three of my favourite things in one crumbly package. The surprisingly subtle combination of cheese and Marmite always reminds me of eating slightly squashed sandwiches with my dad in the dank-smelling aquarium of London Zoo on Saturday afternoons – not the most salubrious of venues, I grant you, but mercifully out of the rain. And there's nothing like watching an enormous electric eel as you munch your lunch – especially if you're seven.

Moving on, these healthily proportioned scones are so deliciously savoury that they can take the place of sandwiches – or you could make them bite-size with a 3cm cutter, rolling them out to just 1.5cm thick, for a rather more elegant effect. Although I prefer the flavour of a nutty Cheddar, which goes particularly well with the pumpkin seeds, the Red Leicester gives a more striking visual effect. Either way, they're best served with plenty of cold, unsalted butter.

150G PLAIN WHITE FLOUR, PLUS A LITTLE
   EXTRA FOR ROLLING OUT
200G PLAIN WHOLEMEAL FLOUR
I HEAPED TEASPOON BICARBONATE
   OF SODA
2 HEAPED TEASPOONS CREAM OF TARTAR
100G BUTTER, CHILLED

75G MATURE CHEDDAR OR RED LEICESTER,
   GRATED
I TABLESPOON MARMITE, MIXED TO A PASTE
   WITH A LITTLE HOT WATER
175ML BUTTERMILK, PLUS A LITTLE EXTRA
15G PUMPKIN SEEDS

1. Preheat the oven to 190°C/gas mark 5 and line a baking sheet with baking parchment. Combine the flours, bicarbonate of soda and cream of tartar in a mixing bowl, then grate in the butter. Rub in until you have fine breadcrumbs, then stir in the cheese.

2. Stir in the Marmite paste, then add enough buttermilk to make a soft dough (you probably won't need it all) and bring together into a ball.

3. Gently roll out the dough on a lightly floured surface until about 2.5cm thick, then cut out scones using an 8cm cutter. Arrange on the baking sheet, brush with a little buttermilk, and top with the seeds.

4. Bake for 20 minutes, until golden, then allow to cool on a wire rack.

Crumpets

MAKES 12

Elizabeth David is very stern on the subject of commercially produced crumpets, writing in *English Bread and Yeast Cookery* that 'terrible travesties of them can still be bought in England, although they are more commonly sold packeted by grocers or supermarkets than by bakers. Perhaps indeed they are delivered direct from a plastics recycling plant, and have never been near a bakery.' At which point I must hang my head, and admit I love crumpets in all their forms – including the bought kind.

In fact, my feelings for crumpets run very deep indeed, so I was quite upset the first time I had a go at making them: doughy, heavy and almost entirely bereft of holes as they were, I blamed myself until I examined the picture accompanying the recipe, by a well-known food personality, and realized his looked pretty rubbish too.

I bitterly bemoaned my failure on Twitter, and the lovely blogger Kavey Eats came to the rescue, sending me a link to a recipe road-tested by her husband Pete. It took me a couple of goes, and some small tweaks, but finally I cracked it – and realized that homemade crumpets are actually well worth the effort, as long as you can trust the recipe. Light and fluffy, you can make them a few days ahead, and then just toast to order.

Remember, if your crumpet doesn't leave a buttery ring behind on the plate when you pick it up, you haven't added enough butter. You'll need food rings of a vaguely crumpety size for this recipe.

115G PLAIN FLOUR
115G STRONG WHITE FLOUR
1 TEASPOON SALT
1½ TEASPOONS CASTER SUGAR
1 X 7G SACHET OF FAST-ACTION
　DRIED YEAST

150ML WARM MILK
150ML WARM WATER
1 TABLESPOON MELTED BUTTER, PLUS EXTRA
　TO GREASE
1 TEASPOON BICARBONATE OF SODA
SOFT BUTTER, TO SERVE

1.　Sift together the flours and stir in the salt, sugar and yeast. Add the milk, water and melted butter and mix well, using a food mixer or a vigorously wielded wooden spoon, until smooth. Cover with clingfilm and put somewhere warmish and draught-free for a couple of hours, until bubbly.

2.　Heat the grill to medium-high. Lightly grease a heavy-based frying pan with butter, and do the same with your crumpet rings (this minimizes the sticking, although I've never yet achieved a completely clean edge). Put the pan on a medium-high heat.

3.   Dissolve the bicarb in 2 tablespoons of warm water and stir into the batter: this will knock a bit of the air out, but don't worry.

4.   When the frying pan is hot, add the rings to the pan, making sure they sit flat, and spoon 1cm of batter into each one. After a few minutes you should, all being well, see bubbles appearing on the top of each crumpet. Cook until the tops look dry, then push them out of the rings (run a knife around the side if necessary, remembering they'll be hot), flip them over and toast on the top until light golden. Cool on a rack and repeat until you've used up all the remaining batter.

5.   To serve, toast or grill until golden brown, and top with vast amounts of butter.

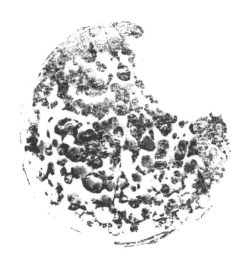

Mini quiches

Quiche, that fabulous egg custard confection so roundly abused by supermarkets, is far too rich and substantial for teatime – if it isn't, you're doing it wrong. It's a meal in itself, with a few salad leaves to salve the conscience. These tiny versions take a little bit of a liberty with the concept, because they're not deep enough to allow for a proper wobbly filling, but they are still delicious, and won't spoil your appetite for the cake to follow (assuming you exercise some self-control).

They also make nice little canapés – although I've gone for two classic teatime sandwich flavours, ham and mustard, and cucumber and cream cheese (well, courgette and creamy cheese, anyway), it's easy to ring the changes with the fillings to make them smarter. Smoked salmon and chive, or black olive and tomato, spring to mind. I've given two flavour options here – if you want to make both, you'll need twice as much pastry.

FOR THE PASTRY
225G PLAIN FLOUR, PLUS EXTRA FOR
    DUSTING
1 TABLESPOON ENGLISH MUSTARD
    POWDER AND 1 TABLESPOON
    MUSTARD SEEDS (FOR THE HAM AND
    MUSTARD OPTION)
A PINCH OF SALT
120G BUTTER, CHILLED, PLUS EXTRA
    TO GREASE
1 EGG WHITE

FOR THE HAM AND MUSTARD
2 EGGS, PLUS 1 YOLK
100ML DOUBLE CREAM
SALT AND PEPPER
30G SHREDDED HAM

FOR THE COURGETTE AND GOAT'S CHEESE
½ A SMALL COURGETTE, CUT INTO THIN
    RIBBONS WITH A PEELER
SALT AND PEPPER
OLIVE OIL
2 EGGS, PLUS 1 YOLK
100ML DOUBLE CREAM
75G SOFT GOAT'S CHEESE, CRUMBLED

1. To make the pastry, sift the flour and mustard powder (if using) into a mixing bowl along with a pinch of salt, and grate in the butter. Rub in with your fingertips, then add the mustard seeds (if using) and enough iced water (about 1½–2 tablespoons) to bring together into a dough. Wrap in baking parchment and chill for 15 minutes. Lightly grease a 12-hole muffin tin with butter.

2. Roll out the pastry on a lightly floured work surface to about 3mm thick and cut out 8cm circles to line the tins. Line each with a circle of baking parchment and weight down with baking beans. Put back into the fridge for 30 minutes to chill, and preheat the oven to 190°C/gas mark 5.

3.	Meanwhile, if you're making the courgette and goat's cheese tarts, put the courgette ribbons into a colander, scatter with ½ teaspoon of salt and toss. Leave in the sink to drain for 20 minutes, then rinse and pat dry. Heat 1 tablespoon of olive oil in a frying pan and fry the courgettes for about 5 minutes, until softened. Set aside.

4.	Bake the pastry cases for 15 minutes, then remove the beans and paper. Lightly whisk the egg white until frothy and brush over the inside of each pastry case. Return to the oven and bake for another 5 minutes.

5.	Briefly whisk together the eggs and cream until just mixed and season well. For the courgette and goat's cheese tartlets, divide the courgette ribbons between the pastry cases and fill with the custard mixture, then top with the crumbled goat's cheese. For the ham and mustard, put a few strands of ham into each case, then fill with the custard. Bake for about 10 minutes, until the custard is just set, but still slightly wobbly, then cool on a wire rack.

Sweet

Earl Grey tea loaf

MAKES ONE 21CM LOAF

Jane Grigson informs me in *English Food* that loaves made with tea were a favourite at church and chapel gatherings based around the soothing virtues of a nice cup of tea, rather than the demon drink. So popular were they at funerals, she claims, that in Yorkshire they're sometimes called 'slow-walking bread'. All of which makes it sound like a depressing excuse for a cake, which is unfair – its charms may be subtle, but if we all ate chocolate brownies every day, what a dull world it would be.

In fact, I decided not to mention it in the title, because it sounds rather joyless, but this is that magical thing, a fatless loaf (well, if you excuse the egg yolk). The plump, tea-sodden fruit prevents it from being dry – I think it actually improves after a few days, which makes it a godsend for time-pressed hosts – and, although it's even nicer spread generously with butter, it's perfectly lovely on its own. Weight-watchers, take note.

100G CHOPPED MIXED PEEL	1 TABLESPOON CLEAR HONEY
100G GOLDEN SULTANAS	1 EGG
100G CURRANTS	225G WHOLEMEAL SELF-RAISING FLOUR
200ML HOT EARL GREY TEA	A PINCH OF SALT

1.   The night before you want to make this loaf, combine the mixed peel and dried fruit in a bowl and pour over the hot tea. Cover and leave to soak overnight.

2.   Preheat the oven to 180°C/gas mark 4 and grease and line a 21cm loaf tin with baking parchment. Stir together the honey and egg and add to the flour in a mixing bowl, along with a pinch of salt. Add the fruit and its soaking liquid, and mix well.

3.   Spoon into the prepared tin and bake for about 50–60 minutes, until golden on top and a skewer inserted comes out clean. Cool on a wire rack, and serve sliced, with butter or jam. Wrapped well or in an airtight tin, this loaf keeps for up to 5 days.

Welsh cakes

MAKES ABOUT 15

I discovered these early one wet morning at the Abergavenny Food Festival a few years ago, after an absurdly uncomfortable night in a tent. As we were wandering around the damp little high street, searching for a breakfast spot that wasn't heaving with hungry foodies, I spotted a chap cooking them on the street. Rich, meltingly soft, and crunchy with sugar, my first Welsh cake knocked the soggy beans on toast that eventually followed into a cocked bonnet.

Vegetarians should be reassured that these little drop scones can be made with double the amount of butter in place of the lard, but pig-eaters should give the authentic version a go – you won't taste it in the finished cake, but it gives them a wonderful lightness. And, if you're swayed by such things, it contains 20 per cent less saturated fat than butter, so it's really not the villain we're led to believe.

Traditionally, these would have been cooked on bakestones, which conjures up thoughts of those hot stones you're sometimes presented with at Japanese restaurants to cook steak on, but actually refers to cast-iron griddle pans that are heated over the fire. A sturdy frying pan makes an excellent substitute.

225G SELF-RAISING FLOUR, PLUS A LITTLE
   EXTRA FOR DUSTING
75G CASTER SUGAR, PLUS A LITTLE EXTRA
   FOR SPRINKLING
½ TEASPOON GROUND MIXED SPICE
A PINCH OF SALT

50G BUTTER, CHILLED
50G LARD, CHILLED, PLUS A LITTLE EXTRA
   FOR COOKING
50G SULTANAS OR CURRANTS
2 EGGS, BEATEN

1. Put the flour, sugar, mixed spice and a pinch of salt into a mixing bowl. Grate in the butter and lard and rub into the flour with your fingertips. Stir in the sultanas, and add just enough beaten egg to bring it to a dough – you might not need it all.

2. Roll out the dough on a lightly floured surface until about 1cm thick. Cut out rounds using a 6cm cutter (or about that).

3. Grease a large, heavy-based frying pan with a little lard (kitchen paper is helpful here) and put over a medium-high heat. When hot, cook the Welsh cakes in batches for about 4 minutes on each side, until golden, crisp and cooked through.

4. Sprinkle with sugar and serve immediately, or, when cool, put into an airtight container – I like them warm, and usually reheat them in a toaster, but beware, their small size can lead to the kind of fiddling around with a knife that threatens the smug joy a homemade Welsh cake usually comes topped with. Better to warm them in a low oven or under the grill.

Bakewell jam tarts

MAKES ABOUT 24

Jam tarts are one of those things that seem to have disappeared quietly into the ether – a staple of childhood parties, they sat somewhere on the scale of excitement between the worthy bread and butter, and the sugar-rush of lurid joy that included iced gems, French fancies and wagon wheels.

You know where you are with a jam tart – except here, where it's naughtily mated with its Derbyshire cousin to produce a sort of Bakewellized hybrid of a beast, more interesting than the standard Mr Kipling number, but still simple enough to find favour with an expert tasting panel made up of my niece and nephew, aged four and two respectively. These are best eaten on the day of baking.

(Interestingly, the good folk of Bakewell would argue that actually the tart often labelled as their particular speciality bears little relation to the Bakewell pudding proper, which features puff pastry and frangipane, and is served as a dessert, rather than a teatime treat. But there we are.)

200G PLAIN FLOUR, PLUS A LITTLE
   EXTRA FOR DUSTING
175G GROUND ALMONDS
65G CASTER SUGAR
200G BUTTER, CHILLED AND DICED,
   PLUS A LITTLE EXTRA SOFT BUTTER
   FOR GREASING

1 EGG, SEPARATED
200G RASPBERRY JAM
50G FLAKED ALMONDS, TOASTED

1. Sift the flour and ground almonds into a mixing bowl and stir in the sugar. Rub the butter into the dry ingredients using your fingertips. Add the egg yolk (setting the white aside for later) and 1 tablespoon of iced water if necessary to bring the mixture together into a dough. Wrap in baking parchment and chill for half an hour.

2. Grease two 12-hole tart tins with butter and preheat the oven to 180°C/gas mark 4. Roll the chilled pastry out on a lightly floured work surface to a thickness of about 5mm, then cut out circles using a 6–7cm cutter and use to line the tart tins. Chill for another 15 minutes.

3. Cut out 24 circles of baking parchment to fit the tart tins, and use them to line each piece of pastry, weighted down with baking beans. Blind bake for 15 minutes, then remove the beans and paper. Lightly whisk the egg white until frothy and brush over the inside of each pastry case. Bake for another 5 minutes, cool for 2 minutes in the tin, then finish cooling on a rack.

4. Put the jam into a pan with 3 tablespoons of water and bring to the boil. Simmer for about 5 minutes, then take off the heat and pour into the tart cases. It will set as it cools. After 10 minutes, sprinkle each tart with flaked almonds.

Seed cake

MAKES ONE 21CM LOAF

Seed cake belongs to a vanished world of high teas and boarding-school tales – it's the kind of thing you can imagine them tucking into after a lacrosse match in an Angela Brazil story, rather than the Kit-Kats and orange squash that passed as a match tea in my day. In fact, it's a far, far older recipe, name-checked in 1577's *Five Hundred Points of Good Husbandry*, and, according to Jane Grigson, mentioned in nearly all 'early 18th-century manuscript books'.

Geraldene Holt gives a lovely quote from Thomas Hardy in her excellent book of cakes, describing a seed cake as 'so richly compounded that it opened to the knife like a freckled buttercup', but in truth, most modern palates can't cope with quite that much caraway, with its powerful aniseed flavour, so add more at your peril. (I note, however, that a 1904 recipe given in Florence White's fascinating *Good Things in England* calls for just 'a few caraway seeds', so perhaps Hardy was guilty of a little romanticism on this point.) Whatever the truth, if you'd like it to look a little, well, seedier, you could always stir in a couple of spoonfuls of poppy seeds or similar – very popular in central European baking.

150G BUTTER, AT ROOM TEMPERATURE, PLUS EXTRA TO GREASE	A PINCH OF SALT
150G CASTER SUGAR	185G PLAIN FLOUR
3 EGGS, LIGHTLY BEATEN	1 TEASPOON BAKING POWDER
2 TEASPOONS CARAWAY SEEDS	30G GROUND ALMONDS
	1 TABLESPOON MILK

1. Preheat the oven to 180°C/gas mark 4. Grease a 21cm loaf tin and line with baking parchment.

2. Cream the butter and sugar together in a food mixer, or with a wooden spoon, until fluffy, then gradually beat in the eggs, followed by the seeds and a pinch of salt.

3. Sift the flour, baking powder and ground almonds into the bowl and fold in, followed by the milk. Spoon the mixture into the prepared tin.

4. Bake for about 50 minutes, until a skewer inserted into the cake comes out clean. Leave in the tin for 5 minutes, then turn out and cool on a rack.

Digestive biscuits

MAKES 16

The original digestive biscuits seem to have emerged in the early nineteenth century, and were very plain affairs made of 'brown wheaten flour', butter, water and yeast, intended to promote digestive health, which is not a claim many would make for its modern incarnation. *The Oxford Companion to Food* throws up the delightful fact that 'the biscuit has no particular digestive properties and is banned from sale under that name in the USA'.

These homemade digestives are a compromise between the worthy originals and the blandly sweet mass-market version, which have been sadly compromised by a recent, tragically misguided reduction in saturated fat, suggesting that the manufacturers concerned lack confidence in the British public's ability to identify a treat when they see one. Although they're good dunkers for tea, I like them best with some thinly sliced, nutty Cheddar. Particularly adventurous eaters might wish to combine the two.

150G PLAIN WHOLEMEAL FLOUR, PLUS A
   LITTLE EXTRA FOR DUSTING
80G FINE OATMEAL
45G SOFT BROWN SUGAR
¼ TEASPOON BICARBONATE OF SODA
A PINCH OF SALT

90G CHILLED BUTTER, PLUS A LITTLE SOFTENED
   BUTTER TO GREASE
1 EGG YOLK
4 TABLESPOONS MILK
150G DARK OR MILK CHOCOLATE (OPTIONAL)

1.   Preheat the oven to 180°C/gas mark 4 and line a baking tray with baking parchment. Put the flour, oatmeal, sugar and bicarbonate of soda into a mixing bowl and add a generous pinch of salt. Grate the butter into the bowl, then use your fingertips to rub it into the mixture.

2.   Beat the egg yolk and milk together and stir into the mixture until you have a soft dough. Roll out on a lightly floured surface to about 5mm thick. Using a 7cm cutter, cut out 16 biscuits and put them on the baking tray. Chill for 15 minutes.

3.   Bake for about 20 minutes, until golden. Leave on the tray for 5 minutes, then move to a wire rack to cool completely. If you're making chocolate biscuits, break the chocolate into pieces and put into a heatproof bowl over a pan of simmering water to melt, making sure the bottom of the bowl dosen't touch the water. Dip one side of each cooled biscuit into the melted chocolate and put aside to set.

Gingerbread gentlemen (and ladies)

MAKES 10

Medieval gingerbread was just that – breadcrumbs bound together with spiced honey – but these days it tends more towards the biscuit in texture. Dorothy Hartley claims in *Food in England* that a firmer version was a popular gift 'in the jousting period', 'rather like expensive chocolates today'. (If you have a yen to hark back to the days of the wimple and woad, Hugh Fearnley-Whittingstall has a recipe online from some festive River Cottage shindig. They have a texture rather like that of a treacle tart.)

As I have fond memories of gingerbread men so stubbornly sturdy that it would take most of a Sunday to chew their limbs off, these stout chaps are of the hard variety, rather than the soft, dark sort sold at German Christmas markets. Such things teach valuable patience and determination, in my opinion.

225G SELF-RAISING FLOUR, PLUS A LITTLE
   EXTRA FOR DUSTING
85G SOFT LIGHT BROWN SUGAR
2 TEASPOONS GROUND GINGER
1 TEASPOON GROUND MIXED SPICE
A PINCH OF SALT

115G BUTTER
4–5 TABLESPOONS MILK
50G CRYSTALLIZED GINGER, FINELY CHOPPED
20G CURRANTS, FOR DECORATION
WRITING ICING, FOR DECORATION
   (OPTIONAL), OR 75G ICING SUGAR, SIFTED

1. Preheat the oven to 200°C/gas mark 6 and line two baking sheets with baking parchment. Sieve the flour into a mixing bowl and stir in the sugar, spices and a pinch of salt. Grate in the butter, and rub it into the dry ingredients.

2. Stir in the milk and the crystallized ginger until the mixture comes together into a dough. Dust a work surface with flour and roll out the dough to about 5mm thick. Cut out gingerbread men and arrange on the baking sheets, spaced slightly apart. Decorate with currants: 2 for the eyes and 3 buttons, pushing these well into the dough. Chill for 15 minutes.

3. Bake for about 17 minutes, until golden, then cool on a rack. When cool, if you're feeling artistic, draw on smiles with writing icing, or a mixture of sifted icing sugar and a little boiling water, made into a stiff paste.

Chestnut and chocolate brownies

MAKES ABOUT 16

Of all the recipes I've written in the last few years, chocolate brownies remain my firm and unwavering favourite, which is strange, because I'm not really much of a chocolate lover. I like it of course – who doesn't? – but not with the kind of passion suggested by those humorous fridge magnets. (If they made 'crazy hot buttered toast gal' versions, I'd be first in line.) Anyway, suffice to say I'm not sure the recipe in *Perfect* can be improved upon – but I firmly believe that this gluten-free version is at least its equal. It's a lighter, crumblier style of brownie that makes an excellent dessert as well as a teatime treat – chill before serving for ultimate squidgy deliciousness.

Because of the relatively small quantity of flour involved, brownies are fairly easy to adapt using standard gluten-free flour anyway, but this faintly sweet chestnut flour, available at Italian grocers, adds a subtle nuttiness that works like a dream with the pecans. Trust me, you'll be fighting the coeliacs for these babies. (As an aside, the rest of the chestnut flour can be put to excellent use in things like Tuscan *castagnaccio* cake, or nutty-tasting pasta.)

250G DARK CHOCOLATE, BROKEN INTO PIECES	60G CHESTNUT FLOUR
275G UNSALTED BUTTER, AT ROOM TEMPERATURE	½ TEASPOON BAKING POWDER
	A PINCH OF SALT
230G SOFT LIGHT BROWN SUGAR	60G COCOA POWDER
3 EGGS, PLUS 1 YOLK, LIGHTLY BEATEN	70G PECANS, ROUGHLY CHOPPED

1. Preheat the oven to 180°C/gas mark 4 and line a 23cm square baking tin with baking parchment.

2. Set a bowl over, but not touching, a pan of simmering water, and add 200g of the chocolate. Melt, stirring occasionally, then take off the heat.

3. Meanwhile, beat the butter and sugar together in a mixer until light and fluffy, and chop the rest of the chocolate into small pieces.

4. With the mixer still running, gradually add the eggs, beating well between additions to ensure they're thoroughly incorporated before pouring in any more. Leave to mix on a high speed for 5 minutes, until the batter is silky and puffed up.

5. Gently fold in the melted chocolate and chopped chocolate with a metal spoon, followed by the sifted flour, baking powder, salt, cocoa powder and nuts.

6. Spoon the mixture into the tin, and bake for about 25 minutes. Test with a skewer; it should come out sticky, but not coated with raw mixture. If necessary, put the tin back into the oven for another 3 minutes, then test again. Prepare a roasting tin of iced water.

7. When the brownies are ready, remove the tin from the oven and place in the cold water bath. Leave to cool for an hour before cutting into squares.

Picnics and other outdoor feasts

'Wherever it is done, picnicking can be one of the supreme pleasures of outdoor life' – James Beard

Whether or not food really does taste better outdoors – and I seem to remember reading a few summers ago that there's no scientific basis for this oft-repeated claim – it certainly feels like it. Perhaps it's the beauty of the surroundings (you never hear people waxing lyrical about lunch in a lay-by, do you?), perhaps it's the novelty of the situation, or maybe it's just the fact that, away from the everyday business of the home, it's easier to focus on the food, but whatever the truth of the matter, picnics are a gift to the aspiring host.

Appetites sharpened by fresh air and a brisk trot to the picnic site (which, quite apart from the views to gaze sleepily at after lunch, is why a hilltop is such an excellent idea, as long as you're not the one carrying the basket), spirits buoyed in anticipation, you could provide cheese and pickle sandwiches and still receive rave reviews. Embrace the idea with both arms whenever the weather permits.

The nature of picnics

For all their studied informality, a good picnic, as opposed to drinks and crisps in the park after work, demands meticulous organization: after all, it's not like you can just pop back inside if you've forgotten anything. If that sounds daunting, however, take comfort in the fact that much of the idea's charm lies in its very simplicity. Properly, picnics should be wholly or largely eaten with fingers, in various attitudes of delicious languor – I firmly believe that no lobster mayonnaise could taste as good on a wind-licked beach as a generously stuffed brown crab sandwich.

Outdoors, people want what is often called 'honest' food – by which I think they mean the kind of uncomplicated fare that you dream of when you're feeling too far from home. Flaky sausage rolls, squidgy brownies, cheese and oatcakes: that's the stuff you crave in the open air. Even that famed gastronome Brillat-Savarin demands little from such a *déjeuner sur l'herbe*, describing the picnicker pulling from a knapsack 'very calmly and contentedly…cold chicken and golden encrusted rolls, packed for him perchance by loving hands, and…the wedge of Gruyère or Roquefort which is to be his whole dessert'.

Picnics also have the inestimable benefit of having a long tradition of what the Americans would call 'potluck' – where everyone brings a share of the food. This makes things even easier for the host, who can just end up providing drinks, but an email chain to establish who's bringing what is probably a wise idea unless you want to end up with nine quiches and a tart.

Food

Although we've hopefully established that lugging a salmon en croûte back to the river bank is probably misguided, some simple food works better than others on a picnic. In theory, the free and easy nature of the occasion means that anything goes, but, depending on the weather and the nature of the expedition, there are a few things it's helpful to bear in mind.

Anything you'd usually keep cool until just before serving is an obvious no-no – jellies, custards, creamy coleslaws and hard cheeses are generally a bad idea, as are delicate salads or anything else that isn't likely to take kindly to being jiggled about in a picnic hamper. Discount any foods that would be better served piping hot (most things with a sauce, for example, and, in my opinion anyway, rice) or very cold – never take ice cream to a picnic, however much you like the idea of lounging around eating Cornettos in the sun. Choose a spot with a likely ice cream van instead.

Even things usually served at room temperature can let you down after a few hours in a warm picnic bag: chocolate, for example, should be treated with caution. A lovely ripe Brie or Camembert, by contrast, or some cured ham, will only benefit from basking in the sun for a while. (Not too long, of course: then things start to get unpleasantly sweaty.)

Lastly, even if you are taking along a table and a full set of cutlery, food that requires carving or boning should be left at home: jiggly tables and joints of meat are a comedy waiting to happen. Aim for as much that can be eaten by hand as possible – and pack a goodly lot of wet wipes.

Drink

This is a hard one, given that most drinks are best served hot or very cold, contravening the rules set out above – which is where a nice ale or cider comes into its own. I'd also strongly suggest ample quantities of soft drink: homemade lemonade (pages 167, 293), elderflower cordial, or even something redolent of childhood picnics – in my case Orangina 'et sa pulpe', which wasn't allowed at home, but ran freely on our annual French camping holiday.

If you're set on wine, something light in alcohol is usually a good bet for the afternoon – perhaps a sweet and sour Riesling; refreshingly acidic Muscadet, Picpoul de Pinet or Vinho Verde; crisp English wine or even a neat little Provençal rosé.

Bubbles always feel appropriately light-hearted of course, but, unless you can keep it well chilled and drink it out of real glasses, champagne only works for the thrill of it – its rich complexity is often a bit serious for picnics in any case. A decent cava, prosecco or even, dare I say it, a lively, off-dry Asti Spumante will suit the mood much better. Or, of course, there's always lager: those stubby little Belgian bottles are easier on the eye than cans, and, if you take some lemonade or ginger beer as well, you can make shandies, just like you're in the world's best beer garden.

All of the above, of course, need to be kept as cold as possible for maximum refreshment value. A coolbox is obviously ideal, but they're generally unwieldy enough to only be suited to the kind of picnics you unpack from the back of a car. If you're walking or cycling, invest in those freezable wine bottle sleeves, or wrap the bottles in damp newspaper and arrange them snugly in a bag with some ice packs. A Thermos flask full of ice is also a very handy thing to take, if you can carry it.

For red wine drinkers, Elizabeth David believed 'a stout…wine such as a Macon or a Chianti, which cannot be unduly harmed by the journey in the car' to be the obvious choice for a picnic. Call me faint-hearted, but the idea of polishing off a bottle of Chianti on a sunny afternoon makes me come over all woozy – if it must be red, I'd much prefer a lightly chilled Beaujolais, or silky Pinot Noir.

Coffee is a nice thing to offer, if you're going all out, and a flask of the iced stuff is much more tempting than anything warm that's been sitting around for a while – I make it a bit milkier than usual, adding a little brown sugar to make it into a halfway house between a sophisticated drink and a milkshake. But as digestifs go, you can't beat Mrs Hilda Leyel's sage advice in her 1936 work, *Picnics for Motorists*: 'if a liqueur is wanted, cherry brandy is a very appropriate one'. Just don't try to get back into your motor afterwards.

Equipment

Wicker picnic baskets are hopelessly impractical, but nothing beats the ceremonial lifting of the lid for sheer al fresco glamour. I use mine if we're picnicking near the car, or in a local park, but as I can't carry it for more than about ten minutes without starting to whinge, I generally prefer to divide the goodies between a backpack and a few sturdy shopping bags or bicycle panniers.

Disposable plates, cups and cutlery are grave sins indeed – not only are they an environmental disaster, but they always look ugly. No drink tastes good out of a paper cup, and I've never found a paper plate sturdy enough to hold much more than a pile of crisps. Most picnics don't need them anyway – you can eat one thing at a time with your hands, and drink straight from the bottle: this is not an occasion for prissiness.

Personally I've never had a glass break on a picnic, despite my lamentable record at home, so I tend to just pack our normal crockery and tumblers for smarter occasions, but there are some excellent sturdy plastic versions around. Just think about what kind of picnic you usually have before investing – it really doesn't require specialist equipment.

Here's a list of the basics I consider essential for a full-blown picnic – if you're just taking a round of sandwiches and an apple with you, obviously feel free to disregard most of them:

* Corkscrew and/or bottle opener
* A rug or two (preferably with waterproof backs if you're buying from new)
* Napkins and wet wipes
* Salt and pepper (I store them in twists of foil if space is tight)
* Condiments (mustard is a must at picnics, and is easily decanted into one of those mini jars you find at hotel breakfasts, or that hold travel-sized lotions and potions; salad dressings can be stored in jam jars)
* A sharp knife, for cutting pies, etc.
* A rubbish bag
* A large umbrella if the weather looks capricious (it can be useful to do a bit of advance research as to suitable places to retreat to in the local area should the picnic have to be abandoned)
* Games to work up an appetite for pudding: boules, French cricket, frisbees, or just a pack of cards, depending on likely levels of indolence

Chilled cucumber and sorrel soup

SERVES 6

Soup seems a very posh thing for a picnic, but in reality, as long as you don't mind sharing the Thermos cup with your friends, or taking spare cups along, it's an easy way to add a touch of class to proceedings with very little effort. This mild and tangy soup deals in serious refreshment – it must be served very cold, when the weather is very hot, for you to reap the full benefit, and its intense flavour means it's best enjoyed in shots, rather than mugfuls.

Sorrel, which grows wild throughout Europe, has a sharp, lemony flavour, and is occasionally found in greengrocers and good supermarkets in the summer months, but I tend to get mine at the local farmers' market, where it's sold alongside the salad leaves. If you are of a foraging bent, it tends to be found in long grass – meadows or at the edge of woodland are good places to try your hand – and looks very much like spinach. As ever, though, check a reputable guide for more information before tasting it.

2 CUCUMBERS
2 SPRING ONIONS, FINELY SLICED
400ML BUTTERMILK OR SINGLE CREAM

A LARGE HANDFUL OF SORREL LEAVES,
    WASHED
SALT AND PEPPER

1. Peel the cucumbers, cut in half lengthways, scoop out the seeds with a teaspoon and discard. Chop the flesh roughly, then put into a blender with the spring onions.

2. Add 350ml of buttermilk and whiz until smooth – if your cucumbers were particularly large, you may need to add more buttermilk to loosen the soup. Add the sorrel and blend again, then season to taste, remembering that chilling dulls the flavours, so erring on the side of more rather than less.

3. Chill before serving – if it separates, don't worry, just shake it well and it will come back together.

Smoked trout, watercress and new potato frittata

SERVES 4

The frittata is the saviour of many a leftover – you can rediscover your appetite for just about anything by imprisoning it in egg, and lightly caramelizing the top – but it's also the ideal vehicle for fiddly ingredients at picnics. Delicate trout, peppery watercress and waxy little boiled potatoes are the very essence of a British summer, but sometimes you can't be bothered with knives, forks or even plates – and the frittata, cut into stout wedges, is perfectly happy to be eaten with fingers. You could try swapping the trout for crumbled goat's cheese if you're not a fish lover.

500G SMALL NEW POTATOES, HALVED
SALT AND PEPPER
3 TABLESPOONS OLIVE OIL
8 EGGS

100G WATERCRESS, STALKS REMOVED, LEAVES ROUGHLY CHOPPED
2 HOT-SMOKED TROUT FILLETS, FLAKED

1. Cook the potatoes in a large pan of well-salted water for about 10 minutes, until tender. Drain and put back into the hot pan to dry.

2. Heat the olive oil in a medium non-stick frying pan over a medium-high heat. Beat the eggs together in a bowl, season and stir in the watercress and flaked trout.

3. Put the potatoes into the pan, spreading them out evenly. Pour in the egg mixture, which should almost fill the pan, and cook for about 15 minutes until it's just starting to set in the middle of the top. Preheat the grill to medium while it's cooking.

4. Put the pan under the grill and cook for about 5 minutes, until the top is firm and slightly browned. Allow to cool slightly, or completely, before serving.

Scotch eggs

I could write a long and self-indulgent essay on the subject of the Scotch egg – its resolutely English origins (London's Fortnum & Mason claim it as their own invention, although even this is disputed), sad decline into petrol station fare, and glorious resurrection at the manicured hands of the gastropub – but I shan't; suffice to say that, if you haven't made them before, you really will be astounded at how quick and easy they are. Once you've mastered the technique, there's virtually nothing you can't wrap an egg in and deep-fry. If it holds together, it's good to go, as the examples that follow should amply demonstrate.

Although cutting into a softly boiled egg is one of life's simplest pleasures, I prefer mine rather more solid for a Scotch egg, especially if they're to be eaten cold. You can adjust the cooking time to suit your tastes – Heston recommends cooking the egg for just 1 minute 45 seconds exactly for his runny-centred recipe.

Classic pork egg

MAKES 6

Keen-eyed *Guardian* readers may notice this is subtly different from the recipe which appeared in my 'Perfect' column for that paper – here I've allowed myself a bit more licence by using bacon for a hint of smoke, which handily supplies the fat in place of the sausagemeat.

8 EGGS, AT ROOM TEMPERATURE
400G MINCED PORK
200G SMOKED RINDLESS STREAKY BACON,
   FINELY CHOPPED
A PINCH OF MACE
2 TEASPOONS ENGLISH MUSTARD
2 TEASPOONS CHOPPED THYME LEAVES

3 FRESH SAGE LEAVES, FINELY CHOPPED
SALT AND PEPPER
A SPLASH OF MILK
100G PLAIN FLOUR, PLUS EXTRA FOR DUSTING
100G DRIED PANKO BREADCRUMBS
1.2 LITRES VEGETABLE OIL, FOR FRYING

1. Put 6 eggs into a pan large enough to hold them in a single layer and cover them with cold water. Bring to the boil, then turn down the heat and simmer for 5 minutes. Meanwhile, prepare a large bowl of iced water, and when the eggs are done, drop them straight in.

2. Mix together the pork, bacon, mace, mustard and herbs, and season well.

3. Meanwhile, arrange three shallow bowls on your work surface: the first containing the remaining 2 eggs, beaten with a splash of milk, the second the flour, seasoned with salt and pepper, and the third the breadcrumbs. Carefully peel the eggs and roll each one in flour.

4. To assemble the eggs, divide the meat mixture into three balls, then divide each ball in half. Cut out two 20cm squares of clingfilm, and put one square on the work surface. Dust lightly with flour, then put a ball of mixture on top and flour lightly. Put the second square of clingfilm on top, then roll out the mixture until you have a circular piece large enough to encase an egg.

5. Lift off the top piece of clingfilm and put an egg in the centre of the mixture, then bring up the edges of the bottom piece of film to encase the egg. Coax the mixture together, using your hands, until you have a smooth ball.

6. Roll the ball first in flour, then in egg, shaking off any excess, then in breadcrumbs. Repeat the egg and breadcrumb stages, then chill while you make the remaining eggs. Refrigerate them all for 20 minutes.

7. To cook, heat a large pan of oil (it should be no more than a third full) to 160°C – a breadcrumb should sizzle as it hits it, but not darken immediately. Carefully lower in the eggs and cook in three batches for 7 minutes, making sure you get the oil back up to temperature between batches. Drain on kitchen paper and season.

Spicy chickpea egg

MAKES 6

The marriage of a British picnic classic with the flavours of Moorish Spain might seem an unwise and potentially disastrous one, but I'm pretty sure I haven't created a monster here. In fact, left in the fridge for my resolutely carnivorous housemates to polish off, they proved as popular as the meat version – although I couldn't help agreeing that they might also be nice with a little cooking chorizo mixed in with the chickpeas…

8 EGGS, AT ROOM TEMPERATURE

3 TABLESPOONS OLIVE OIL

1 RED ONION, FINELY CHOPPED

4 CLOVES OF GARLIC, CRUSHED

2 CARROTS, PEELED AND GRATED

1 RED PEPPER, DESEEDED AND FINELY CHOPPED

2 X 400G TINS OF CHICKPEAS, DRAINED

2 TEASPOONS SWEET SMOKED PAPRIKA

2 TEASPOONS CHILLI FLAKES

SALT AND PEPPER

A SPLASH OF MILK

100G FLOUR, PLUS EXTRA FOR DUSTING

100G DRIED PANKO BREADCRUMBS

1 TEASPOON CAYENNE PEPPER

1.2 LITRES VEGETABLE OIL, FOR FRYING

1. Put 6 eggs into a pan large enough to hold them in a single layer and cover them with cold water. Bring to the boil, then turn down the heat and simmer for 5 minutes. Meanwhile, prepare a large bowl of iced water, and when the eggs are done, drop them straight in.

2. Heat 2 tablespoons of olive oil in a frying pan over a medium heat and cook the onion, garlic, carrots and red pepper for about 5 minutes, until softened. Meanwhile, use a stick blender or potato masher to roughly crush the chickpeas with 1 tablespoon of olive oil.

3. Stir the smoked paprika and chilli flakes into the vegetables and cook for another minute, then combine them with the chickpeas and season generously to taste. Allow to cool. Meanwhile, arrange three shallow bowls on your work surface: the first containing the remaining 2 eggs, beaten with a splash of milk, the second the flour, seasoned with salt and pepper, and the third the breadcrumbs and cayenne pepper, well mixed. Carefully peel the eggs and roll each one in flour.

4. To assemble the eggs, divide the chickpea mixture into three balls, then divide each ball in half. Cut out two 20cm squares of clingfilm, and put one square on the work surface. Put a ball of mixture on top and flour lightly. Put the second square of clingfilm on top, then roll out the mixture until you have a circular piece large enough to encase an egg.

5. Lift off the top piece of clingfilm and put an egg in the centre of the mixture, then bring up the edges of the bottom piece of film to encase the egg. Coax the mixture together, using your hands, until you have a smooth ball.

6. Roll the ball first in flour, then in egg, shaking off any excess, then in breadcrumbs. Repeat the egg and breadcrumb stages, then refrigerate while you make the remaining eggs. Refrigerate them all for 20 minutes.

7. To cook, heat a large pan of oil (it should be no more than a third full) to 160°C – a breadcrumb should sizzle as it hits it, but not darken immediately. Carefully lower in the eggs and cook in three batches for 7 minutes, making sure you get the oil back up to temperature between batches. Drain on kitchen paper and season.

Kedgeree egg

MAKES 6

My reasoning for this went something like – kedgeree is great with eggs, deep-fried *arancini* are almost better than the leftover risotto they're intended to use up … so why not see if I can fuse the two in one utterly glorious package? This is one Scotch egg that I think is better served warm, or at least at room temperature – and the usual prohibitions about the dangers of cooked rice compel me to warn you to refrigerate the rice to allow it to cool down as quickly as possible before use. It only takes one bout of food poisoning for you to realize that, rare as it may be, it's just not worth the risk, especially if you're catering for the less stoutly stomached.

250G SMOKED HADDOCK	2 TABLESPOONS MEDIUM CURRY POWDER
2 TABLESPOONS OLIVE OIL	SALT AND PEPPER
4 SPRING ONIONS, FINELY SLICED	8 EGGS, AT ROOM TEMPERATURE
2 GREEN CHILLIES, DESEEDED AND FINELY CHOPPED	A SPLASH OF MILK
	100G FLOUR, PLUS EXTRA FOR DUSTING
300G RISOTTO RICE	100G DRIED PANKO BREADCRUMBS
2 CARDAMOM PODS, CRUSHED	1.2 LITRES VEGETABLE OIL, FOR FRYING

1. Put the fish into a shallow pan over a low heat and cover with boiling water. Allow it to sit for 10 minutes, then drain, reserving the cooking water. When cool enough to handle, remove the skin and flake the fish. Put the cooking water, made up to 1 litre with more water, into a large saucepan and bring to the boil. Leave over a low heat.

2. Meanwhile, heat the oil in a large, heavy-based pan over a medium heat, and add the spring onions and chillies. Soften for a couple of minutes, then add the rice and stir well to coat with oil. Add the spices and cook for a minute or so, until the rice is translucent, then turn up the heat.

3. Add a ladleful of the boiling haddock cooking water to the pan (it should sizzle as it hits the pan – if not, turn up the heat) and cook, stirring, until it has evaporated. Add another and cook, stirring, until it has nearly all evaporated, then repeat until the rice is creamy and rather softer than you might normally expect from an authentic risotto. When ready, mix in the flaked haddock and season well to taste. Remove the cardamom pods and discard. Refrigerate until cool.

4. Put 6 eggs into a pan large enough to hold them in a single layer and cover them with cold water. Bring to the boil, then turn down the heat and simmer for 5 minutes. Meanwhile, prepare a large bowl of iced water, and when the eggs are done, drop them straight in.

5. Arrange three shallow bowls on your work surface: the first containing the remaining eggs, beaten with a splash of milk, the second the flour, seasoned with salt and pepper, and the third the breadcrumbs. Carefully peel the eggs and roll each one in flour.

6.   To assemble the eggs, divide the rice mixture into three balls, then divide each ball in half. Cut out two 20cm squares of clingfilm, and put one square on the work surface. Dust lightly with flour, then put a ball of mixture on top and flour lightly. Put the second square of clingfilm on top, then roll out the mixture until you have a circular piece large enough to encase an egg.

7.   Lift off the top piece of clingfilm and put an egg in the centre of the mixture, then bring up the edges of the bottom piece of film to encase the egg. Coax the mixture together, using your hands, until you have a smooth ball.

8.   Roll the ball first in flour, then in egg, shaking off any excess, then in breadcrumbs. Repeat the egg and breadcrumb stages, then refrigerate while you make the remaining eggs. Refrigerate them all for 20 minutes.

9.   To cook, heat a large pan of oil (it should be no more than a third full) to 160°C – a breadcrumb should sizzle as it hits it, but not darken immediately. Carefully lower in the eggs and cook in three batches for 7 minutes, making sure you get the oil back up to temperature between batches. Drain on kitchen paper and season.

Superior sausage rolls

MAKES ABOUT 25

The sausage roll is picnic and party food par excellence – flaky, savoury and delicious warm or cold, it's a hit with all ages, and always disappears at such a gobsmackingly rapid rate that I generally make two batches, just to be sure I get one myself. (After all, no one's ever regretted having leftover sausage rolls in the house.)

This is a version inspired by an apricot and almond sausagemeat stuffing we always have at Christmas, but if you'd prefer a more classic filling, feel free to substitute a couple of teaspoons of chopped sage, and perhaps the grated zest of 1 lemon in place of the dried fruit, nuts and ginger.

FOR THE PASTRY
225G PLAIN FLOUR, PLUS EXTRA TO DUST
A PINCH OF SALT
1 TEASPOON SWEET SMOKED PAPRIKA
175G COLD BUTTER
50ML ICED WATER
VEGETABLE OIL, TO GREASE
1 EGG, BEATEN WITH A LITTLE WATER
   AND SALT

FOR THE FILLING
400G PORK MINCE
200G SMOKED RINDLESS STREAKY BACON,
   FINELY CHOPPED
50G DRIED APRICOTS, FINELY CHOPPED
50G FLAKED ALMONDS, TOASTED IN A DRY
   PAN UNTIL GOLDEN
1 TEASPOON GROUND GINGER
FINELY GRATED NUTMEG, TO TASTE
SALT AND PEPPER

1. Sift the flour, salt and paprika into a large bowl and grate in the butter. Rub in with your fingertips, then add just enough iced water to make a dough that comes cleanly away from the bowl but isn't sticky. Wrap in baking parchment and chill for 30 minutes.

2. Preheat the oven to 220°C/gas mark 7. Lightly grease a large baking tray and line it with baking parchment. Mix together the filling ingredients, seasoning generously.

3. Roll out the pastry on a lightly floured surface to a thickness of about 5mm and cut into three long strips. Divide the meat into three, and roll each into a sausage about the same length as the strips.

4. Place each sausage slightly off-centre on the pastry, and brush one edge of the pastry with egg wash. Bring the other edge over the sausage and press down with the back of a fork to seal. Repeat with the other two, then cut into 4cm lengths and arrange, well spaced, on the baking tray. Brush with egg wash.

5. Bake for 25 minutes, until golden, then allow to cool on the tray.

Spinach, feta and egg pies

MAKES 6

Filo is one of the few varieties of pastry that I always buy – I've finally mastered the kind used for strudel, but the crisper, flakier kind beloved by my Turkish neighbours is just so much easier to buy, and freezes brilliantly, making it a very useful thing to keep in the house.

Based loosely on the classic Greek *spanakopita*, these pretty little pies look fancy, with their baked eggs against the vivid green of the spinach, but they're incredibly easy to make, and always go down a treat at picnics. You could also make one large pie instead, layering the whole pastry sheets, buttered as below, in a 20cm deep tart tin, adding the filling, then folding the overhanging pastry back over the top – less portable perhaps, but perfect for a garden picnic.

500G FROZEN WHOLE LEAF SPINACH
1 TABLESPOON OLIVE OIL
3 SPRING ONIONS, FINELY SLICED
2 CLOVES OF GARLIC, CRUSHED
75G FETA, CRUMBLED
JUICE OF ½ A LEMON

FINELY GRATED NUTMEG, TO TASTE
SALT AND PEPPER
75G BUTTER, MELTED
6 SHEETS OF FILO PASTRY
6 EGG YOLKS

1. Preheat the oven to 180°C/gas mark 4. Put the spinach into a pan of boiling water and cook until thawed, then drain in a colander, pressing down well to squeeze out any remaining water.

2. Heat the oil in a frying pan over a medium heat and sauté the spring onions and garlic for 3 minutes until softened. Add the spinach, then turn up the heat and fry for another 3 minutes to completely dry the spinach out. Take off the heat and stir in the cheese, lemon juice and a little grated nutmeg. Season to taste and set aside.

3. Grease a 6-hole muffin tray with butter. Put the filo sheets in a pile on a clean work surface and cut each into four. Stack these quarters and cut in half again. Cover with a damp tea towel to keep them from drying out while you line the tins.

4. Brush a square of filo with butter and put into one of the holes of the muffin tray. Repeat with another four squares, putting each one slightly out of kilter with the one below so the hole is completely lined with a fan of pastry. Repeat with the other five holes.

5. Spoon the mixture into the pastry and bake for 30 minutes, then use a spoon to poke a hole in the filling of each pie, and put an egg yolk into each hollow. Bake for another 15 minutes, then season and allow to cool before serving.

Chicken, chorizo and pepper pies

MAKES 6

If there were a picnic top trumps, the hand-held pie would rival the Scotch egg in the all-important portability and deliciousness categories. You can make your own pork pies, of course, but better, I think, to concentrate on the kind of pies that really benefit from being homemade. Mass-produced shortcrust pastry can become soggy when refrigerated, whereas you can pack these up crisp from the oven and enjoy them at their best.

FOR THE PASTRY
225G PLAIN FLOUR, PLUS EXTRA TO DUST
A PINCH OF SALT
1 TEASPOON SMOKED PAPRIKA
175G COLD BUTTER
50ML ICED WATER
VEGETABLE OIL, TO GREASE
1 EGG, BEATEN WITH A LITTLE WATER
    AND SALT

FOR THE FILLING
4 CHICKEN THIGHS
1 CELERY STALK, CHOPPED
1 CARROT, CHOPPED
1 BAY LEAF
4 PEPPERCORNS
2 TABLESPOONS OLIVE OIL
½ AN ONION, CHOPPED
½ A GREEN PEPPER, DESEEDED AND DICED
½ A RED PEPPER, DESEEDED AND DICED
75G CURED CHORIZO, SKINNED AND DICED
75G CRÈME FRAÎCHE

1. Sift the flour, salt and paprika into a bowl, and grate in the butter. Rub in with your fingertips, then add enough iced water to make a dough that comes cleanly away from the bowl. Wrap in baking parchment and chill for 30 minutes.

2. Put the chicken thighs into a large pan with the celery, carrot, bay leaf and peppercorns and cover with cold water. Bring to the boil, then lower the heat and simmer until the chicken is cooked through (about 20–30 minutes, depending on the size of the thighs). Remove the chicken and set aside to cool, then bring the liquid to the boil and cook until reduced by half to make a stock. Strain, discarding the vegetables.

3. Preheat the oven to 220°C/gas mark 7. Pick the meat off the chicken and discard the skin and bones. Cut the chicken meat into small cubes. Heat the oil in a frying pan over a medium heat and add the onion and peppers. Cook for about 5 minutes, until soft, then turn up the heat slightly, add the chorizo dice and sauté until they begin to crisp and release their oil. Stir in the chicken, followed by 50ml of the reduced stock, and then the crème fraîche.

4. Lightly grease a 6-hole muffin tray with oil. Roll out the pastry on a lightly floured surface to about 7mm thick, then, using a 9cm cutter, cut out six circles of pastry to line the holes, along with six slightly smaller lids. Make sure you don't stretch the pastry – try dropping the muffin tray on to the work surface from elbow height to encourage it into the holes.

5. Divide the filling between the pies and brush the rims with egg wash. Put the lids on, and press down with the back of a fork to seal well. Snip a small hole in each lid to let out steam, and brush the tops with egg wash. Bake for about 25 minutes, until golden, and allow to cool in the tray for 15 minutes before transferring to a rack to cool completely if eating cold.

Green potato salad

MAKES 6

Potato salad is a classic for a reason – and, although the joy of the first new season potatoes, dressed simply with a little butter, has become something of a sacred mantra amongst food writers, I secretly prefer them like this. Butter may be good, but come summer, mayonnaise is even better, especially when it's bright green.

This salad, while delicious eaten straight from the bowl when no one's looking, also transports very well. Don't make the mayonnaise until the day itself, or the herbs will lose some of their glorious colour, and consider substituting a mustard vinaigrette, replete with the same herbs, if the weather's very hot and you're carrying it a long way; homemade mayo has a nasty tendency to split.

500G NEW POTATOES
SALT AND PEPPER
2 TABLESPOONS WHITE WINE VINEGAR
3 TABLESPOONS OLIVE OIL
1 EGG YOLK
125ML VEGETABLE OIL
50ML EXTRA VIRGIN OLIVE OIL

A SQUEEZE OF LEMON JUICE
1 TEASPOON DIJON MUSTARD
1 TABLESPOON CAPERS, ROUGHLY CHOPPED
A GENEROUS MIXED HANDFUL OF FRESH
   TARRAGON, CHIVES AND FLAT-LEAF
   PARSLEY, FINELY CHOPPED

1. Put the potatoes into a large pan and cover with cold, salted water. Bring to the boil and simmer for about 15 minutes, depending on size, until tender. Meanwhile, whisk together the vinegar and olive oil to make a vinaigrette, and season.

2. Drain the potatoes well, then cut in half, or, if particularly large, into quarters. Toss together with the vinaigrette and leave to cool.

3. To make the mayonnaise, whisk the egg yolk for a minute, using a food mixer or electric whisk, then add a pinch of salt and continue to beat well for 30 seconds, until thick and sticky. Start adding the vegetable oil, a little at a time, whisking well, and making sure it's all well incorporated before adding any more or your mayonnaise will split.

4. Whisk in the olive oil in the same way, then, once it's all incorporated, whisk the mayonnaise for another 30 seconds until thick and glossy. Add a squeeze of lemon juice and the mustard and mix well.

5. Stir in the capers and the chopped herbs (there should be enough to turn the mayonnaise green – if your handful now seems skimpy, add more), then lift the potatoes out of the vinaigrette with a slotted spoon and put into a serving bowl. Toss with the mayonnaise and serve.

Peach and tomato salad

SERVES 4

It may sound a bizarre combination (well, it certainly did to me), but I don't think you need me to tell you how to prepare a classic tomato vinaigrette, or drizzle a few ripe plum tomatoes with extra virgin olive oil and basil leaves, so instead, I offer up this more unusual take on the tomato salad, inspired by a dish in Lindsey Bareham's mind-bogglingly comprehensive *Big Red Book of Tomatoes*.

I'm a firm believer in the idea that there's no point buying fresh tomatoes until about May, and, as really juicy peaches won't be with us until the end of that month, this is a brief, but wholeheartedly summery pleasure. Enjoy it while you can.

200G BABY PLUM TOMATOES, HALVED
2 RIPE PEACHES, HALVED, STONED AND
   THINLY SLICED
JUICE OF ½ A LEMON

SALT AND PEPPER
EXTRA VIRGIN OLIVE OIL
A SMALL BUNCH OF FRESH MINT, LEAVES
   CHOPPED

1. Put the tomatoes and peaches into a serving bowl and squeeze over the lemon juice. Season and drizzle with extra virgin olive oil.

2. Sprinkle with the mint and serve.

Green salad

SERVES 4

Not one of those plates of impeccably dressed lettuce found in the least pretentious of French restaurants, but a mélange of some of the season's finest green ingredients, which travel far better than any fragile variety of leaf.

Unlike fresh peas, which are only worth buying if you're sure they're super fresh (their natural sugars quickly convert to starch upon picking), broad beans in the pod should be snapped up as soon as you see them. Look for small, crisp pods – very young beans won't need shelling as below, but as soon as they develop that tough, pale green coat, it's worth a few minutes' fingernail work to enjoy them at their best. If you can't find fresh ones, however, the frozen variety will do.

SALT AND PEPPER
4 STALKS OF ASPARAGUS
300G SHELLED BROAD BEANS
200G PODDED PEAS
I COURGETTE
JUICE AND ZEST OF ½ A LEMON

EXTRA VIRGIN OLIVE OIL
100G FETA, CRUMBLED
A SMALL BUNCH OF FRESH BASIL, LEAVES TORN
I TEASPOON CHILLI FLAKES (OPTIONAL)

1. Bring a large pan of salted water to the boil and add the asparagus. Cook for 2 minutes, then add the beans. Cook for another minute, then add the peas and cook for a further minute. Drain and cool under running water, or plunge into a large bowl of iced water. (The asparagus should still have some crunch to it.)

2. Chop the asparagus into 1cm lengths, and use a vegetable peeler to cut the courgette into thin ribbons lengthwise. Combine all the vegetables and toss with the lemon juice and zest and a generous glug of extra virgin olive oil.

3. Add the cheese and basil, and the chilli flakes if using, then season lightly and toss together just before serving.

Picnic loaves

Many of the best picnic dishes aren't much to look at from the outside – Scotch eggs and pies, for example, are only revealed in their full glory when you bite into them, and this trio of stuffed loaves works on the same principle. Like many of the best superheroes, beneath their dull exterior lurks something quite extraordinary…well, if you get excited by sandwiches anyway. Which I really do.

More conventional sandwich recipes can be found on pages 169–76.

Scandinavian

SERVES 4–6

I EGG, AT ROOM TEMPERATURE
I ROUND CRUSTY WHITE LOAF, ABOUT
   400G
I50G CREAM CHEESE
5 CORNICHONS, THINLY SLICED

A SMALL BUNCH OF DILL, CHOPPED
¼ OF A RED ONION, FINELY CHOPPED
I50G SMOKED SALMON, SLICED
I PICKLED BEETROOT, SLICED
SALT AND PEPPER

1. Put the egg into a small pan and cover with cold water. Bring to the boil, then turn down the heat and simmer for 6 minutes. Plunge into iced water and leave to cool.

2. Meanwhile, cut the top off the bread to make a small lid. Scoop out the soft crumb inside with a spoon or using your hands, leaving a thin layer of bread around the edges. (You can, of course, blitz the crumb in a food processor and freeze as breadcrumbs.)

3. Mix together the cream cheese, cornichons, dill and red onion. Carefully peel the egg and slice.

4. Line the base of the loaf with the smoked salmon, followed by a layer of beetroot, the cheese and, finally, the egg, pushing it all down to ensure it fits if necessary. Season and replace the lid. Wrap well for transportation. Cut into wedges to serve.

Mediterranean

SERVES 4–6

This is probably the classic version of the picnic loaf: the olive oil in the pesto and the griddled vegetables will soak into the bread, with predictably lovely results. Because of this, you'll need to make it at least four hours in advance, to give the ingredients a chance to get to know each other before serving.

1 COURGETTE	50G FRESH BASIL, LEAVES ONLY
1 SMALL AUBERGINE	20G GRATED PARMESAN
1 RED PEPPER, HALVED AND DESEEDED	100ML EXTRA VIRGIN OLIVE OIL
OLIVE OIL	125G MOZZARELLA
SALT AND PEPPER	1 ROUND CRUSTY WHITE LOAF, ABOUT 400G
1 TABLESPOON PINE NUTS	

1. Cut the courgette and aubergine into thin lengthways slices, and each half pepper into two flat slices. Heat a griddle pan over a medium-high flame, and toss the vegetables with seasoned olive oil.

2. Cook the vegetables in batches for about 3 minutes on each side, until softened and beginning to char. Set aside.

3. Toast the pine nuts in a dry pan until beginning to colour, then put them, along with the basil, Parmesan and extra virgin olive oil, into a food processor and pulse briefly until you have a coarse pesto. Slice the mozzarella.

4. Cut the top off the bread to make a small lid. Scoop out the soft crumb inside with a spoon or using your hands, leaving a thin layer of bread around the edges. (You can, of course, blitz the crumb in a food processor and freeze as breadcrumbs.)

5. Line the base of the loaf with a thick layer of pesto, then a layer of aubergine, then a layer of mozzarella. Season, then top with courgettes, then red pepper and finally, any leftover pesto. Replace the lid and wrap tightly in clingfilm. Put into the fridge, weighted down with a plate and a tin, or whatever works for you, and leave for at least 4 hours, or overnight, before serving – bring to room temperature before you slice.

The New Yorker

SERVES 4–6

Loosely based on the Reuben sandwich, but without the American-style salt beef, which can be difficult to find here – although feel free to substitute it if you have a source, and prefer it to the spicier pastrami. (Note that the corned beef called for by native recipes bears little relation to the stuff sold here in tins.)

I call this a picnic loaf, but because of the melted cheese element, it's better served warm: if you have a culinary blowtorch, you'll find it easier to use that than the grill to melt the cheese. Best for picnics at home – or just lunch!

1 ROUND WHOLEMEAL OR RYE LOAF,
  ABOUT 400G
100G SAUERKRAUT, DRAINED
150G PASTRAMI, THINLY SLICED
60G EMMENTHAL OR GRUYÈRE,
  THINLY SLICED

FOR THE RUSSIAN DRESSING
4 TABLESPOONS THICK SOURED
  CREAM OR CRÈME FRAÎCHE
1½ TABLESPOONS STRONG HORSERADISH
  SAUCE
½ TEASPOON WORCESTERSHIRE SAUCE
1½ TABLESPOONS TOMATO KETCHUP
1 TABLESPOON FINELY CHOPPED FRESH
  PARSLEY OR CHIVES
¼ OF A SMALL ONION, VERY FINELY CHOPPED
1 LARGE GHERKIN, FINELY CHOPPED
TABASCO SAUCE (OPTIONAL)
SALT AND PEPPER

1. Slice the top off the loaf and scoop out the inside with a spoon, leaving a thin layer of bread round the crust and saving the innards for breadcrumbs.

2. Mix together all the ingredients for the dressing, seasoning to taste – you can add more of anything if you like.

3. Preheat the grill to medium. Spoon a third of the dressing over the base of the loaf, followed by half the sauerkraut. Top with a thick layer of pastrami, and then the cheese.

4. Put the loaf under the grill for 2–3 minutes to melt the cheese, being careful not to burn the top of the loaf. Top with the remaining sauerkraut and dressing, then squash on the lid of the loaf. Wrap tightly until ready to serve.

Coconut and cardamom ice

MAKES ABOUT 25 SQUARES

The fresh flavour of cardamom works like a dream with the coconut – but, whether you include it or not, this is a British classic. Tooth-rottingly sweet, it's in the grand tradition of childhood treats – just enough will always be the square that makes you feel a teensy bit queasy. There are few nicer things to munch on the beach, though, and it will certainly give you energy for a foolhardy dip in the sea, or chasing the dog away from someone else's picnic.

250ML CONDENSED MILK
5 CARDAMOM PODS, CRUSHED
225G ICING SUGAR, SIFTED, PLUS EXTRA
   TO DUST

200G DESICCATED COCONUT
PINK FOOD COLOURING

1. Put the condensed milk and the cardamom pods into a pan and heat gently, stirring constantly, until just simmering, then take off the heat and set aside to infuse for 45 minutes.

2. Put the icing sugar and coconut into a large bowl and stir together. Remove the cardamom pods from the milk and discard, then pour the milk into the bowl and mix well – it should be stiff and dough-like in consistency.

3. Divide in half, and put into separate bowls. Add a few drops of food colouring to one of the bowls, and work in well until evenly coloured.

4. Dust a work surface with icing sugar, and shape the white dough into a rough rectangle about 1.5cm thick (a rolling pin may be helpful). Do the same with the pink dough, and place on top. Transfer to a board and leave to set overnight.

5. Cut into squares and store in an airtight container.

Barbour bars (aka fruity flapjacks)

MAKES ABOUT 12 BARS

Forgive the slightly twee, Boden catalogue-esque name, but the premise of this recipe was to find an energy-rich snack sturdy enough to stand up to being shoved into a coat pocket and taken on a long and muddy walk, only to emerge triumphant just when you start to feel that, frankly, if the pub isn't around the next corner, you'll sit down on the grass and weep. After much experimentation, I think I've cracked it – stuffed full of good things, it's a smug version of Kendal mint cake. If you don't have, or don't fancy, some of the fruits or nuts, feel free to leave them out, and make up the total weight with more of the others.

250G BUTTER
125G SOFT BROWN SUGAR
5 TABLESPOONS CLEAR HONEY
300G ROLLED OATS
75G DESICCATED COCONUT

25G CHOPPED MIXED PEEL
70G DRIED APRICOTS, CHOPPED
70G DRIED FIGS, CHOPPED
50G SKIN-ON ALMONDS, CHOPPED
50G PUMPKIN SEEDS

1.   Preheat the oven to 180°C/gas mark 4. Put the butter, sugar and honey into a large pan over a medium heat and melt, stirring to mix.

2.   Lightly grease a 23cm square baking tin. Tip the remaining ingredients into the pan with the butter and sugar mixture, and stir well so they're all coated.

3.   Spoon the mixture into the tin and press it all down firmly with the back of a spoon to compact it. Bake for 40 minutes, until golden, then allow to cool completely in the tin before cutting into 12 bar shapes – this is important or they will crumble. Wrap tightly in foil before transporting.

Whisky and ginger fruit cake

MAKES ABOUT 12 BARS

It may be a Christmas classic, but really, fruit cake never tastes better than outdoors: I think because it's so very dense and sweet you need a fresh breeze to fully appreciate the flavours. This is a sticky, spicy little number which is particularly good on a winter walk, or after a day mucking about on boats. As usual, if you don't like glacé cherries, or mixed peel, simply make up the weight with more of some of the other dried fruits.

I can hear people wondering what on earth they should do with the rest of a bottle of ginger wine – to which I say, send it my way, or, alternatively, discover the joys of the whisky mac, perhaps the finest cold cure known to man.

250G CURRANTS	1 TEASPOON GROUND MIXED SPICE
250G SULTANAS	70G GROUND ALMONDS
100G CHOPPED MIXED PEEL	125G BUTTER, SOFTENED
100G GLACÉ CHERRIES, CUT IN HALF	75G DARK MUSCOVADO SUGAR
100G DRIED PRUNES, CHOPPED	50G SOFT LIGHT BROWN SUGAR
65ML WHISKY	4 EGGS, BEATEN
85ML GINGER WINE	A PINCH OF SALT
110G PLAIN FLOUR	100G PECANS, ROUGHLY CHOPPED
½ TEASPOON BAKING POWDER	25G GLACÉ GINGER, ROUGHLY CHOPPED

1. Put the dried fruit into a large bowl with the whisky and ginger wine, stir and cover. Leave to soak overnight.

2. Preheat the oven to 160°C/gas mark 3, and grease and double-line a 20cm round springform cake tin with baking parchment.

3. Sift together the flour, baking powder, mixed spice and ground almonds. In another bowl, beat the butter and sugars together until light and fluffy, then gradually beat in the eggs, a little at a time.

4. Fold in the flour mixture, along with a pinch of salt, then stir in the pecans and glacé ginger, and the soaked dried fruits with all their soaking liquid. Spoon the mixture into the prepared tin and smooth the surface, scooping out a small dent in the middle to prevent it doming in the oven.

5. Bake for 1 hour 10 minutes, then check – if it's browning too rapidly, cover with foil. Bake for another 30 minutes, then check whether it's done by inserting a skewer into the middle. If it comes out clean, the cake's ready; if not, put it back into the oven and check every 10 minutes until it's done.

6. Leave to cool completely in the tin. If you're not eating it immediately, you can feed it like a Christmas cake by poking a few small holes in the surface with a skewer and pouring over a little whisky or ginger wine over every week – but you're unlikely to regret tucking in sooner.

Barbecues

Given how much easier the lot of a cook has become in the last couple of centuries,* why do we still persist in the practice of cooking food over open flames? The answer, apart from the fact that it's jolly nice to stand around in the sunshine, watching your lunch gently singe, is that, like our prehistoric ancestors, we enjoy the taste of burnt food. Only slightly burnt, mind – although my family does demand its sausages with the kind of carbon crust which would send health writers into a carcinogenic tailspin – but still with the kind of mouthwatering dollop of smoke you can only get from the timeless marriage of meat juice and hot coals.

Fire would have been the only cooking method available to the humans who, 1.8 million years ago, first decided they fancied eating that antelope toasted and, thanks to its intense heat, it's still a method capable of producing some of the most flavourful results. I like to tell myself as I'm cycling past the local strip of *ocakbasi* charcoal grill restaurants with my mouth open that I'm the helpless pawn of millions of years of genetic inheritance, but I'm probably just greedy.

It's no surprise, then, that most things seem to taste better when cooked over coals, but although I wouldn't dream of getting all snooty about the old friends that have sustained me through so many damp and merry afternoons, there is more to barbecuing than burgers, bangers and the odd orange chicken wing. Almost every culture on earth has some tradition of grilling, so there's really no need to confine yourself to stuff that looks like it's gone six rounds with the St Tropez. Once you've got your *batterie de cuisine* in place, the world really is your barbecued oyster – preferably smothered with Cajun butter and cheese, New Orleans-style.

* Actually we've had ovens since 29,000 BC, and if you think turkeys are big, thank your lucky stars you've never had to roast a mammoth.

Equipment

Although I hesitate to recommend those disposable terrors that burn everything in sight, including the grass, or punt, you stand them on (I speak from bitter experience) before disappearing into landfill, just about anything else goes: indeed the best barbecue I've ever eaten from appeared to have been made from the wheel of a truck. If you're in the market for a new model, it's useful to invest in one with a lid and adjustable air vents, so you can dip your toe into the low and slow world of American barbecue.

Personally I prefer to use coals to gas, because it makes the thing far more portable, and feels more excitingly caveman-like, but you'll get a smoky flavour with both, so if you lack patience and like dry-clean-only clothes, the cleaner, faster wonders of gas might be a better choice. (Whatever you plump for, however, never leave it uncovered between cook-outs: if there's one thing that British summertimes can be relied upon to provide, it's rain, and water and ash will destroy your barbecue faster than an inebriated guest in high heels.)

Purists insist on lump charcoal made from hardwood in the traditional fashion, on the basis that it burns at a higher temperature than the re-formed briquettes, and is easier to control. I'm not enough of an expert to know if they speak the truth, but I do always seek out the British sustainable stuff — it's quite widely available now, and manufacturers claim that, although it's a bit more expensive, you'll use less of it. It certainly has the smug factor going for it.

A long-handled pair of tongs is absolutely essential if you don't fancy finding out what you'd smell like chargrilled, as is a sturdy spatula for flipping burgers and other more fragile items. For a long time I dismissed those fish-shaped grill cages as a classic gimmick in the same mould as the egg slicer, but actually they make turning a school of sardines an awful lot easier.

Less excitingly, you'll find a fierce brush for cleaning the grill afterwards worth its weight in bristles (rubbing the grill with the cut side of a lemon, or half an onion, is also handy for getting the gunk off).

Heed those scary summertime salmonella adverts, and bring out a meat thermometer to check things are done before serving: if you don't own one, you could just cut every piece open to check, but mauled merguez might not impress the mother-in-law (although food poisoning tends to be even less of a crowd-pleaser, so please opt for one approach or the other).

Cloches, to keep food covered before cooking, are essential if you're plagued by flying beasts (or persistent felines), and a table near the barbecue, for food, tools and, of course, a drink, is handy if you've got the room. I often end up piling plates on the floor, which doesn't always go down well with my fussier guests.

Technique

Forget noxious gels and firelighters: the best way to start a barbecue is to make a chimney of coal – you can buy special metal cylinder starters for the purpose, or craft your own if you're handy with the welding torch. Simply pile the coals inside, then light the bottom with some old newspaper: in about fifteen minutes, they'll have a rosy glow to gladden your hungry heart.

Cylinder or not, wait until the coals are an even, ashy grey colour before you even start to think about cooking anything. To assess their heat (a worthwhile exercise: you wouldn't just stick something in the oven without checking the temperature), place your hand above them, about the same height as the food would be – remembering that the grill itself will be hot – and start counting. If you have to move it after a couple of seconds, you have a hot grill, perfect for searing steaks and the like. If you can stand three seconds, it's medium-hot, or four, medium – both good for general grilling – while five or more qualifies as a low heat, best for slower, gentler cooking.

Lastly, men aren't better at barbecues – they're just better at standing in the garden swallowing beer and occasionally poking at the coals while all the hard work goes on inside, so, ladies, grab yourself a drink and some tongs and be proud to call yourself a feminist.

Setting the scene

You don't need outdoor space to host a barbecue: increasing numbers of parks and beaches have dedicated barbecuing areas, although it's wise to check before setting out – you may be forced to retreat miserably to a pub if you fall foul of local regulations. A picnic rug will do just as well as a table and chairs, as long as your menu doesn't require too much in the way of cutlery.

Fairy lights in bushes or trees always look pretty, if you've got the battery-operated sort (or a long extension lead that isn't going to trip people up on their way to the loo), but you can't beat a sprinkling of candles for atmosphere. Storm lanterns are perfect protection from the wind, but you can also substitute clean jam jars, which are far less likely to shatter in the heat than ordinary glasses. The only really specific tip I'd give is that, if you're barbecuing in the evening, you should try to provide some blankets for the cold-blooded – there's nothing nicer than a garden full of people chatting and drinking long into the night (unless you live next door to it).

Mexican barbecue

SERVES 6

We don't tend to associate barbecues with cuisine south of the border – but even the most clichéd of Mexican dishes benefits from a touch of charcoal. Fajitas and tacos stuffed with chargrilled steak and vegetables, smoky quesadillas – even nachos can be stuck on a baking tray on the barbie if you really must.

In Mexico itself, barbecuing is big news: coastal regions specialize, unsurprisingly, in seafood, serving up fish you've never even dreamt of with a squeeze of lime, and Sundays are a popular time for big family *parrilladas*, or grills, all over the country. (In the north, they also go in for roasting entire kids, minus the head and the hooves, but you'll run up against certain practical difficulties if you try to do that in this country.)

Grilled onglet with green sauce

SERVES 6

I don't know why we don't barbecue more steak in the UK – it's the closest you'll get to a super-hot restaurant grill at home, and far quicker than chicken, sausages and all those other barbecue staples which need cooking through on a heat source that, however handy you are with the firelighters, will always be just a little unreliable. Perhaps it's the expense – we still tend to think of barbecues as a repository for cheap meat – but unless you plan to follow the honourable British tradition of burning everything to a cinder, this is an idea that deserves to be buried as deep as a novelty naturist apron.

Nevertheless I've gone for flavoursome but thrifty onglet, or skirt steak, a popular cut across the Channel, but strangely difficult to find here: indeed, it's sometimes still known as 'butcher's steak', as it was what the man himself would take home to eat with his own family. And eating what the professionals eat is generally a good idea – especially when it's this tasty. Onglet is sometimes found in supermarkets, but you're more likely to track it down at a proper butcher's or farmers' market, or online. Give it a go, it's well worth it.

2 TABLESPOONS CUMIN SEEDS	1 TEASPOON SALT
3 GREEN JALAPEÑO OR OTHER	1 TEASPOON GROUND BLACK PEPPER
MEDIUM-HOT GREEN CHILLIES, DESEEDED	200ML VEGETABLE OR OLIVE OIL
3 CLOVES OF GARLIC, ROUGHLY CHOPPED	6 X 120G ONGLET STEAKS (SKIRT STEAK)
2 HANDFULS OF FRESH CORIANDER	6 LARGE TORTILLAS, TO SERVE (SEE PAGE 298)

1. Put the cumin seeds into a dry frying pan over a medium-high heat and toast for a couple of minutes, shaking the pan, until fragrant. Put into a food processor with the chillies, garlic and coriander and whiz to a purée, then add the salt, pepper and oil and whiz briefly to combine.

2. Put the steaks into a large zippable bag and add the marinade. Refrigerate for at least 4 hours or overnight, then bring to room temperature while the barbecue heats.

3. Sear for 3 minutes on each side, then let them rest for 5 minutes before serving, cut into strips. (Be careful to cut across the grain of the meat – the ridges and furrows – rather than with them, or it will be tough.)

Corn on the cob with smoky spiced butter

SERVES 6

I always find that corn gets pushed to the side of the grill to make way for the meat and ends up being ready at about the time when you want to start clearing the plates, so I sneakily boil it first, and just put it on the grill to finish off. You might want to skip that stage if you've got strict vegetarians coming over: they tend not to fancy stuff that's been grilled in close proximity to steak, however deliciously charred the results.

3 EARS OF CORN, CUT IN HALF
SALT
100G SALTED BUTTER, SOFTENED
1 CHIPOTLE CHILLI, SOAKED IN BOILING
   WATER FOR 15 MINUTES, THEN DRAINED
   AND ROUGHLY CHOPPED

1 CLOVE OF GARLIC, CRUSHED
6 LIME WEDGES

1. Put the corn into a large pan of salted boiling water and cook for 6 minutes.

2. Meanwhile, put the butter, chilli and garlic into a food processor and whiz until smooth and well combined. Form into a sausage shape, wrap in clingfilm and refrigerate.

3. Barbecue the corn for about 10 minutes, until charred, then serve with the chipotle butter and wedges of lime.

Bean burgers

MAKES 6

Unapologetic retro chic, these – but it wouldn't be Mexican without some beans somewhere. The addition of chunks of salty cheese (feta standing in for the *queso fresco* that I fondly imagine would be used in the Yucatan, once they'd stopped laughing at the very idea of *hamburguesas de frijoles*) and a little spice lifts them above the dry, crumbly versions of yore – they should be crisp on the outside and creamy within.

I shan't lie, however: thanks to its parsimonious fat content, the bean burger is always going to be more delicate than its meaty cousin, so make sure you oil the grill well before cooking, and be very careful when turning them over. Alternatively, you can fry them in a lightly oiled pan and then simply put them on to the barbecue for a minute before serving, for that smoky flavour – or, if you've got strict vegetarians coming, and only one grill, cook them entirely in the pan, they'll be just as good. I like them topped with mashed avocado.

2 TABLESPOONS VEGETABLE OIL, PLUS
    EXTRA FOR GREASING
I ONION, CUT INTO SMALL DICE
4 CLOVES OF GARLIC, CRUSHED
I–2 GREEN CHILLIES, DESEEDED AND
    FINELY CHOPPED
I TEASPOON GROUND CUMIN
3 X 400G TINS OF BEANS, DRAINED – I LIKE
    A MIXTURE OF PINTO AND BLACK, BUT FEEL
    FREE TO EXPERIMENT

A GENEROUS HANDFUL OF FRESH CORIANDER,
    CHOPPED
75G CORNMEAL
75G FETA, CRUMBLED
WEDGE OF LIME
SALT AND PEPPER
I EGG, BEATEN

1. Heat the oil in a large frying pan over a medium heat and gently fry the onion for about 6 minutes, until softened but not browned. Add the garlic and chillies and cook for another 3 minutes, then stir in the cumin and cook for a further minute.

2. Add the drained beans and allow them to heat through before taking the pan off the heat and roughly mashing the contents (a potato masher works well): you should still be able to see some whole beans in there. Allow to cool slightly.

3. Stir in the coriander, cornmeal, feta and a squeeze of lime juice and season to taste, remembering that the cheese is quite salty. Add the egg and mix in well, then form the mixture into 6 burgers and put on a plate. Cover and chill for at least 30 minutes, then cook for about 5 minutes on each side on a well-greased grill, brushing them with oil before turning them over.

Mexican chocolate banana split

SERVES 6

Forget the Swiss and the Belgians – for my money, the best chocolate in the world comes from Mexico. They like it sweet and slightly spicy, just like this rich and lovely sauce, which, poured over ice cream and sticky bananas, makes a deliciously unsophisticated end to the meal.

I sometimes skip grilling the bananas and just make the dish in the traditional fashion, with uncooked fruit – but if you're more patient than me, it does give them a nice smoky flavour.

6 BANANAS
150ML DOUBLE CREAM
100G DARK CHOCOLATE, BROKEN INTO
   CHUNKS
½ TEASPOON GROUND CINNAMON

½ TEASPOON CHILLI FLAKES
A DASH OF VANILLA ESSENCE
500ML TUB OF VANILLA ICE CREAM, TO SERVE
6 TABLESPOONS FLAKED ALMONDS, TOASTED

1. Wrap each banana, skin and all, in foil.

2. To make the sauce, heat the cream in a pan until simmering, then take off the heat and add the chocolate, cinnamon, chilli flakes and vanilla essence. Leave to sit for a minute or so, then stir well to combine into a smooth chocolate sauce.

3. When you've finished your main course, tuck the foil-wrapped bananas into the embers and leave them there until you're hungry: they should be soft and sticky after about 15 minutes.

4. Put each into a bowl, then open the foil and cut the banana in half lengthways. Put a couple of scoops of ice cream in the middle, drizzle with chocolate sauce and scatter with flaked almonds.

Satay fest

Who doesn't love food on a stick? It's a pleasure as elemental as sticking Hula Hoops on your fingers and pretending you're some sort of bejewelled medieval potentate – you never grow out of it. Back to the point, satay is a speciality of south-east Asia, to be found sizzling away at night markets and hawker stalls all over the region, although in my experience modernity hasn't been especially kind to the dish: the last lot I had in Singapore tasted strongly of lighter fluid. But perhaps I was just unlucky. In any case, it was an awful lot nicer than the re-formed bits of salty chicken that generally pass for satay in this country.

All the satay recipes that follow could, indeed should, be prepared a few hours in advance to allow them to wallow in the marinade, and of course, the sorbet will need time to freeze – so you'll have nothing to do when your guests arrive but light the barbecue and pass round the drinks. Cold lager would be apt.

If you're using wooden skewers, you'll need to soak them in water for half an hour so they don't burn when they hit the grill. Each recipe makes enough for six skewers.

Thai pork skewers

SERVES 4–6

Pork is a meat that I think barbecues brilliantly: like lamb, it has enough natural fat to keep it juicy, however fierce the heat, although, unlike lamb, you do need to make sure it's cooked through before serving. This sweet, slightly spicy marinade will caramelize on the grill to create a seriously delicious crust.

I TEASPOON CORIANDER SEEDS

½ TEASPOON CUMIN SEEDS

I TEASPOON SALT

2 STALKS OF LEMONGRASS, PEELED AND
  CHOPPED

I DRIED RED CHILLI, CHOPPED

I TEASPOON TURMERIC

I TABLESPOON SOFT LIGHT BROWN SUGAR

150ML COCONUT CREAM

I TEASPOON FISH SAUCE

400G PORK NECK OR SHOULDER, CUT INTO
  BITE-SIZE CHUNKS

1. Toast the coriander and cumin seeds in a dry pan over a high heat until fragrant, stirring so they don't burn. Put into a pestle and mortar along with the salt, lemongrass and chilli and grind to a rough powder, then mix in the turmeric and sugar.

2. Put the coconut cream into a bowl and stir in the spice powder and fish sauce to make a paste. Add the pork chunks and stir well to coat. Cover and refrigerate for at least 3 hours.

3. Thread the pieces on to pre-soaked skewers, squashing them on well: you shouldn't be able to see any stick.

4. Grill, turning occasionally, for about 10–12 minutes, until cooked through.

Classic chicken satay with peanut sauce

SERVES 4–6

It wouldn't be a true satay fest without the version we first took to our hearts – although I'd humbly hope that this bears little resemblance to that suspiciously juicy buffet favourite, served with its mandatory sachet of peanut butter. Make it with thigh meat, rather than breast, if you want your skewers to taste of marinated chicken, not just marinade.

2 CLOVES OF GARLIC
2CM PIECE OF GINGER, PEELED
3 TABLESPOONS KECAP MANIS
    (INDONESIAN SOY SAUCE, AVAILABLE
    FROM SPECIALIST SHOPS AND LARGER
    SUPERMARKETS – YOU CAN APPROXIMATE IT
    BY MIXING EQUAL PARTS DARK SOY SAUCE
    AND SOFT LIGHT BROWN SUGAR)
1 TABLESPOON SOY SAUCE
600G CHICKEN THIGH FILLETS, SKINNED
    (ABOUT 8 FILLETS, IF YOU'RE DOING IT
    YOURSELF), CUT INTO BITE-SIZE PIECES

FOR THE PEANUT SAUCE
150G SALTED ROASTED PEANUTS
2 RED CHILLIES, DESEEDED AND CHOPPED
1 CLOVE OF GARLIC, PEELED AND CHOPPED
4 SHALLOTS, PEELED AND CHOPPED
1 TEASPOON SHRIMP PASTE
1 TABLESPOON VEGETABLE OIL
300ML COCONUT MILK
1 TABLESPOON LIME JUICE

1. Mash together the garlic and ginger to make a paste. Scrape this into a large bowl and stir in the kecap manis and soy sauce.

2. Add the chicken pieces and stir to coat. Cover and refrigerate for at least 3 hours.

3. Meanwhile, to make the peanut sauce, put the nuts into a dry pan over a medium-high heat and toast, stirring, until beginning to colour.

4. Put them into a food processor and pulse to roughly chop, then add the chillies, garlic, shallots and shrimp paste and whiz until you have a fine purée.

5. Heat the oil in the pan on a medium-high heat and fry the paste, stirring frequently, until the shallots and garlic lose their raw scent. Pour in the coconut milk and cook for a few minutes to thicken slightly, then stir in the lime juice and keep at room temperature until ready to serve.

6. Thread the chicken pieces on to pre-soaked skewers, pushing them together so you can't see any stick between them.

7. Grill for 8–10 minutes, until cooked through, and serve with the peanut sauce.

Vietnamese-style prawn skewers

SERVES 4–6

These are fiercely aromatic and utterly addictive, and I could quite happily eat three or four skewers on their own – they taste completely and happily of holidays. Thread the prawns individually on to pre-soaked cocktail sticks and this also makes a very fine canapé.

2 SHALLOTS, CHOPPED

3 CLOVES OF GARLIC, CHOPPED

3 LEMONGRASS STEMS, PEELED AND
   CHOPPED

2 TABLESPOONS FISH SAUCE

2 TABLESPOONS LIME JUICE

2 TABLESPOONS VEGETABLE OIL

18 LARGE RAW TIGER PRAWNS, SHELLED
   AND DEVEINED

FOR THE DIPPING SAUCE

2 TABLESPOONS CASTER SUGAR

100ML WATER

2 CLOVES OF GARLIC, CRUSHED

2 TABLESPOONS FISH SAUCE

2 TABLESPOONS LIME JUICE

½ A RED CHILLI, DESEEDED AND FINELY
   CHOPPED

1. Put the shallots, garlic and lemongrass stems into a food processor and whiz to a purée. Stir in the fish sauce, lime juice and vegetable oil, then tip into a bowl and add the prawns. Stir to coat, then cover, chill and leave to marinate for 2 hours.

2. To make the dipping sauce, stir the sugar into the water until dissolved, then add the rest of the ingredients and stir well.

3. Thread the marinated prawns on to four pre-soaked wooden skewers, and grill for 3 minutes on each side. Serve immediately, with the dipping sauce.

Javanese lamb satay

SERVES 4–6

Any mention of Java always puts me in mind of that wonderfully overblown 1960s disaster film *Krakatoa, East of Java*, widely ridiculed both for its special effects and for the fact that the volcano in question is actually west of that Indonesian island. I don't remember any mention of the local food on screen, however, which is a shame, because it sounds pretty interesting: sweet and spicy, and always served with a liberal dollop of Indonesia's beloved thick and treacly *kecap manis* soy sauce.

I TABLESPOON TAMARIND PASTE
3 CLOVES OF GARLIC, CHOPPED
3 SHALLOTS, CHOPPED
5CM PIECE OF GINGER, PEELED
   AND CHOPPED
I TABLESPOON DARK BROWN SUGAR
I TABLESPOON SOY SAUCE
I TEASPOON GROUND CORIANDER
I TABLESPOON VEGETABLE OIL
300G BONELESS LAMB SHOULDER,
   CHOPPED INTO BITE-SIZE CHUNKS

FOR THE DIPPING SAUCE
125ML KECAP MANIS (SEE PAGE 237)
2 TABLESPOONS LIME JUICE
I RED CHILLI, DESEEDED AND
   FINELY CHOPPED

1. Mix the tamarind paste with 3 tablespoons of boiling water. Put into a food processor with the remaining ingredients, apart from the lamb and dipping sauce ingredients, and whiz to make a paste. Put the lamb pieces into a bowl, add the paste, and stir well. Cover, refrigerate and leave to chill for at least 3 hours.

2. To make the dipping sauce, stir together all the ingredients and taste – you may wish to add a little more lime juice if you're averse to sweet flavours.

3. Thread the lamb on to soaked wooden skewers, packing the pieces on tightly, and grill for about 8–10 minutes, turning, until charred and almost cooked through. Serve with the dipping sauce.

Thai-style crisp salad

I've called this Thai-style because while I've no idea whether they go in much for cabbage and pink radish in Phuket, they'd certainly recognize the salty-sour dressing, which makes a refreshing contrast to the smoky, sweet flavours of chargrilled meat. It can happily be made a few hours in advance and refrigerated.

2 TABLESPOONS LIME JUICE

2 TEASPOONS SUGAR

A PINCH OF SALT

2 TABLESPOONS FISH SAUCE

I CUCUMBER, CUT INTO BATONS

150G RADISHES, SLICED

I CARROT, GRATED

½ A RED CABBAGE, SHREDDED

A HANDFUL OF FRESH MINT, CHOPPED

A HANDFUL OF FRESH CORIANDER, CHOPPED

1. Put the lime juice, sugar, salt and fish sauce into a bowl and whisk together to make a dressing.

2. Toss the dressing with the salad ingredients until they are well coated, then cover until ready to serve.

Coconut and lemongrass sorbet

SERVES 4–6

The perfect palate cleanser – creamy without being cloying, aromatic without demanding too much from your tastebuds after that whistlestop tour round the smoking grills of south-east Asia. Because I have a sneaking fondness for the piña colada (only on holiday, mind), I'd hazard a guess that it's also pretty good served in a glass with a splash of rum – hell, why not throw in a pineapple garnish while you're at it?

150G CASTER SUGAR

1 TABLESPOON LIME JUICE

750ML COCONUT MILK

4 STALKS OF LEMONGRASS, BRUISED

1. Put the sugar into a pan with 150ml of water and set over a medium heat. Stir until the sugar has dissolved, then bring to the boil.

2. Add the lime juice and turn down the heat. Simmer for 5 minutes, then allow to cool slightly.

3. Put 175ml of the resulting syrup into a pan (discarding the rest), along with the coconut milk and lemongrass stalks. Heat to a simmer, then take off the heat and leave to infuse for 30 minutes.

4. Remove the lemongrass stalks and churn the sorbet in an ice cream maker if you have one. Otherwise, put it into a freezerproof container and freeze until it's almost solid (this will take about 3 hours). Use a fork to scrape it into a food processor, then whiz until slushy. Return to the container and freeze again until solid.

Big Moor-ish bake

SERVES 6

As the name suggests, I've taken a bit of a liberty with the flavours of North Africa here – yoghurt and grilled lamb is a combination you're more likely to come across in Turkey or Greece, but the spices are definitely Moorish. The distinctly European apricot tart can be excused, meanwhile, because it's the kind of thing you might well come across in one of Morocco's many excellent French pâtisseries. (And also, of course, because it's incredibly moreish.) The gin fizzes are not in the least North African, I admit, but are a handy way of using up the rosemary syrup you're left with after making the tart. So let's just call it Moorish in spirit. You can make the tart and the aubergine salad, and marinate the lamb, up to a day ahead, leaving you very little to do at the last minute except barbecue and drink gin.

Rosemary gin fizzes

If you're not baking the apricot tart, you can make a more classic gin fizz by replacing the syrup with 2 teaspoons of caster sugar, and leaving out the rosemary garnish: it'll still be delicious. The egg white gives it a wonderful frothiness and, if you don't have any immediate desire to make custard or ice cream (more fool you), they can be bought separately in chilled cartons from most supermarkets.

PER PERSON
I LEMON
50ML GIN
2 TEASPOONS ROSEMARY SYRUP
  (SEE PAGE 248)

I EGG WHITE
ICE, TO SHAKE
CHILLED SODA WATER, TO TOP
A SMALL SPRIG OF ROSEMARY

I. Put a tumbler into the freezer for 30 minutes. Peel a thin ribbon of lemon rind if you like, and reserve as a garnish. Juice the lemon and strain out any pips.

2. Put the lemon juice into a cocktail shaker with the gin, rosemary syrup and egg white. Take the glass out of the freezer. Fill the shaker with ice.

3. Shake vigorously for a minute, then strain into the glass and top up with soda water. Garnish with the reserved lemon rind, if using, and a sprig of rosemary.

Spiced shoulder of lamb

SERVES 6

When I tested this recipe out during Euro 2012, my guinea pigs were incredulous – they refused to believe that a whole shoulder of lamb could go on to the barbecue at kick-off, come off at half-time, and be carved ready to spice up the tedious post-match analysis. OK, so I had to nip off a couple of times during the first half to turn the thing over, but I'm not much of a football fan, so I didn't miss anything. Thankfully for my professional pride it was absolutely perfect: charred on the outside, rare in the middle, and wonderfully smoky.

I'm wary of giving an exact cooking time, as barbecues, and joints, can vary, so I'd advise deploying a meat thermometer to judge when it's done to your liking.

4 CLOVES OF GARLIC, CRUSHED

2–3 TABLESPOONS DRIED CHILLI FLAKES

3 TEASPOONS GROUND CUMIN

3 TEASPOONS GROUND CORIANDER

I TEASPOON CARAWAY SEEDS, CRUSHED
    IN A PESTLE AND MORTAR

2 TEASPOONS SALT

1.8–2KG SHOULDER OF LAMB

300G GREEK YOGHURT

2 TABLESPOONS EXTRA VIRGIN OLIVE OIL

6 FLATBREADS

1. Mix together the garlic, spices and salt. Rub this all over the lamb, massaging it in well, then cover and leave to marinate at room temperature for at least 2 hours (you can leave it overnight if you prefer, in which case refrigerate, and bring to room temperature before cooking).

2. Once the barbecue is ready for cooking, add the lamb, cover and cook for about 40 minutes, turning a couple of times. Bear in mind that because of the fat in the meat, if you try to start cooking on a barbecue that's too hot, it will simply burn, so be patient and wait until the coals are an even grey colour.

3. Take the lamb off the barbecue, cover and leave to rest somewhere warm for about 30 minutes. Mix together the yoghurt and oil and season well.

4. While you're carving the meat, put the flatbreads on to the barbecue to toast. Serve the meat on a platter surrounded by flatbreads, and pass around the yoghurt for dolloping.

Aubergine and tomato salad

SERVES 6

Aubergines work very well on the barbecue, but if you cook them along with the lamb it won't leave you much time to make the salad, so I prefer to do it in advance in the oven. Barbecue fiends who don't object to lighting the thing twice in a day could do step 1 on a covered grill instead.

1KG RIPE TOMATOES
3 LARGE AUBERGINES
3 TABLESPOONS OLIVE OIL
6 CLOVES OF GARLIC, THINLY SLICED
1 TEASPOON GROUND CUMIN
A PINCH OF SUGAR

½ A LEMON
SALT AND PEPPER
A HANDFUL OF FRESH FLAT-LEAF PARSLEY,
   ROUGHLY CHOPPED
A HANDFUL OF FRESH CORIANDER, ROUGHLY
   CHOPPED

1. Preheat the oven to 220°C/gas mark 7. Cut the tomatoes in half and prick the aubergines several times with a fork. Put them into a lightly oiled roasting tin and cook for about 45 minutes, until soft and lightly charred.

2. When the aubergines are cool enough to handle, strip them from their skins and roughly chop the flesh. You can skin the tomatoes too if you want, but, in the spirit of rusticity, I just chop them.

3. Heat the rest of the olive oil in a large pan over a medium heat and cook the garlic until softened. Add the cumin and cook, stirring, for another minute, then tip in the tomatoes and their juices, plus a pinch of sugar, and cook for 5 minutes.

4. Stir in the aubergine, along with a good squeeze of lemon juice, and season to taste. Allow to cool to room temperature.

5. Just before serving, stir in the chopped herbs.

Apricot and rosemary frangipane tart

SERVES 6

This lovely tart positively glows golden with fruit – I like to keep it hidden until dessert, to maximize the wow factor as I set it down on the table, but there's some truth to the argument that I'm an enormous show-off. Rosemary always reminds me of holidays in the south of France, where it grows wild in enormous dusty clumps, scenting the forest in the midday heat, but if you don't share my affection for it, feel free to leave it out.

FOR THE PASTRY
325G PLAIN FLOUR, PLUS EXTRA
   FOR DUSTING
50G GROUND ALMONDS
125G CASTER SUGAR
A PINCH OF SALT
125G BUTTER, CHILLED
2 EGGS AND 1 EGG YOLK

FOR THE TART
300G CASTER SUGAR
2 SPRIGS OF ROSEMARY
6 APRICOTS
100G BUTTER, AT ROOM TEMPERATURE
2 EGGS
200G GROUND ALMONDS
4 TABLESPOONS APRICOT JAM
CRÈME FRAÎCHE OR GREEK YOGHURT,
   TO SERVE

1. To make the pastry, put the flour, ground almonds and sugar into a large mixing bowl with a pinch of salt, and grate in the butter. Rub it in with your fingertips, then stir in the eggs and yolk until well combined. Wrap in clingfilm and chill for 30 minutes.

2. Roll the pastry out on a lightly floured surface to a thickness of about 5mm and use to line a 22cm loose-bottomed tart tin, gently pressing it into the sides rather than stretching it. Prick the base several times with a fork, then line with foil or baking parchment, and fill with baking beans. Put back into the fridge to chill for 20 minutes. Meanwhile preheat the oven to 200°C/gas mark 6.

3. Blind bake the pastry case for 15 minutes, then remove the beans and paper and bake for another 5–10 minutes. Allow to cool. Turn the oven down to 180°C/gas mark 4.

4. Put 200g of caster sugar into a wide saucepan over a medium-low heat along with 200ml water and the rosemary. Stir until dissolved, then bring to a simmer.

5. Meanwhile, cut the apricots in half down their length and remove the stones and any stalks. Put them, cut side down, into the pan in one layer, and turn the heat down. Simmer gently for about 5–10 minutes, until softened, being careful they don't turn mushy. Scoop out with a slotted spoon and set aside, along with some of the rosemary needles. Keep the syrup if you fancy making the rosemary gin fizzes on page 244.

6. Make the frangipane by beating together the remaining caster sugar with the butter, then beating in the eggs and ground almonds. Spoon into the pastry case and top with the apricot halves, skin side up, keeping the rosemary needles for later.

7.   Bake for about 45–50 minutes, until the filling has set, checking towards the end to ensure the pastry isn't burning. If the edges are turning too brown, cover them carefully with foil. Heat the jam in a small pan with 1 tablespoon of water, and when the tart comes out of the oven, brush the glaze on top and scatter with a few of the reserved rosemary needles.

8.   Allow to cool to room temperature, then remove from the tin and serve with crème fraîche or Greek yoghurt.

Mediterranean fish grill

SERVES 6

Chargrilled seafood, all crisp scales and singed shells, is the quintessential taste of Mediterranean holidays – served with a little bread, and some cold wine, it makes the perfect light lunch to fuel another afternoon's lounging in the shade, or divebombing into the pool. The best I ever had was a plate of smoky sardines, cooked on a huge barbecue at a beach restaurant forty minutes' hot and spiky walk from the more fashionable bit of St Tropez, and washed down with a carafe of salmon-pink local rosé that matched my fingernails: at that moment, nothing could have been more perfect.

Fish loves hot, quick cooking, which makes it ideal barbecue fodder – and it doesn't even need to marinate for hours first. Make sure you grease the grill well before you start cooking, however, as it does have a tendency to stick.

Garlic and parsley prawns

SERVES 6

You may query the point of the marinade when you're just going to discard the shells – but trust me, if you dig in with your fingers you'll get plenty of the delicious garlicky stuff, while the prawns inside will remain beautifully moist. And, from a theatrical point of view, you can't deny that these magnificent beasts look far more impressive with their armour intact.

5 CLOVES OF GARLIC, CRUSHED
A BUNCH OF FRESH FLAT-LEAF PARSLEY,
   FINELY CHOPPED

150ML OLIVE OIL
A PINCH OF SALT
18 RAW TIGER PRAWNS, SHELL ON

1. Put the garlic, parsley and olive oil into a bowl and whisk together with a generous pinch of salt. Add the prawns, cover and refrigerate until you're ready to cook.

2. Grill for 2 minutes, then serve.

Squid and chorizo skewers

SERVES 6

Another outing for one of my favourite combinations: sweet, tender squid and oily spicy sausage. It's easiest to thread the squid on to the skewers lengthways, then skewer the tentacles separately, divided by a chunk of chorizo.

1 LEMON
1 TABLESPOON OLIVE OIL
6 SMALL SQUID, CLEANED

SALT
12 THICK SLICES OF COOKING CHORIZO

1. Zest the lemon and mix the zest, and the juice of half the lemon, with the oil. Toss the squid in the oil with plenty of salt.

2. Thread the squid and chorizo on to skewers. Grill for 2 minutes on each side and serve immediately, before the squid go rubbery.

Grilled sardines

The simplest things are often the best, and these little fish need no other adornment than salt and a spritz of lemon. Summer on a plate. Make sure you oil them well before cooking, and, if you have one, this is a moment for a grill cage – sardines are annoyingly prone to sticking.

6 SARDINES, CLEANED AND GUTTED
4 TABLESPOONS SEA SALT FLAKES
OLIVE OIL, TO DRIZZLE

FRESHLY GROUND BLACK PEPPER
1 LEMON, CUT INTO 6 WEDGES

1. Put the sardines into a colander, sprinkle with salt and leave for 30 minutes.

2. Drizzle the fish with olive oil and grind black pepper over the top. Grill for about 3 minutes on each side, and serve with a wedge of lemon to squeeze over.

Griddled fennel

SERVES 6

Fennel is a great favourite in the south of France, where its aniseedy flavour pops up in everything from liqueurs to soaps, but I think it really comes into its own with fish. The solid bulbs are very amenable to barbecuing, although if you wanted to make this in advance, you could cook them on a hot griddle pan instead.

2 LARGE FENNEL BULBS,
CUT INTO QUARTERS
2 TABLESPOONS OLIVE OIL

1 TABLESPOON CHILLI FLAKES
1 TABLESPOON COARSE SALT
1 LEMON

1. Put the fennel into a bowl and toss with the oil, chilli flakes and salt.

2. Grill for about 10 minutes on each side, until softened and beginning to char.

3. Toss with lemon juice just before serving.

Potato and olive salad

I had to have one potato salad in a chapter on barbecues, and this rather smart version seemed to fit the bill perfectly. Leave the skins on the potatoes – and, if you can, make it a little in advance and serve just slightly warm, so the potatoes have had time to absorb a bit of the dressing.

1KG NEW POTATOES
SALT AND PEPPER
5 TABLESPOONS EXTRA VIRGIN OLIVE OIL
2 TABLESPOONS SHERRY VINEGAR

¼ OF A RED ONION, FINELY CHOPPED
100G PITTED BLACK OLIVES, ROUGHLY
   CHOPPED

1. Cut the potatoes in half and put into a large pan. Cover with cold, well-salted water, bring to the boil and simmer for about 15 minutes, until tender.

2. Meanwhile, whisk together the oil and vinegar and season well. Stir in the red onion.

3. Drain the potatoes and toss in the dressing. Add the olives and serve.

Grilled peaches

If you're lucky enough to have found a source of dangerously ripe stone fruit, I'd advise you to do nothing more than have a napkin handy, but this is a very nice way with the slightly more robust specimens one is often stuck with in this country, and exceedingly good with something cold and creamy.

6 RIPE PEACHES, NECTARINES OR PLUMS
25G UNSALTED BUTTER

3 TABLESPOONS DEMERARA SUGAR
2 SPRIGS OF FRESH ROSEMARY OR THYME

1. Halve and stone the fruit and divide it between two large squares of foil. Dot with butter, and sprinkle with the sugar and the rosemary needles or thyme leaves. Fold the foil to enclose.

2. Put the parcels on the grill and cook for about 15–20 minutes. Serve with a dollop of crème fraîche or ice cream.

Special occasions

Such is the reassuringly timeless and universal nature of human greed that celebration, whether to mark the end of the harvest, or the birth of a child, has always come catered. Even mourners need to eat – *The Oxford Companion to Food* gives a wonderful example of a gloomy message from the wrappings of a traditional British funeral biscuit:

'When ghastly Death with unrelenting hand,
Cuts down a father! brother! or a friend!
The still small voice should make you understand,
How frail you are – how near your final end.'

And if that doesn't give you an appetite . . .

Here, tempted as I am to dip my toe into the sugar-coated world of wedding feasts and christening cakes, I'm going to reluctantly confine myself to some of the special occasions that crop up every year for many of us – because, whether you celebrate Easter or Christmas or not, you certainly get some time off for them, and that's excuse enough for a feast as far as I'm concerned.

Of course, with the – possible – exception of the plum pudding ice cream, you don't have to save these recipes for the occasion they were designed for: I'd wolf down rib of beef and Stilton sauce, or even toffee apples any day of the year.

Setting the scene

The same rules really apply as in Cooking to Impress (see page 98), but you've got licence to go a little over the top with the decor. The normal rules of good taste go out of the window on special occasions, at Christmas in particular. In addition to the usual household decorations, a scattering of baubles down the centre of the table looks festive, but unless you have a huge table, they can get in the way of serving plates. Instead, pile them up in glass vases or bowls: I like a gaudy mixture of glittery metallic ones, but I'll leave such details up to you. Tie napkins up with slim tinsel or Christmassy-coloured ribbon, or stick a small fir twig inside the napkin rings if you have them. Twinkly fairy lights, although I think they set the scene all year, seem particularly appropriate here: the plugless versions, available from Ikea among other places, look lovely coiled up in glass bowls.

Christmas dinner for two

SERVES 2

Christmas just isn't the same without friends and family, according to the more saccharine elements of the media — and they're right. It's much, much more relaxing. However fond you are of your nearest and dearest, there can be no one who, in the maelstrom of wrapping paper and absurdly large birds, hasn't fleetingly imagined another kind of more peaceful festivity, which doesn't involve sitting through *The Snowman* five times, or getting into a long and protracted argument about how long the turkey needs to cook for.

Whether you're a duo by choice, or necessity, this unashamedly luxurious feast is made for two — and I promise that you won't miss the plum pudding one little bit.

Beetroot-cured sea bass

SERVES 2

You could of course simply go for salmon here, but a white fish picks up the vivid pink of the beetroot so beautifully it would be a bit of a shame. Look for small, thick fillets that will be easier to slice thinly – and because it needs to be made twenty-four hours ahead, that's one less thing to get you out of your armchair on Christmas Day.

½ A SMALL RAW BEETROOT
ZEST OF ½ A LEMON
2 TABLESPOONS FRESH DILL, ROUGHLY
   CHOPPED
25G CASTER SUGAR
20G SALT

PEPPER
2 SMALL SEA BASS FILLETS
   (ABOUT 100–125G EACH)
100G WATERCRESS, COARSE STEMS REMOVED,
   LIGHTLY DRESSED WITH OLIVE OIL,
   TO SERVE

1. Peel, trim and coarsely grate the beetroot (you may wish to use rubber gloves for this), and mix with the lemon zest, dill, sugar, salt and a grinding of pepper.

2. Spread half the mixture in a small baking dish and add the fish, skin side down. Spread the remaining mixture on top, and cover with clingfilm. Weight down the dish with a plate and a few tins, or whatever fits, and leave in the fridge for 24 hours.

3. Rinse the fish well, and pat dry. Slice very thinly, and serve with a watercress salad.

Guinea fowl with chestnut, apricot and brandy stuffing, baked squash and curly kale

SERVES 2

You could have a partridge each, but a bird that requires ceremonial carving is more in the festive spirit, and will also supply a thankfully small helping of the necessary leftovers – I can take or leave family, but Christmas isn't Christmas without curry.

Inspired by French foie gras stuffing, which, ethics aside, is a quite outrageous decadence, this is a main course that should leave you seasonally replete, but just able to fit in a modest mouthful of pudding. I like the sweetness of the roasted squash with the richness of the meat, but if you're a stickler for tradition, you could substitute roast potatoes instead.

1 X 1.1KG FREE-RANGE GUINEA FOWL, UNTRUSSED
SALT AND PEPPER
5 RASHERS OF SMOKED STREAKY BACON OR PANCETTA
50ML DRY WHITE WINE
50ML BOILING WATER
150G CURLY KALE
A KNOB OF BUTTER

FOR THE STUFFING
50G GOOD-QUALITY DUCK LIVER PÂTÉ

50G VAC-PACKED COOKED CHESTNUTS, ROUGHLY CHOPPED
50G READY-TO-EAT DRIED APRICOTS, ROUGHLY CHOPPED
2 TABLESPOONS BRANDY
35G WHITE BREADCRUMBS

FOR THE BAKED SQUASH
1 SMALL PUMPKIN OR BUTTERNUT SQUASH
2 TABLESPOONS OLIVE OIL
2 TABLESPOONS PINE NUTS
3 FRESH SAGE LEAVES, CHOPPED

1. Preheat the oven to 190°C/gas mark 5. Mix together the ingredients for the stuffing and add a little seasoning.

2. Put the guinea fowl into a roasting tin and season well. Fill the cavity with the stuffing, then cover the breast with the bacon.

3. Roast the bird for about an hour and a quarter, until the juices run clear, then remove from the oven and allow to rest.

4. While the bird is cooking, peel and deseed the squash and cut into chunky slices. Toss with oil, season and put into a separate roasting tin. Put into the oven with the guinea fowl for the last 20 minutes of cooking, then add the pine nuts and sage and roast the squash for another 10 minutes.

5. Take the guinea fowl out of the roasting tin. Make a gravy by putting the roasting tin on the hob, and adding the wine. Scrape the bottom of the tin, and add the water. Bring to the boil and simmer for 5 minutes. Season to taste and keep warm.

6. Bring a pan of salted water to the boil and add the kale. Cook for 4 minutes, then drain well. Toss with the butter.

7. Transfer the guinea fowl to a board and carve the breast into thin slices. Remove the legs. Scoop out the stuffing from the cavity and serve alongside the meat, kale and squash.

Panna cotta with mulled sherry syrup

SERVES 2

The ultimate antidote to heavy steamed puddings, these silky little desserts will slip down dangerously easily, even if you honestly believe yourself to be stuffed fuller than your average turkey. The buttermilk adds tanginess, which contrasts pleasantly with the sweetly spicy syrup accompaniment, but if you can't find it, make up the difference with milk instead. Because they need at least four hours to set firm, you can make the whole thing on Christmas Eve if you like: spend the extra time doing something really selfish.

1 GELATINE LEAF
OIL, TO GREASE
150ML DOUBLE CREAM
25G CASTER SUGAR
100ML WHOLE MILK
50ML BUTTERMILK

FOR THE SYRUP
1 UNWAXED ORANGE (ORGANIC ORANGES
   ARE UNWAXED)
1 UNWAXED LEMON
150ML MEDIUM SWEET SHERRY
50G CASTER SUGAR
2 CARDAMOM PODS, CRUSHED
½ A CINNAMON STICK
A PINCH OF GRATED NUTMEG
6 SEMI-DRIED FIGS OR PRUNES

1. Soak the gelatine in cold water for 5 minutes and lightly grease two ramekins. Meanwhile, put the cream and sugar in a pan and set over a medium heat, stirring, until the sugar has dissolved. Bring to a simmer, then take off the heat.

2. Squeeze out the gelatine, then stir it into the cream until dissolved. Strain through a sieve into a jug, then stir in the milk and buttermilk and pour into the ramekins. Chill until set.

3. To make the syrup, use a peeler to remove the outer rind of the orange and lemon in long strips and put into a small pan with the juice of the orange, the sherry, sugar and spices. Heat, stirring, over a medium heat until the sugar has dissolved, then bring to the boil. Boil for about 10 minutes, until syrupy, then add the fruit and allow to cool to room temperature. Remove and discard the citrus rind and whole spices.

4. To serve, dip the ramekins very briefly into boiling water, then put a plate upside down on top of each and turn it over to release the panna cotta. Spoon a little syrup and fruit on top of each.

Alternative Christmas dinner

SERVES 6

This is my fantasy Christmas dinner menu, lurking in the wings should my family ever agree to relinquish their stubborn claim to their rightful three courses of smoked salmon, turkey, and plum pudding and custard. There's nothing groundbreaking here, just the kind of food you might find yourself fancying more than once a year. Enjoy it with my envious compliments.

Potted salmon

SERVES 6

We always start our Christmas feast with smoked salmon, brown bread and butter. No complaints there – decent fish needs nothing more, but, given it's Christmas, this is a more luxurious take on the combination. Very easy to do, it can be made up to a day in advance, and chilled until needed.

400G FRESH SALMON FILLETS, SKINNED
200G SMOKED SALMON
A BUNCH OF FRESH CHIVES, FINELY
    CHOPPED
100G CRÈME FRAÎCHE

I TABLESPOON CAPERS
JUICE OF I LEMON
200G BUTTER
CAYENNE PEPPER, TO SERVE
TOAST, TO SERVE

1. Put the salmon fillets into a shallow bowl and pour over boiling water to cover. Leave to cool completely.

2. Chop the smoked salmon into ribbons, and flake the cool poached fish. Put into a bowl and fold together with the chives, crème fraîche and capers, then add lemon juice to taste. Spoon into six ramekins.

3. Melt the butter in a pan, then pour on top of the ramekins and refrigerate for at least a few hours or overnight. Decorate with a sprinkle of cayenne pepper, and serve with triangles of hot toast.

Rib of beef with Stilton béarnaise, roast potatoes and watercress

SERVES 6

The blue cheese sauce is inspired by that served at London's justly renowned Hawksmoor steakhouses – and if the gods are with you, your roasties should be as crunchy as their fabulous chips. What nicer way to celebrate Christmas than with the kind of meal you'd jump at at any time of year?

3KG BEEF RIB JOINT, AT ROOM
    TEMPERATURE
OLIVE OIL
SALT AND PEPPER
2 BUNCHES OF WATERCRESS

FOR THE ROAST POTATOES
1.2KG FLOURY POTATOES (E.G. MARIS PIPER
    OR KING EDWARDS)
4 TABLESPOONS GOOSE FAT

FOR THE STILTON BÉARNAISE
2 SHALLOTS, FINELY CHOPPED
½ A BAY LEAF
2 TABLESPOONS WHITE WINE VINEGAR
4 EGG YOLKS
250G UNSALTED BUTTER, DICED
150G STILTON, CUBED

1. Preheat the oven to 220°C/gas mark 7. Rub the meat with oil and season, then put it into a roasting tin and cook for 30 minutes.

2. Turn the heat down to 160°C/gas mark 3, leaving the door open briefly to cool it down quickly. Return to the oven and cook for another 80 minutes for medium rare meat, then rest it in a warm place in the roasting tin, covered with foil, for at least 30 minutes.

3. Meanwhile, peel the potatoes and cut in half, or quarter them if large. Put them into a large pan of boiling salted water and parboil for 8 minutes. Spoon the goose fat into a large roasting tin and put on the hob over a medium heat.

4. Drain the potatoes well and return them to the pan with the lid on to dry out. Shake the pan to fluff up the edges of the potatoes, then place them in the roasting tin one by one, turning them in the fat to coat well. Put into the oven and cook until golden and crisp – you can turn the temperature up to 220°C/gas mark 7 again once the meat has come out.

5.   To make the béarnaise, put the shallots, bay leaf and vinegar into a small pan and bring slowly to the boil. Simmer until almost all the liquid has evaporated, then take off the heat and add 2 tablespoons of water. Allow to cool slightly, then strain through a fine sieve and discard the shallots and bay leaf.

6.   Put the egg yolks into a small heavy-based pan over a very low heat and whisk in the vinegar reduction. Add the butter, piece by piece, adding another as soon as the first has melted, whisking well all the time. The sauce will gradually thicken: if it becomes too thick, or scrambles, take off the heat immediately and add a few drops of cold water, a little at a time.

7.   Stir in the cheese until melted, then keep in a warm place until ready to serve.

8.   Toss the watercress with a little olive oil and good salt, and serve with the beef and roast potatoes, with the Stilton béarnaise on the side.

Plum pudding bombe

SERVES 6

Just thinking about this recipe makes me smile: it's the modern equivalent of one of those witty medieval gastronomic tricks like the cockentrice – and rather easier than sewing together a chicken and a pig. As long as you keep it tightly wrapped in the freezer, it can be made weeks in advance, although I wouldn't advise putting the chocolate on until nearer the time.

75G SULTANAS	250ML WHIPPING CREAM
75G CURRANTS	130G GROUND ALMONDS
50G CHOPPED MIXED PEEL	5 EGG YOLKS
25G GLACÉ CHERRIES, QUARTERED	140G CASTER SUGAR
5 TABLESPOONS BRANDY	300G DARK CHOCOLATE, BROKEN UP PIECES
500ML WHOLE MILK	25G WHITE CHOCOLATE, BROKEN UP PIECES

1. Put the dried fruit, peel, cherries and brandy in a bowl, cover and leave to soak for at least 4 hours.

2. Put the milk, cream and almonds in a pan over a medium heat and bring to a simmer. Take off the heat and leave to infuse for 20 minutes, then strain through a fine sieve into a jug, pushing through as much as possible with a spatula. Discard the almond pieces left behind in the sieve and wipe out the pan. Pour the strained milk back into the pan and reheat.

3. Whisk the egg yolks and sugar together in a heatproof bowl, then pour on the hot milk mixture, stirring continuously.

4. Wipe the pan again, then return the mixture and heat very gently, stirring all the time, until it has thickened enough to coat the back of a spoon. Transfer to a metal bowl and place this inside a larger bowl or sink of ice-cold water. Stir regularly until cool. Meanwhile, line a 1 litre pudding basin with lightly greased clingfilm.

5. Use an ice cream maker to churn the mixture until thick, then add the soaked fruit and the brandy and churn for a further 10 minutes, until thickened again. Alternatively, spoon the mixture into the pudding basin and freeze for an hour, then stir the frozen edges and top into the mix and return to the freezer. Repeat three or four further times until frozen, but still soft – once it starts to freeze properly, you can fold the fruit in. Cover and freeze until solid. If using an ice cream maker, spoon the frozen mixture into the lined basin, cover and freeze until solid, preferably overnight.

6. Put the dark chocolate into a large heatproof bowl set above a pan of simmering water and stir until melted. Allow to cool to room temperature, stirring regularly to keep it liquid.

7. Take the bombe out of the freezer, uncover and put a serving plate on top. Invert the basin and slide the bombe out, removing the clingfilm. Pour the melted chocolate over the top, working quickly to spread it all over the surface before it sets. It's easier if you have an assistant to help out with a spatula.

8. Put the plate back into the freezer for about 10 minutes, until the chocolate has set. Meanwhile, melt the white chocolate in a fresh bowl. Once the dark chocolate has set, spoon the white chocolate on top, and return it to the freezer for at least 5 minutes before serving. A sprig of holly on top looks particularly festive (obviously, please don't eat it).

New Year's menu

If Christmas is traditionally a time for family, the dying hours of the year are best spent with friends – and not in a sweaty bar celebrating by doubling its prices for the evening. In my experience, at least, elaborate New Year's Eve plans inevitably disappoint: much better to stick to a rowdy house party (also sweaty, but at least there's a good chance you already know and like the person stepping on your foot), or a more relaxed dinner party. Both often end up looking much the same by about 2 a.m., but dinner does have the benefit of sending the old year off in style.

Given the general mood of indolence that prevails between Christmas and New Year, this menu, which, I warn you, is pretty rich (and thus an excellent start to that January diet), can all be made well ahead, leaving you plenty of time to practise your 'Auld Lang Syne' jig and check your clocks are right before the big moment.

Spiced duck pâté with orange champagne jelly

SERVES 6

Pâté is one of those things that sounds like it ought to be a ridiculous faff to make, but is actually really, really easy – as long as you have a food processor. This rich, smooth number is inspired, very loosely, by Heston Blumenthal's famous meat fruit, a foie gras and chicken liver parfait encased in mandarin jelly, moulded to look exactly like a plump little citrus fruit. I can't aspire to such culinary trickery, but the flavours, I fondly hope, are just as good.

If you can't find duck livers, you can use chicken livers instead, and any decent medium-sweet sparkling wine should do the trick – although, as you'll have quite a bit left over, even allowing for the syllabub topping on the trifle, I'd recommend getting something worth serving with the pâté itself, or as an aperitif. Look for 'demi sec' on the label. Like all the best starters, this can be made a couple of days in advance and taken out of the fridge half an hour before you're ready to serve it.

360G DUCK LIVERS
200G BUTTER, PLUS 2 TABLESPOONS
SALT AND PEPPER
1 LARGE SHALLOT, FINELY CHOPPED
½ TEASPOON CHINESE FIVE-SPICE
150ML MEDIUM-SWEET CHAMPAGNE OR
　SPARKLING WINE

FOR THE ORANGE JELLY
2 LEAVES OF GELATINE
125ML FRESHLY SQUEEZED ORANGE JUICE
ZEST OF 1 ORANGE
50ML MEDIUM-SWEET CHAMPAGNE OR
　SPARKLING WINE

1. Clean the livers and trim off any green bits or membrane. Heat the 2 tablespoons of butter in a frying pan over a medium-high heat, and sauté the livers until golden on the outside but still slightly pink on the inside. Spoon out of the pan, season and set aside.

2. Lower the heat slightly, then add the shallot to the pan and cook for 5 minutes, until softened, stirring in the five-spice for the final minute. Turn up the heat and pour in the champagne, then allow to simmer and reduce to about 2 tablespoons of liquid.

3. Take the pan off the heat and add the rest of the butter to soften it, then tip the butter, shallot and champagne mixture into a food processor. Add the livers, and whiz until you have a smooth purée. Season to taste, remembering that chilling will dull the flavours slightly – err on the side of generosity here.

4. Divide between six small ramekins, smoothing the tops flat, and chill until firm. Meanwhile, make the jelly. Soak the gelatine in cold water for about 5 minutes, until soft. While this is happening, heat the orange juice in a small pan until warm, then squeeze out the gelatine and stir it into the warm juice. Add the zest, gently pour in the champagne, and allow to cool slightly.

5. When the pâtés are set, which won't take long, and the jelly mixture is cool, carefully spoon the jelly on top of the pâtés and refrigerate until set – 3 hours should do it. Serve with crisp toasts and a watercress salad.

Russian fish pie

SERVES 6

Although I am a firm fan of a Friday evening fish pie, topped with fluffy mash, a special occasion demands something a little less homely – like a golden crown of puff pastry. For New Year's Eve, I'd write the new year in pastry trimmings on top of the pie, so you can all dive in with the same happy vigour you intend to apply to the forthcoming twelve months (an idea which works equally well for birthdays, engagements and so on), but you could just stick to a fish or two if you're nervous about digging into the new year before midnight.

I'm not sure if they'd recognize this pie in St Petersburg or Partizansk, but the roe and the rich cream give it a certain air of exoticism, so I couldn't resist. You can make it a good few hours in advance and simply stick it in the oven just before you sit down to eat your starter. It's good with leafy green vegetables – kale, cabbage or spinach would be my picks here.

5 EGGS, AT ROOM TEMPERATURE
20G BUTTER
5 SHALLOTS, FINELY CHOPPED
300ML DRY VERMOUTH
200ML WHITE WINE
400ML FISH STOCK
200ML DOUBLE CREAM
SALT AND PEPPER
700G SALMON FILLET, SKINNED AND
    PIN-BONED
200G PEELED NORTH ATLANTIC PRAWNS
    OR RAW KING PRAWNS

100G SALMON, LUMPFISH OR RE-FORMED
    HERRING ROE
A SMALL BUNCH OF TARRAGON, FINELY
    CHOPPED
A SMALL BUNCH OF FRESH CHIVES, FINELY
    CHOPPED

FOR THE PASTRY
250G PLAIN FLOUR, PLUS EXTRA TO DUST
½ TEASPOON SALT
175G CHILLED BUTTER
2 TEASPOONS LEMON JUICE

1. To make the pastry, put the flour and salt into a mixing bowl and coarsely grate in the chilled butter. Add the lemon juice and enough cold water to bring it together into a firm pastry – about 75ml. Wrap in clingfilm or baking parchment and chill for 15 minutes.

2. Roll the pastry on a lightly floured surface to a rectangle three times as long as it is wide. Fold the bottom edge into the middle, and then the top edge into the middle, overlapping the bottom edge, as if you were folding a letter. Wrap and chill for 15 minutes, then turn out on to the floured surface, turn 90 degrees, so the folds are no longer parallel with the edge of the work surface, and repeat the process. Do this twice more, so four times in total, then put into the fridge for 30 minutes, wrapped, before rolling out to top the pie.

3. Meanwhile, make the filling. Preheat the oven to 190°C/gas mark 5. Put 4 of the eggs into a pan of cold water and bring to the boil, then turn the heat down and simmer for 6 minutes. Cool the eggs in iced water.

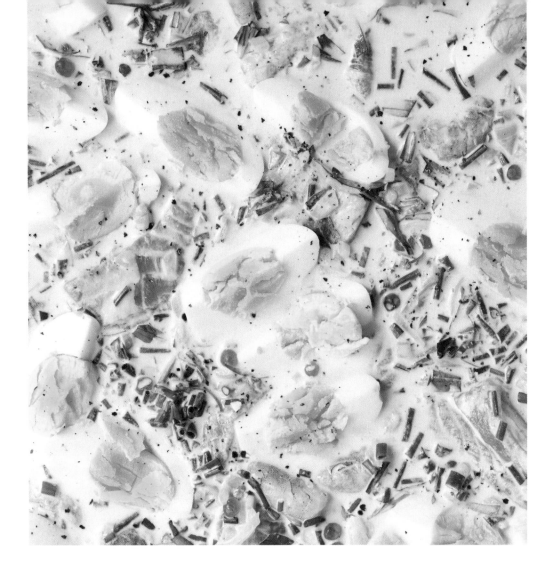

4.   Heat the butter in a medium pan over a medium heat and add the shallots. Soften, then pour in the vermouth and white wine, and turn up the heat. Simmer until it has reduced by half, then add the stock and do the same again. Stir in the double cream and simmer again until the sauce has reduced to the thickness of double cream. Season to taste, then leave to cool.

5.   Shell the eggs and cut into quarters lengthways. Cut the salmon into large chunks. Pat the prawns dry with kitchen paper. Gently fold the seafood, including the fish roe, chopped herbs and egg quarters, into the sauce, and spoon it into a large pie dish. Beat the remaining egg with a little cold water to use as egg wash.

6.   Roll the pastry out on the same lightly floured surface until about 3mm thick and the same size as your pie dish. Brush the rim of the dish with egg wash, then place the pastry on top and press down around the edges to seal. Brush the top of the pie with egg wash, make a small hole in the middle, and cut out any leftover scraps of pastry to use as decoration.

7.   Bake for about 40 minutes, until golden. If making in advance and baking from chilled, allow 50 minutes.

Whisky Mac trifle with champagne syllabub

SERVES 6

I couldn't have a book without a trifle recipe, and, much as I love the simple raspberry and vanilla sort, this spicy, boozy little number seemed more appropriate to see the old year out on. You can make your own ginger cake, or, if time is short, buy a good dark one – once it's soaked with whisky and covered in fruit and cream, no one will be any the wiser.

Syllabubs are an old favourite of the trifle fancier, having, according to Helen Saberi and Alan Davidson's fascinating work on the subject (how can anything be entirely bad in a world where such a book exists?), appeared on top of trifles since 1751. Originally they would have been frothy and foamy, but these days they're more of an alcoholic cream – no less delicious, but with less call for milking a cow directly into a bucket of wine. Note that you can use the same medium-dry sparkling wine here as in the duck pâté (see page 269), if you haven't drunk it all by this point.

90G CASTER SUGAR
2 TABLESPOONS CORNFLOUR
6 EGG YOLKS
875ML DOUBLE CREAM
A FEW DROPS OF ALMOND ESSENCE
200G SPICY GINGER CAKE
5 TABLESPOONS WHISKY
300G FRUIT OF YOUR CHOICE – JARRED
    FIGS OR PITTED CHERRIES IN SYRUP,
    DRAINED, WORK WELL

1 UNWAXED ORANGE (ORGANIC ORANGES
    ARE UNWAXED)
100ML MEDIUM-DRY CHAMPAGNE OR
    SPARKLING WINE
CANDIED PEEL, CHOPPED OR SHREDDED,
    AND TOASTED FLAKED ALMONDS, TO
    DECORATE

1. To make the custard, whisk together 2 tablespoons of the caster sugar with the cornflour and egg yolks in a large, heatproof bowl. Pour 575ml of the cream into a medium saucepan and heat gently until hot but not simmering. Pour on to the egg mixture, stirring continuously, and then very quickly wipe out the pan and pour the mixture back in. Cook over a low heat, always stirring, until thickened enough that it coats the back of a wooden spoon. Stir in a few drops of almond essence, to taste, then pour into a bowl, cover with clingfilm and set aside to cool for about 30 minutes.

2. Cut the ginger cake into 2cm thick slices, and use to line the bottom of a glass bowl. Pour over the whisky and spoon in the fruit. When the custard has cooled slightly, pour it in, then chill until set.

3. To make the syllabub, zest the orange, cut it in half, and squeeze out the juice from one of the halves. Mix this with the remaining sugar and the champagne. Whip the remaining cream until it forms soft peaks. Fold in the orange and champagne mixture and spoon on top of the set custard. Decorate with candied peel and flaked almonds.

Easter feast

SERVES 6

Whether you celebrate Easter with a glut of church services or a clutch of chocolate eggs (although the two are not mutually exclusive, I can assure you), it's a festival that mentally marks the beginning of spring for most of us. However, being that wonderful thing, a movable feast, fixed only as the first Sunday after the first full moon on or after the spring equinox, it can occur any time between 22 March and 25 April, which means that it can involve anything from barbecued lamb to a ceremonial egg hunt in thick snow.

An Easter menu should thus pay lip service to the spring we hope lies ahead, while acknowledging that chocolate alone won't keep us warm until it arrives. I hope this meal, with its fresh North African and Italian flavours, does both. As far as decor goes, a scattering of mini eggs always looks sweet – don't expect them to last until pudding – as do pots of early spring flowers and greenery, or you could try your hand at painting your own eggs if you're feeling particularly crafty, or have sugar-fuelled children to entertain.

Blood orange and almond salad

SERVES 6

If you can find blood oranges, which are in season only from January to March, then you're probably still at the chilly end of Easter, but their tart, almost crimson flesh should bring a breath of Sicilian or Spanish sun to your table nonetheless. If you can't find any, their more common cousins will do just as well, although you'll miss out on some of that seasonal wow factor.

¼ OF A RED ONION, PEELED AND
    THINLY SLICED
A PINCH OF SUGAR
SALT
RED WINE VINEGAR
30G FLAKED ALMONDS
4 BLOOD ORANGES (YOU CAN
    USE ORDINARY ORANGES, BUT
    THEY WON'T LOOK SO PRETTY)

JUICE OF ½ A LEMON
2 TABLESPOONS EXTRA VIRGIN OLIVE OIL
2 BUNCHES OF WATERCRESS, WASHED
    AND TRIMMED

1. Put the sliced onion into a cup or small bowl and add a pinch of sugar and a pinch of salt. Cover with red wine vinegar and leave to sit for at least 15 minutes.

2. Toast the flaked almonds in a dry pan until lightly golden, then set aside to cool.

3. Peel the oranges by cutting the top and bottom off each, then slicing down around the circumference of the fruit, until no white pith is left. Cut into rounds, removing any pith from the centre, and arrange on a platter.

4. Make the dressing by whisking together the lemon juice with any juice left over from preparing the oranges, the olive oil and a pinch of salt.

5. When you're ready to serve, toss the dressing through the watercress until it is well coated, then arrange this on top of the oranges. Scatter with the drained red onion and toasted almonds and serve immediately.

Roast Italian pork belly with polenta and cavolo nero

SERVES 6

Who doesn't love pork belly? Striped with meltingly tender ribbons of fat, it makes the most fabulous crackling – especially when the scored skin is deeply rubbed with toasted fennel seeds and flakes of chilli. This is a spring-like take on the Sunday roast, with a light, tangy gravy, and polenta and Italian cabbage in place of potatoes and root vegetables – although if a roast isn't a roast without your roasties, feel free to substitute them.

A THICK END PIECE OF PORK BELLY (THE
    LAST 6 RIBS, ABOUT 1.5KG)
2 TABLESPOONS DRIED CHILLI FLAKES
2 TABLESPOONS FENNEL SEEDS
1 TABLESPOON SALT FLAKES
4 CLOVES OF GARLIC, CRUSHED
2 TABLESPOONS OLIVE OIL

SALT AND PEPPER
500G EASY-COOK POLENTA
100G BUTTER OR 5 TABLESPOONS OLIVE OIL
300ML WHITE WINE OR DRY VERMOUTH
1.5KG CAVOLO NERO, TRIMMED AND CUT
    INTO RIBBONS
EXTRA VIRGIN OLIVE OIL, TO DRESS

1. The day before you cook the pork, take it out of its wrappings, pat it dry with kitchen paper, and use a sharp knife to score the skin in a diamond pattern if it's not already done, cutting into the fat but not right down to the meat. Put it into a baking dish and leave it uncovered in the fridge – this will dry out the skin and help make it crisp.

2. Preheat the oven to 220°C/gas mark 7. Mix together the chilli, fennel seeds, salt and crushed garlic with the olive oil to make a paste, and rub it all over the pork. Put the pork into the oven for 30 minutes, then turn the heat down to 180°C/gas mark 4 and roast for about another hour to an hour and a half, until the juices run clear. (It should have lovely crackling, but if it's disappointing, you can cheat and pop it under a hot grill for a couple of minutes at this point until it bubbles up.)

3. While the pork is resting, bring 2 litres of generously salted water to the boil in a large, heavy-based pan and sprinkle in the polenta, whisking all the time so you don't get lumps. Continue to cook and stir vigorously (at some point it will thicken sufficiently that you'll end up beating rather than stirring) for another 7–10 minutes. Remove from the heat, beat in the butter or olive oil, season to taste, and keep warm.

4.	Take the pork out of the roasting tin and put on a board for carving. Spoon as much fat from the juices remaining in the tin as possible (or use a gravy separator if you have one) and put the tin on the hob, scraping off all the bits stuck to the bottom. Stir in the wine and 200ml of hot water and bring to the boil. Simmer until slightly reduced, then season to taste and keep warm.

5.	Bring a large pan of salted water to the boil and add the cavolo nero. Cook for about 5 minutes, until just tender. Meanwhile, carve the pork and put on a serving platter. Drain the cavolo nero well, toss with a little extra virgin olive oil and season.

6.	Serve a dollop of creamy polenta with a hunk of pork and crackling and a generous amount of cavolo nero, and pass the gravy round for dousing.

Easter bunny blancmange

SERVES 6

Blancmange, which counted as a definite treat in my 1980s childhood, seems to be remembered less fondly by my contemporaries, which is why I simply billed this as a chocolate rabbit when I tested it out on some – they loved it. (Frankly I can't think why the idea of a milk jelly would be off-putting to people who've never been known to turn down a panna cotta – after all, it's not like I'm offering them the original medieval version, made from shredded chicken and ground almonds.) Any pedants who see a contradiction between the notion of white food and chocolate should please respectfully refrain from pointing this out.

VEGETABLE OIL, TO GREASE
400ML WHOLE MILK
150ML DOUBLE CREAM

50G CASTER SUGAR
200G DARK CHOCOLATE, FINELY CHOPPED
4 GELATINE LEAVES

1. Grease a 600ml rabbit mould with a little vegetable oil. Put the milk, cream and sugar into a medium pan and heat, stirring, until the sugar has dissolved. Bring just to a simmer, then take off the heat and leave to cool for a minute.

2. Tip the chocolate into the pan and leave for a minute or so, then whisk until you have a smooth mixture.

3. Soak the gelatine in cold water for about 4 minutes until softened, then squeeze out the leaves and stir into the chocolate cream to dissolve it completely.

4. Pour the mixture into the greased mould and push a piece of clingfilm on to the surface of the mixture to prevent a skin forming. Allow to cool to room temperature, then chill in the refrigerator until set.

5. To serve, dip the mould very briefly in boiling water, then put a plate on top and quickly turn the plate over so the blancmange slithers out.

Hallowe'en

SERVES 6

I'll leave the gruesome green jellies and spider-shaped biscuits up to you – there are stacks of recipes online, and some friends of mine boast a beautifully unpleasant skull-shaped jelly mould which they use for panna cotta – but here are a couple of recipes to get you going. Decorations, obviously, should involve eyeballs, skeletons and copious amounts of slime.

Pumpkin and worm soup

SERVES 6

I wouldn't advise using the kind of big, watery pumpkins that make such effective jack o' lanterns here: they inevitably taste disappointing. However, if you do have flesh left over from your carving efforts, cut it into small chunks, toss them well with olive oil and seasoning, and bake them along with the pumpkins until they start to caramelize. You can stir a few into each soup before serving. Waste not, want not.

If you can't find a pumpkin, make the soup up to the end of step 2, then add 1kg of cubed butternut squash and simmer for 30 minutes. Blend until smooth. Add the rice noodles, and reheat to serve.

It's difficult to give exact amounts for this recipe, because my medium squash might look pitifully tiny to you (as a guide, I mean a bit smaller than a netball), in which case you'll need a little more coconut cream and chicken stock to fill the monster you've lugged home. Don't worry too much: as long as the soup tastes good in the pan before you add it, it'll all be fine.

1–2 SMALL RED CHILLIES, DESEEDED AND
   ROUGHLY CHOPPED
1 SHALLOT, ROUGHLY CHOPPED
1 CLOVE OF GARLIC, ROUGHLY CHOPPED
1 TABLESPOON CHOPPED FRESH GINGER
2 LIME LEAVES, ROUGHLY CHOPPED
2 STALKS OF LEMONGRASS, PEELED AND
   ROUGHLY CHOPPED
2 TEASPOONS FISH SAUCE

JUICE OF ½ A LIME
1 TABLESPOON VEGETABLE OR GROUNDNUT
   OIL
400ML COCONUT CREAM
200ML CHICKEN OR VEGETABLE STOCK
1 MEDIUM ROUND PUMPKIN OR OTHER
   SQUASH
75G RICE NOODLES
A HANDFUL OF CHOPPED FRESH CORIANDER

1. Preheat the oven to 180°C/gas mark 4. Whiz the chillies, shallot, garlic, ginger, lime leaves and lemongrass in a food processor along with the fish sauce and lime juice to make a paste (this can also be done in a pestle and mortar).

2. Heat the oil in a large frying pan over a medium-high heat and fry the paste until aromatic. Stir in the coconut cream and stock, then taste, adding a little more fish sauce or lime juice if you think it needs it.

3. Cut the top off your pumpkin, and scoop out the seeds and fibrous stuff inside to give you a smooth bowl. Put it into a roasting tin, season, then pour the coconut mixture into the pumpkin to almost fill it – if you need to add a little more coconut cream or stock, do so.

4. Replace the lid and bake for about 1 hour 15 minutes, until the squash is cooked through. Cook the rice noodles according to packet instructions and drain well.

5. Add the noodles to the soup, along with the coriander, and serve at the table in a large dish, encouraging everyone to scoop a good bit of pumpkin out into their bowls along with the noodle soup. (Because of the risk that they'll puncture the skin as they do so, make sure you keep it in the dish, rather than transferring it to a plate.)

Toffee apples

SERVES 6

The ideal way to use up any excess from the inevitable apple-bobbing: the variety is up to you – I like the contrast between a tangy Granny Smith and its crisp, sugary coating – but try to get unwaxed ones if you can, either organic versions, or russet types, to make your life easier. (If you are apple-bobbing first, avoid any fruit with obvious teeth marks, please.)

To make the lurid red apples of yesteryear, add a few drops of food colouring to the toffee after you take it off the heat and swirl to combine. You'll need six lollipop sticks or sturdy twigs to impale the apples on, and a sugar thermometer.

6 SMALL APPLES, STALKS REMOVED
225G CASTER SUGAR
1 TEASPOON CIDER VINEGAR
½ TEASPOON SALT

3 TABLESPOONS GOLDEN SYRUP
10 DROPS OF RED FOOD COLOURING
   (OPTIONAL)

1. Line a baking tray with greaseproof paper. Put the apples into hot water and scrub vigorously to remove as much wax as possible – even if they haven't been waxed before sale, they'll still have a layer of natural wax which might stop your toffee sticking. Dry well and push a stick into the stalk end of each apple. Arrange on the baking tray and put it close to the hob.

2. Put the sugar into a large, heavy-based pan with 50ml water and heat, stirring, until it dissolves. Add the vinegar, salt and golden syrup, swirl in the food colouring if using, and heat until it reaches 150°C.

3. Take the pan off the heat and, working quickly, dip each apple into the toffee and swirl to coat. Put back on the lined tray and leave to set.

Bonfire night

There isn't really any official food for 5 November – history doesn't record what Guy Fawkes might have chosen to commemorate the occasion, although as he spent over a decade in the Spanish army, I might fancifully suggest chorizo rather than the British bangers which have mysteriously become associated with the occasion. (Anyone trying to cook them on a stick in the flames will quickly realize this is an endeavour doomed to disaster, much like the Gunpowder Plot itself.) What generally is required, however, is something warm to munch on while you watch the fireworks – and these recipes should fit the bill nicely.

Sausages with smoky tomato relish

SERVES 6

Although I usually fry my sausages, I find that, if they're to be eaten with fingers, the slightly drier bangers you get from baking are preferable – they're easier to handle, and less liable to squirt hot fat in your eyes when you're trying to watch the fireworks.

12 SAUSAGES

2 TABLESPOONS OLIVE OIL, PLUS A LITTLE
    EXTRA TO GREASE

1 SMALL RED ONION, FINELY CHOPPED

2 CLOVES OF GARLIC, FINELY CHOPPED

1–2 TABLESPOONS SWEET SMOKED PAPRIKA

400G CHOPPED TOMATOES

1 TABLESPOON CIDER VINEGAR

1 TABLESPOON DARK MUSCOVADO SUGAR

SALT AND PEPPER

1. Preheat the oven to 200°C/gas mark 6. Lightly grease a baking dish, and arrange the sausages in one layer inside. Prick each sausage and bake for about 35 minutes, turning once, until well coloured and firm.

2. To make the relish, heat the oil in a medium pan over a medium heat and add the onion and garlic. Allow to soften without colouring, which should take about 7 minutes, then add the smoked paprika and cook, stirring, for another minute. If you're not sure how spicy you want it, add 1 tablespoon to start with: you can always stick in another when it's done.

3. Tip in the tomatoes, vinegar and sugar. Bring to the boil, then turn down the heat and simmer for about 20 minutes, until slightly thickened. Season to taste, and serve hot or cold with the sausages. The relish can be kept in the fridge for up to a week – bring to room temperature before serving.

Bonfire baked potatoes

SERVES 6

If you thought baked potatoes topped with a mountain of cheese were pretty damn perfect, wait till you try these vaguely cowboy-inspired numbers. They're basically an entire meal in one crunchily delicious skin (although you'll need a potato each if you're not serving sausages as well).

2 TABLESPOONS SALT FLAKES
3 LARGE BAKING POTATOES
25G SOFTENED BUTTER
80G RED LEICESTER, GRATED

3 TABLESPOONS SOURED CREAM
A SMALL BUNCH OF FRESH CHIVES, CHOPPED
1 X 400G TIN OF PINTO BEANS, DRAINED
CAYENNE PEPPER (OPTIONAL)

1. Preheat the oven to 220°C/gas mark 7.

2. Put the salt on a saucer. Wash the potatoes, prick several times with a fork, then roll them lightly in the salt. Bake for about an hour. Check to see if they're done – the skins should be crisp, and the insides should yield to gentle pressure (remember they'll be very hot).

3. Once they're done, turn down the oven to 190°C/gas mark 5. Cut the potatoes in half and scoop out the insides into a large bowl. Add the butter, cheese and soured cream and mix well. Stir in the chives and beans, then spoon the mixture back into the potato skins.

4. Return to the oven and bake for 20–25 minutes, until golden. Sprinkle with cayenne pepper, if using, just before serving – you'll need to let them cool down a little if you're eating with fingers.

Cinder toffee

SERVES 6

More prosaically known as 'that stuff inside a Crunchie bar', these honeycomb-like treats are presumably popular on Bonfire Night because of the name – although those who prefer a chewier toffee should consider a batch of the treacle variety, sometimes known, equally mysteriously, as bonfire toffee. The bubbles come courtesy of the reaction between bicarbonate of soda and vinegar, and can be quite spectacular – if they'd allowed us to make cinder toffee at school, I suspect I would have found chemistry rather more interesting.

Any leftover toffee is excellent smashed into smithereens and stirred through ice cream to make hokey pokey: apparently New Zealand's second most popular flavour. (First is vanilla, of course, as it is everywhere. Yet no one under the age of fifty has ever been seen buying it. Spooky.) A sugar thermometer is well-nigh essential for this recipe.

50G SALTED BUTTER, PLUS EXTRA FOR
    GREASING
2 TEASPOONS BICARBONATE OF SODA

I TABLESPOON CIDER VINEGAR
3 TABLESPOONS GOLDEN SYRUP
475G GRANULATED SUGAR

1. Line a smallish baking tin with foil and grease well with butter. Put within easy reach of the hob, along with the bicarbonate of soda.

2. Put the butter, vinegar and 2 tablespoons of water into a large saucepan over a medium heat until the butter has melted. Add the golden syrup and the sugar, and stir until dissolved.

3. Bring to the boil, and heat until the mixture reaches 150°C: be patient, and do not, whatever you do, leave the pan unattended. Stir in the bicarb, and immediately take off the heat. Pour into the tin, and leave to set.

4. Once cooled and set, you can break up the toffee by dropping the tin on to the work surface from elbow height a few times.

Parties

Whether to celebrate a birthday, or to welcome a new house, a new baby or a new year, parties are the most straightforwardly joyous of occasions, both to attend and, I think, to host. The whole point of a party is, quite nakedly, to have fun (not necessarily naked): really, there's no onus on you to do anything but pick a date and a venue, and invite a few nice guests. Everything else will largely look after itself: people bring drinks, they often bring nibbles, and, most importantly, they provide the entertainment. Or, rather, they are the entertainment.

That said, once you've started planning a party, it can be quite difficult to stop. You spend countless evenings taste-testing potential wines, lose entire weekends in the pursuit of the perfect playlist, buy at least three new outfits before deciding to go for an old favourite instead — see, even the preparation is bona fide fun. For this reason, I favour house parties: you get much more control over the minutiae if you do it yourself, rather than trusting in a bar's choice of beer or music. I can't deny that clearing up the morning after is less amusing, but you won't regret it. Unless someone's been sick in your bed, of course.

Think about how much time you have to organize the party and who you want to invite, and make your decisions accordingly: if you're rushed off your feet, or don't want people dancing around your new flat with mulled wine, then it might be best to go for a pre-dinner drinks event, with an end time: 7–9 p.m. for example. Make this very clear on the invitation, or you're liable to find yourself nipping out for more supplies at 11 p.m. and wondering if the corner shop also sells Shake n' Vac.

If you, or a lot of your friends, have small children, however, it might be wiser to make it an afternoon event one weekend, perhaps even a picnic in the garden, or a local park, where they can be turned loose to amuse themselves.

When planning a party for a really special occasion — a big birthday, or an engagement, say — do send out invitations well in advance, or at the very least a 'save the date' to your nearest and dearest. You don't have to start thinking much further than this until a few weeks beforehand, but it's important to reserve the A-Team before the rival invitations come in.

You may think your flat or house is too small for a big party. Unless you live in one of those snooker-table-sized flats in Knightsbridge, I suspect you're wrong. You'll be amazed at how many people you can cram in when they're all milling about chatting, rather than sitting down being precious about personal space — and bear in mind that parties ebb and flow: at an evening bash, you'll have the pre-dinner crowd who are popping in before going elsewhere, the all-nighters, and then, around 10.30 p.m., those who've come from somewhere else, so they won't all rush the bar at once.

Practicalities

Move as much furniture out of the way as possible, leaving a few chairs or a sofa pushed against the wall for people who suddenly find themselves in the midst of a deep conversation. Although, unless your friends are really wild, you don't have to hide any breakables, I would move them on to higher shelves, away from flailing arms and terrible dance moves.

Discreetly tuck away that champagne you're saving to enjoy with a few close friends, because at some point in most parties someone will go on a scavenger hunt. I know, I've done it myself. (Sorry, Chris.) Bear in mind that every single available and vaguely flat surface will play host to someone's sticky drink at some point, so put protective mats or magazines on that beautifully polished walnut ottoman you inherited from Great Aunt Winnie. ('Hello, French polishers … ?')

From long experience parties seem to flow best if you set all the drinks out on one surface, with a large bin and a recycling bin underneath, but still in sight. You will inevitably end up fishing a few crisps out of the latter and some glass from the ordinary bin, and at some point in the evening, people will just start leaving drinks everywhere, but it will make your job ever so slightly easier the next morning.

Remember to leave two or three corkscrews and bottle openers handy: it won't stop people asking you for one, but you might have a better chance of actually gratifying their request.

If you're serving lots of cold drinks, and don't have much room in the fridge, consider hiring an ice bucket from the same wine merchants or supermarket where you get your booze: they come filled with ice, and, unless you have a massive chest freezer and 100 ice cube trays, this can work out surprisingly cost-effectively. Alternatively, there's always the old beer-in-the-bathtub option or, if it's cold outside, simply stick the drinks in the garden or on the balcony and bring them in in batches.

Also, I can't recommend glass hire strongly enough. Big wine merchants and supermarkets usually offer it for free, especially if you're prepared to return the glasses clean, with a breakage charge of about £1 a glass. In an average case of 100 (remember, guests often use more than one glass in the course of a party), I'd expect two or three losses, which isn't a bad return – they do tend to be quite sturdy things, and people are far more careful with real glasses than they might be with horrible (and expensive) plasticky things.

Lastly, on the less glamorous side, lay in lots of kitchen paper, bin bags, loo roll, soft drinks and local taxi numbers.

Catering

If you're having a shortish party, you'll just need a few nibbles – people will be going on to eat afterwards, so you'll only spoil their appetite if you start handing round sausages. Holding a party without anything to eat is criminal, however: even a few crisps are better than drinking on an empty stomach.

An all-evening bash demands something a bit more substantial: you can just opt for a pizza delivery (usually better than the supermarket alternative) or a big platter of salami and ham, but it's not much more trouble to make up a few loaves of garlic bread in advance. Not only will people linger longer when they're not feeling faint with hunger, but they're less likely to get so drunk you need to put them to bed on the sofa with a washing-up bowl next to their head.

Rather than just ripping open packets of crisps and nuts, like you're in the pub, take the trouble to put them into big serving bowls: I truly believe people behave better if you've taken a bit of trouble over such things.

Drinks-wise, many online merchants have tools to help you calculate how much you'll need: don't forget to take into account the fact that most people will bring a bottle unless you order them not to (and why would you?). I usually allow a generous bottle of wine per person for an all-evening bash, on the basis that many people will drink less but a hardcore few will drink considerably more. In my group of friends, about 25 per cent of people will opt for beer instead, especially if the weather's warm, but, of course, yours may differ.

Even if you aren't providing spirits, it's a good idea to buy a few mixers, both in case someone turns up with gin, and as a soft option. Tonic water, fruit juice and lemonade are all suitably versatile, and leaving a big bottle of squash near the sink never did any harm.

If you just want to offer people a glass of fizz on arrival, or to toast whatever you're celebrating, a bottle contains six glasses (or seven if you're on a tight budget). By all means go for champagne if you like, but I think many of the entry-level *grandes marques*, or big names, are overpriced – you can often get a much nicer own-label variety for a few pounds less, so it's worth reading critics' recommendations, or checking out things like the *Decanter* wine magazine's awards site to see what's done well in recent taste tests.

For a big party, I prefer to buy a good prosecco or a sparkling wine from the New World or another region of France: prosecco in particular is lighter and fruitier than most champagnes, which makes it more suitable for glugging all evening.

When opening a bottle of fizz, have the glasses ready nearby. Remove the foil and, holding the bottle firmly in one hand, gently twist and remove the wire cage holding the cork in place, and replace it with a palm – the pressure inside the bottle is equal to that of the rear tyre of a double-decker bus, so it deserves a bit of respect. Gripping the cork with your weaker hand, use your stronger arm to twist the bottle until you feel the cork start to loosen. Allow it to gradually ease its way upwards until it emerges with a gentle pop (some people claim that any noise louder than a maiden's sigh is terribly vulgar, but they're killjoys), then get to work. It's easiest to pour glasses a third full, wait for the foam to die down, then complete the operation: for a big table of flutes, you can save time by pouring the first third a little in advance, and topping them up as people arrive.

Two punches

I wouldn't advocate making cocktails for big parties, unless you want to spend your entire evening with your hands welded to the shaker. Punches, however, are a different matter: they get the party going like nobody's business. If you're turbo-charging them with extra spirits, do warn people . . . a party can always peak too soon.

Winter punch

SERVES 10–20 (DEPENDING ON HOW MANY GLASSES THEY HAVE)

People have been spoiled for mulled wine by about 5 December: there are too many pubs serving thin, aggressively sweet versions to allow yours to be greeted with the proper enthusiasm. In any case, I think warm cider's much nicer: and if you'd prefer to make it less alcoholic, either leave out the rum, or dilute the whole thing with apple juice.

2 ORANGES (BUY ORGANIC ONES IF
    POSSIBLE: THEY'RE UNWAXED)
8 CLOVES
2 LITRES MEDIUM-DRY CIDER (DON'T GO
    FOR THE CHEAPEST YOU CAN FIND: YOU'LL
    REGRET IT THE NEXT DAY)

5 CINNAMON STICKS
500ML DARK RUM

1.   Give the oranges a good scrub in hot water to remove the wax, then cut one of them in half. Stick it with the cloves, and put it into a large pan along with the cider and cinnamon.

2.   Cover and bring very slowly to a simmer over a gentle heat. Meanwhile, slice the remaining orange thinly.

3.   When the punch comes to a simmer, turn off the heat and stir in the rum and slices of orange. It's now ready to serve. With caution.

Alcoholic lemonade

SERVES 10–20 (DEPENDING ON HOW MANY GLASSES THEY HAVE)

Anyone who came of age in the 1990s will have fond(ish) memories of Hooch: the original teenager-friendly alcopop, sadly long since overtaken by more aggressively marketed rivals. I seem to remember it being so sugary that an evening 'on the Hooch' left your teeth feeling distinctly furry – this is a rather more sophisticated version for those of us no longer in the first flush of youth. I'm afraid it has none of the tongue-staining properties of the original.

Put a serving jug in the freezer for half an hour before you serve this to ensure it's well chilled. If you're making it ahead of time you can store it in another container in the fridge, then decant it into the frozen jug and add the ice just before serving. For a longer, more refreshing drink, top up with soda water.

8 UNWAXED LEMONS (ORGANIC ONES
ARE ALWAYS UNWAXED), CUT INTO
ROUGH CHUNKS
300G CASTER SUGAR

500ML GIN, CHILLED
ICE CUBES, TO SERVE
SPRIG OF FRESH MINT, TO SERVE

1.   Put the lemons into a blender or food processor along with 50g of sugar and 250ml of water. Blitz until smooth.

2.   Pour the juice through a sieve into a chilled jug and tip the lemon pulp back into the blender. Add another 50g of sugar and another 250ml of water and repeat the process until all the sugar has been used up.

3.   Discard the pulp and stir the gin into the jug. Fill with a generous number of ice cubes, stick a sprig of mint in the top and serve.

Nibbles

It's a truth universally acknowledged that alcohol brings on an almost supernatural craving for salty, fatty foods – you don't see many people ordering a salad pitta in the kebab shop on a Friday night. Unless it's with a side order of chips and garlic sauce anyway. The recipes below are unapologetically designed with this appetite in mind. If you're more health-conscious you can serve the dips with carrot sticks, cucumber batons and radishes rather than crisps, but from experience I usually find these, almost untouched, when clearing up the next morning, while every other bowl has been licked clean. Perhaps your friends are better people, however. More ideas for nibbles can be found on page 60–61.

Parmesan thins

MAKES ABOUT 40

Crisp, buttery and almost criminally cheesy, these are the grown-up equivalent of a day-glo orange Wotsit. Quite honestly, I'd serve both to cater for all tastes; but perhaps save the cheese puffs for later in the evening, when people have left their airs and graces with their shoes by the side of the dance floor (aka sitting-room).

180G FINELY GRATED PARMESAN OR
   OTHER STRONG, HARD CHEESE
50G BUTTER, AT ROOM TEMPERATURE
100G PLAIN FLOUR

A LARGE PINCH OF SALT
1 TABLESPOON MILK
SMOKED PAPRIKA, TO SPRINKLE

1. Beat together the cheese and butter until well combined, then stir in the flour and a large pinch of salt. Sprinkle the milk over and bring together into a dough.

2. Roll the dough into two sausages about 4cm in diameter, and wrap in clingfilm. Chill for at least 30 minutes, or until ready to cook. Preheat the oven to 180°C/gas mark 4.

3. Cut the sausages into slices about 3mm thick. Space well apart on lined baking sheets, chill for 15 minutes, then bake for about 15 minutes until crisp and golden.

4. Sprinkle with smoked paprika and cool on a rack. Store in an airtight container.

Devils on horseback

MAKES 26

A remnant of the old savoury course which used to conclude every proper British dinner (our forebears must have had digestive systems crafted from wrought iron), this is, in my opinion, a far superior dish to its angelic counterpart, made from fried oysters. Sweet, salty, and just a little bit greasy, they're particularly good at Christmas parties.

26 STONED PRUNES

75ML BRANDY

13 RASHERS OF THIN-CUT STREAKY SMOKED
BACON OR PANCETTA

1. Put the prunes into a bowl and cover with the brandy. Leave to soak for at least an hour.

2. Preheat the oven to 200°C/gas mark 6. Stretch each rasher of bacon out with the back of a knife, then cut it in half. Drain the prunes. Put a prune at one end of each rasher, roll up tightly, and secure with a cocktail stick.

3. Bake for about 12 minutes, until the bacon is crisp, and allow to cool down slightly before serving; the prunes get very hot.

Sticky sausages

MAKES 20

I fell upon these glorious things at my very first grown-up New Year's Eve party — although the blurry photographic evidence suggests the champagne made more of an impact at the time, they stuck in my mind and a few years later, when I'd graduated to holding my own parties, I badgered my friend Emma to ask her mum for the recipe. To be honest, they don't really need one, although I've attempted to codify the magic here. Basically, you're looking for the ideal mix of sweet and sticky and hot and tangy, but as long as hot sausages are involved, you can't really go wrong.

3 TABLESPOONS HONEY

4 TABLESPOONS HOI SIN SAUCE

1 TABLESPOON ENGLISH MUSTARD POWDER

20 COCKTAIL SAUSAGES

2 TABLESPOONS MUSTARD SEEDS

1. Preheat the oven to 200°C/gas mark 6. Mix together the honey, hoi sin sauce and mustard powder, and put the sausages into a lined baking tray. Pour over the marinade and toss well, then shake over the mustard seeds.

2. Bake for about 30–35 minutes, until browned and cooked through.

Homemade tortilla chips and guacamole

MAKES ABOUT 60 CHIPS

These are infinitely more interesting than most bought tortilla chips, and, as they're baked rather than fried, healthier too. You can also make them with ten ready-made corn tortillas instead, which are available online or from larger supermarkets, but these tend to be expensive, so it's worth mastering the art of tortilla making, even if the results look a little more rustic than your average Dorito – the flavour is far, far better. Load them up with guacamole or the fresh salsa on page 152.

500G FINE MAIZE FLOUR
600ML WARM WATER
I TEASPOON SALT
GROUNDNUT OIL, TO COOK
SALT
CAYENNE PEPPER

FOR THE GUACAMOLE
1–3 FRESH GREEN CHILLIES, DEPENDING
 ON HEAT, AND YOUR TASTE, DESEEDED
 AND FINELY CHOPPED

2 SPRING ONIONS, THINLY SLICED
A HANDFUL OF FRESH CORIANDER, ROUGHLY
 CHOPPED
SALT
3 RIPE AVOCADOS (HASS, THE KNOBBLY BROWN
 ONES, TEND TO BE THE CREAMIEST AND MOST
 FLAVOURSOME)
I RIPE MEDIUM TOMATO, CUT INTO 3MM DICE
JUICE OF I LIME

1. Put the flour, water and salt into a large bowl and stir together, then cover and leave for quarter of an hour.

2. Preheat the oven to 180°C/gas mark 4. Scoop out a ping-pong-ball-sized lump of dough: it should be the consistency of play-dough – not sticky, but not crumbly. Add more water, or more flour, to bring it to this texture if required.

3. Cut out two 20cm squares of clingfilm. Put one square on to the work surface, place the ball of dough in the middle, then top with the other square. Flatten the ball with a frying pan, then roll it out as thinly as possible. Repeat with the others, and meanwhile heat a dry frying pan over a medium-high heat.

4. Cook the tortillas for about a minute on each side, until the edges begin to curl, then set aside.

5. Cut each tortilla into about six triangles, and brush each triangle on both sides with oil. Put into baking trays and sprinkle with salt. Bake for about 15 minutes, tossing a couple of times, until crisp, then sprinkle with cayenne pepper and allow to cool: they'll crisp as they do so.

6. Meanwhile, make the guacamole. Put a teaspoon each of the chilli, spring onion and coriander into a pestle and mortar, along with a pinch of coarse salt, and grind to a paste.

7. Peel the avocados and remove the stones. Cut into cubes, then mash to a chunky paste, leaving some pieces intact. Stir the chilli paste into the avocado, then gently fold in the tomatoes and the rest of the onions, chilli and coriander. Add lime juice and salt to taste. Serve immediately, or cover the surface with clingfilm and refrigerate.

Smoky almonds

MAKES 150G

The combination of nuts and smoke is a dangerously moreish one. These Spanish-inspired numbers go extremely well with a well-chilled glass of bone-dry sherry, but they'll disappear equally swiftly when served with anything from lager to lemonade, so it's worth erring on the generous side. They keep well in an airtight container for several days.

1 EGG WHITE
2 TEASPOONS SOFT LIGHT BROWN SUGAR
1 TEASPOON SALT

1 TEASPOON SWEET SMOKED PAPRIKA
150G ALMONDS

1. Preheat the oven to 180°C/gas mark 4 and line a baking tray with foil. Beat the egg white until foamy, then add the sugar, salt and smoked paprika and whisk again to combine.

2. Toss the nuts with the egg white mixture, then lift on to the baking tray with a slotted spoon. Bake for about 17 minutes, then leave to cool for 5 minutes before breaking up any clumps. Allow to cool completely before storing in an airtight container.

Padrón peppers

MAKES 300G

These small green peppers, which look rather like large chillies to the uninitiated, are absolutely delicious lightly charred and sprinkled with salt. Their appearance isn't entirely deceptive: although they have a mild, almost sweet flavour, the odd one is surprisingly fiery, which makes eating them a game of culinary Russian roulette. Not that they're hot enough to actually kill you, you understand, just to send you in search of a cooling glass of water. Put an empty bowl nearby, or you'll find your table littered with discarded stalks.

2 TABLESPOONS OLIVE OIL
300G PADRÓN PEPPERS

COARSE SALT, TO SERVE

1. Heat the oil in a large frying pan over a high heat and add the peppers. Fry, stirring, for about 5 minutes, until they begin to char.

2. Toss in a good pinch of salt and tip into a bowl.

Dips

Dips are a party classic for good reason – you can prepare them well in advance and simply stick them out with some breadsticks, crisps, or crudités at the appointed time. People seem to like an interactive nibble, but they do tend to congregate around them, so if you make more than one batch, try to spread them out around the party, or you'll have a traffic jam on your hands.

This trio should hopefully be an improvement on the quartets of dips that seemed so sophisticated (to me at least) in the 1990s – although I'm afraid that if you want that orange tikka number, you're on your own. Note there are also dips on pages 63 and 152–3.

Spinach and Parmesan dip

MAKES 500G

Americans really know how to make a dip – as usual, the secret is cheese, and lots of it. This one may be criminally rich, but it's not as if you're eating it with a spoon (stop that!) and anyway, it's got spinach in it, so it must be healthy, right?

400G CHOPPED FROZEN SPINACH, THAWED
1 TABLESPOON OLIVE OIL
1–3 CLOVES OF GARLIC (ERR ON THE SIDE
    OF CAUTION IF YOU INTEND TO DO
    SOME MATCHMAKING, OR INDEED
    SEDUCTION, AT YOUR PARTY), CRUSHED

100G FULL-FAT CREAM CHEESE
50ML MILK
50G PARMESAN, FINELY GRATED
A PINCH OF FINELY GRATED NUTMEG
SALT AND PEPPER

1. Drain the thawed spinach thoroughly in a sieve, pushing it hard to squeeze the last of the water out.

2. Heat the oil in a frying pan over a medium-high heat. Fry the garlic for 3 minutes, until softened but not coloured, then add the spinach and stir well to combine with the garlic and oil. Cook for another couple of minutes, stirring, then add the cream cheese, milk and Parmesan and cook for about 2–3 minutes, until well mixed and thick – if you'd prefer a looser texture, you can add a little more milk, but be careful, as a dip that's too loose will simply fall off your crisps or pieces of bread.

3. Add the nutmeg and season to taste. Good served warm or at room temperature.

Smoky black bean dip

When offered the option at burrito vans and restaurants, I invariably go for black beans – they sound more Mexican than refried beans, and they taste damn good. (Sometimes, in the queue, I rashly decide I'm going to ring the changes and go for pinto, but somehow, I never quite have the courage of my convictions.) You can use almost any bean you like here, though. Chillies in spicy adobo sauce can sometimes be found in the speciality food sections of supermarkets, and can also be bought online. They add a distinctive flavour to the dip, so do try to find them if you can: a fresh chopped chilli won't be quite the same.

1 X 400G TIN OF BLACK BEANS, DRAINED
2 CLOVES OF GARLIC, PEELED AND
   ROUGHLY CHOPPED
3 SPRING ONIONS, CHOPPED
A SMALL BUNCH OF FRESH CORIANDER,
   ROUGHLY CHOPPED

1 CHILLI IN ADOBO (SEE ABOVE)
½ TEASPOON SWEET SMOKED PAPRIKA
JUICE OF ½ A LIME
SALT AND PEPPER

1.   Combine all the ingredients in the food processor and whiz until puréed, but not absolutely smooth.

2.   Season to taste, adding a little more paprika or lime juice if you think it needs it. Particularly good with tortilla chips.

Provençale tapenade

Not strictly a dip, this – my dad used to run up vast batches of it when my parents lived in France, and we'd all dig in with thin slices of baguette, but, as well as being great on crostini and the like, it also works well with breadsticks and plain crisps. Anything salted will be overkill with the black olives, capers and anchovies, though.

100G BLACK OLIVES, STONED
4 ANCHOVIES
1 TABLESPOON CAPERS

1 PLUMP CLOVE OF GARLIC, CRUSHED
A SQUEEZE OF LEMON JUICE
A DASH OF OLIVE OIL

1.   Put the olives, anchovies, capers and garlic into a food processor and whiz until you have a smooth purée.

2.   Add a squeeze of lemon juice and a dash of olive oil and taste. Add a little more lemon juice if necessary, then refrigerate until ready to serve.

More substantial food

See also the pesto cake salé on page 313, which makes a very tasty nibble, birthday or not.

Flammekueche

MAKES 2

I first encountered this Alsatian speciality (the French *département*, not the dogs – although I'm sure they're very talented chefs) at a German wine fair, where merry folk were devouring vast wooden trays of the stuff along with the local Riesling. *Flammekueche* is the dialect name: in French they're known as a *tarte flambée*, and in German *Flammkuchen*. To my mind, this neatly reflects the character of this lovely region – officially it's French, but quite often it feels German. (Unsurprising, given it swapped ownership four times in seventy-five years.)

A *flammekueche* is actually very much like a pizza except, instead of tomatoes and mozzarella, it's topped with cream, onions and bacon – perfect with beer or a crisp white wine. Tradition has it that, when peasants used to make their bread once a week or fortnight, this was also baked in the hot oven by way of celebration: all it needs is a bit of spare bread dough. The wood-fired ovens are so fierce that the real thing is often deliciously charred, but you can still make a very tasty version at home, especially if you splash out a bit and add cheese (frugal peasants, look away now). Note, this must be eaten with fingers, preferably while still so blistering hot that it's painful to tear.

You can make the dough in advance (keep it in the fridge once proved), and simply stretch it out to order. Quark, a fresh very low-fat cheese, is available in most supermarkets – check near the cottage cheese – but if you can't find it, use another 200g of crème fraîche instead.

10G FRESH YEAST OR 1 TEASPOON FAST-
   ACTION DRIED YEAST
½ TEASPOON CASTER SUGAR
320ML WARM WATER
500G STRONG WHITE BREAD FLOUR,
   PLUS MORE FOR ROLLING
1 TEASPOON SALT
OIL, TO GREASE
A KNOB OF BUTTER
2 ONIONS, FINELY SLICED

180G SMOKED BACON LARDONS
200G QUARK, AT ROOM TEMPERATURE
200G CRÈME FRAÎCHE, AT ROOM TEMPERATURE
SALT AND PEPPER
WHOLE NUTMEG, FOR GRATING
CORNMEAL, TO DUST
180G REBLOCHON CHEESE, RIND REMOVED,
   THINLY SLICED (OPTIONAL)

1. To make the dough, mash together the yeast and sugar with a fork, then stir in the warm water. Leave to sit for 5 minutes, until beginning to froth.

2. Put the flour into a mixing bowl or the bowl of a food mixer. Add the yeast mixture and mix gently, using a wooden spoon or a food mixer, until it comes together into a dough, then add the salt. If using a food mixer, turn the speed up and mix for another 5 minutes; by hand, knead for 10 minutes. Put into a large, lightly oiled bowl, and cover. Leave in a warm place for about an hour and a half, until doubled in size.

3. Preheat the oven to maximum. Put the butter into a heavy-based frying pan over a medium-high heat. Add the onions and cook until softened, then add the lardons and cook until beginning to crisp. Transfer the onions and lardons to a plate and leave to cool. Mix together the Quark and crème fraîche, season well and grate in a little nutmeg.

4. Dust a baking tray with cornmeal, and divide the dough in two balls. Put one on the tray and flatten it, then use your fingertips to knock the air out of it. Stretch it out with your fingertips to make a rough rectangle, thin in the middle and thicker around the edges.

5. Spread it with half the crème fraîche mixture, and scatter with half the onions and lardons. Cook for 8 minutes, then, if using the Reblochon, arrange it on the top and cook for another 2 minutes, until melted. If not, cook for 10 minutes in total.

6. Cut into squares and serve immediately, while it's still hot, then repeat with the rest of the dough.

Vietnamese summer rolls

MAKES 10

I can't understand why, although the British have welcomed its Chinese counterpart with open arms (soggy spring rolls and chips were a school speciality), the far superior Vietnamese summer roll has never made inroads here. I suspect it may be because it's not deep-fried. Nevertheless, these make an excellent drinking companion: spicy, squidgy and starchy, they even come complete with that old pub classic, the salted peanut.

(Although, what with the dipping sauce, this isn't one for a posh party ... make sure you provide napkins nearby. You can also use quarter rounds of rice paper, available from oriental supermarkets.)

50G DRY RICE VERMICELLI NOODLES

200G COOKED, SHELLED KING PRAWNS

I LITTLE GEM LETTUCE, LEAVES SEPARATED
AND SHREDDED

5 SPRING ONIONS, SHREDDED FINELY
LENGTHWAYS

½ A CUCUMBER, CUT INTO THIN SLICES
LENGTHWAYS

25G SALTED PEANUTS, CHOPPED

A SMALL BUNCH OF FRESH CORIANDER,
LEAVES ROUGHLY CHOPPED

A SMALL BUNCH OF FRESH MINT, LEAVES
ROUGHLY CHOPPED

10 RICE FLOUR PANCAKES

FOR THE DIPPING SAUCE

JUICE OF 2 LIMES

3 TABLESPOONS FISH SAUCE

2 TEASPOONS SOFT LIGHT BROWN SUGAR

4 TABLESPOONS RICE WINE VINEGAR

I RED BIRD'S-EYE CHILLI, FINELY CHOPPED

I CLOVE OF GARLIC, FINELY CHOPPED

1. Cover the noodles with boiling water and leave to soak for about 5 minutes, until soft. Drain well. Meanwhile, prepare the other ingredients and set out around a clean, dry chopping board or plate. Fill a shallow bowl, large enough to fit the rice flour pancakes, with warm water.

2. To assemble the summer rolls, soak a pancake in the warm water for a minute or so, until soft and elastic. Shake well, and put on the board or plate. Put a couple of prawns 2cm away from the left edge of the pancake, then top with a pinch of noodles, some lettuce, spring onion, cucumber, a few peanuts and finally some coriander and mint sprigs. Don't be tempted to overfill the pancake, or it won't roll up properly. It might take you a couple of goes to get the quantity right.

3. Fold the bottom third of the pancake upwards over the filling, and do the same with the top. Then carefully fold the left edge right over the filling and tuck underneath. Continue rolling the pancake up into a tight sausage, making sure the bottom is still securely tucked in. Put on a plate and continue with the remaining rolls. Refrigerate for up to 2 hours, until ready to serve.

4. To make the dipping sauce, whisk together all the ingredients. Serve with the rolls, and some napkins.

Pink lemonade jelly

SERVES 8–10

I'm pleased jellies have come back into fashion in recent years: their wonderful wobbliness never fails to gladden the heart and, although you can get all retro ironic with a Sex on the Beach version, or try to give the jelly airs and graces by sticking champagne in there, for me, it's essentially a childish pleasure.

This wonderful summery one fits the bill perfectly: despite the name, it's actually a deep, fruity red colour – and is, of course, best enjoyed with ice cream.

250G RIPE STRAWBERRIES, HULLED
125G CASTER SUGAR
ZEST AND JUICE OF 1 LEMON

7 GELATINE LEAVES
500ML SPARKLING LEMONADE
OIL, TO GREASE

1. Set aside a few small fruit to use as garnish and put the rest into a saucepan with the sugar, lemon zest and juice and 250ml of water. Bring to a simmer, then cook for about 5 minutes, depending on ripeness, until the fruit is soft.

2. Pour into a jelly bag, if you have one – if not, line a sieve with a double thickness of muslin, pour in the mixture, then gather the top of the muslin together with an elastic band to make a bag – and suspend over a bowl. Leave to drain, then squeeze any remaining juice out; you want as much as possible.

3. Soften the gelatine in cold water for 5 minutes while you warm the strawberry juice in a small pan. Squeeze out the gelatine leaves and stir into the juice until dissolved, then carefully pour in the lemonade, trying not to let it foam too much.

4. Pour into a lightly greased 1 litre jelly mould and chill in the fridge for about an hour, then add the remaining strawberries and chill until set.

Gin and tonic sorbets

MAKES ABOUT 30 SHOTS

This recipe was a last-minute addition, inspired by a friend's impromptu thirtieth birthday party – we served them after dinner, in wide shot glasses, and they went down a treat. In fact, we're still finding the sticky evidence in nooks and crannies around the house some months later.

On reflection, we decided that making a sorbet to get the party started, instead of a big bowl of noxious vodka jelly, is probably one of the more welcome signs of age, although whether it encouraged any more sophisticated behaviour is unclear.

If you don't have time to make sorbet (and, of course, they do need to be done a few hours ahead to allow them to freeze), then serving a shot glass of bought lemon or lime sorbet, topped with well-chilled gin or vodka, would probably have a similar effect.

300G CASTER SUGAR	75ML GIN
300ML WATER	BITTERS OF YOUR CHOICE
2 LIMES	400ML TONIC WATER, CHILLED

1. Put the sugar into a pan with the water and heat, stirring, until it dissolves. Bring to the boil, then reduce the heat and simmer for a minute. Take off the heat, leave to cool, then chill.

2. Zest the limes into the syrup, then stir in their juice, the gin and a dash or two of bitters until well mixed. Gently pour in the tonic water, trying not to create too much froth, and stir carefully to combine.

3. Put into an ice cream maker and churn according to instructions. Alternatively pour into a strong plastic box and put in the coldest part of the freezer. After an hour and a half it should have frozen round the edges – take it out and beat vigorously with a fork, electric whisk or in a food processor until you have a uniformly textured icy slush. Put back into the freezer and repeat at least twice more every hour and a half, then freeze for at least another hour.

4. To serve, take out of the freezer and leave to soften for 10 minutes, then scoop into shot glasses and hand out immediately.

Birthday cakes

Birthday cakes should, strictly speaking, be whatever the celebrant's favourite cake is every other day of the year: if they always go for lemon drizzle in cafés, then baking them a chocolate cake, just because it's their birthday, is downright cruel. Birthdays are not a time for forcible re-education, however much you feel they're missing out with their weird preferences – just humour them on their special day. That said, I can't pretend to be able to offer every single possible preference, and, as chocolate seems to be the most universally popular, I've plumped for that. Although if anyone's baking one for me, I'd like coffee and walnut, please.

For people who eschew the sweet, I've also included a savoury alternative, which, coincidentally, just happens to go much better with a celebratory glass of fizz.

Chocolate and rose* layer cake

MAKES ONE 18CM CAKE

This towering four-tier cake is inspired by the spectacular layer cakes of the American south – and in terms of sheer drama, it can't really be beaten. I made it for my flatmate's thirtieth, and kept it hidden in my bedroom the night before, to present to her before work – and just the sight of it, looming out of the darkness, made me smile every time I woke up. (Which was frequently: the heady smell of chocolate is not conducive to a restful night's sleep.)

Part of the cake's fabulous flamboyance is the contrast between the icing and the sponge, so, even if you're not normally a food-colouring kind of a person, I'd strongly advise relenting this once: you can get some very good natural varieties these days, and unless you're baking for the Queen, it's only their birthday once a year. Note that rosewater varies in strength, so add it very gradually to taste.

FOR THE CAKE
250G DARK CHOCOLATE, BROKEN INTO
    SMALL PIECES
350G BUTTER, SOFTENED, PLUS EXTRA
    TO GREASE
350G CASTER SUGAR
300G SELF-RAISING FLOUR
50G COCOA POWDER
2 LEVEL TEASPOONS BAKING POWDER
A PINCH OF SALT
6 EGGS, BEATEN
2 TABLESPOONS MILK

FOR THE ICING AND DECORATION
250G BUTTER, SOFTENED
400G ICING SUGAR, SIFTED
2 TABLESPOONS MILK
A PINCH OF SALT
ROSEWATER, TO TASTE
PINK FOOD COLOURING
CRYSTALLIZED ROSE PETALS

1. Preheat the oven to 180°C/gas mark 4 and grease and line four 18cm sandwich tins at least 5cm deep (if you only have two you can bake the cake in two batches).

2. Put the chocolate into a heatproof bowl over a pan of simmering water and allow to melt. Remove and leave to cool for 5 minutes. Meanwhile, put the butter and sugar into a food mixer with a whisk attachment, or use electric hand beaters, and beat until light and fluffy.

3. Sift the flour, cocoa powder, baking powder and a pinch of salt into a bowl. Mix together the eggs and milk and beat into the butter and sugar, a little at a time, making sure each addition is fully mixed in before adding any more. If the mixture threatens to curdle, add a little flour.

4. Fold in the dry ingredients, then mix in the melted chocolate and stir to combine well. Divide between the tins, level the tops, and bake for 25 minutes. Let the cakes cool in their tins for 5 minutes, then loosen the edges with a knife and turn out on to a cooling rack. Make sure they are completely cool before icing.

5.   To make the icing, beat together the butter with half the icing sugar, then, when the mixture is smooth, add the rest of the sugar along with the milk, salt, rosewater, and a couple of drops of food colouring. This varies according to brand, so you may need to add more to get the colour you desire. Taste and add more rosewater if necessary.

6.   When the cake is cool, put one layer on to a board or plate and spread with a quarter of the icing, making sure it's particularly thick around the edges. Continue to layer in this way, then top the cake with the remaining icing, smoothing it down well with a palette knife.

7.   Decorate with crystallized rose petals. To make these yourself, wash and gently dry the petals from an organically grown rose. Whisk 2 egg whites until frothy in one bowl and put 50g of caster sugar into another. Dip each petal first into the egg white, shaking off any excess, then into the sugar. Place on a tray lined with baking parchment and leave to dry. Alternatively, stick in zillions of candles and serve with due fanfare.

✳   If roses don't tickle your fancy (and I've never met a man wise enough to truly appreciate their delicate flavour), then it's simplicity itself to change the flavour of the icing to whatever does. (You may wish to alter the colour accordingly, although chocolate and coffee will obviously provide their own alternative.) Simply replace the rosewater with:

*   Coffee – 80ml cooled espresso (and no milk)
*   Chocolate – 100g plain chocolate, melted and cooled
*   Orange – zest and juice of 1 orange (and no milk)
*   Mint – 1 teaspoon peppermint extract
*   Vanilla – 1 teaspoon vanilla extract
*   White chocolate – 100g white chocolate, melted and allowed to cool slightly

Pesto cake salé

The first time my dad presented me with a slice of cake liberally studded with what looked like currants, but which, on closer inspection, turned out to be pieces of black olive, I recoiled – was that a chunk of ham lurking beneath the crust? Once I got over the cake thing, and realized this was actually what we in Britain would call a bread or a loaf, despite it being clearly no such thing, I managed to open my mind wide enough to recognize that here was an idea of no little genius.

Traditionally served cut into chunks with the aperitif in France, the savoury cake is also the perfect choice for the person in your life who always orders cheese rather than pudding, and can never be prevailed upon to share a bag of sweets at the cinema. For such salty-toothed types, the ritual of the birthday cake must be an annual gift of disappointment – and the sight of everyone else tucking in with gusto a bitter pill to swallow on their special day.

Although I've seen cake salé made with everything from tuna to goat's cheese and coriander, I was particularly pleased with the lurid green of this one, which should leave no one in any doubt of its emphatic savouriness.

150ML OLIVE OIL, PLUS EXTRA TO GREASE
50G PINE NUTS
100G PARMESAN, GRATED
100G GRUYÈRE, GRATED
85G FRESH BASIL, LEAVES ONLY

250G PLAIN FLOUR
1 TEASPOON BAKING POWDER
150ML MILK
4 EGGS, BEATEN

1. Preheat the oven to 200°C/gas mark 6 and grease a 22cm loaf tin with oil. Line with baking parchment, and oil this too.

2. Toast the pine nuts in a dry pan until beginning to colour, then put into a food processor along with the cheeses and the basil leaves. Whiz to a purée, then add the olive oil and whiz again.

3. Sift the flour and baking powder together into a mixing bowl. Whisk together the milk, eggs and the olive oil and pesto mixture, then fold quickly into the dry ingredients.

4. Spoon into the prepared loaf tin and bake for 45–50 minutes, until a skewer inserted into the centre comes out clean. Cool in the tin for 5 minutes, then transfer to a wire rack to cool completely.

Useful resources

Drinks

When it comes to drinks matching, as mentioned on page 17, in the Cooking to Impress chapter, the best option is always to chat to an expert in the form of a wine merchant or similar. If you don't have any such gems near you, the internet makes a decent substitute: wine writer Fiona Beckett's website, matchingfoodandwine.com, is an amazing resource of suggestions, for spirits, beer, cider and even soft drinks as well as the wine in the name.

If you're really keen, the Beer Academy, beeracademy.co.uk, and various wine schools and merchants including the venerable Berry Bros. & Rudd (bbr.com), run courses on the subject. Books on wine necessarily date quickly, but I've found Jancis Robinson's *How to Taste* consistently useful from a drinker's perspective.

Newspaper and magazine buying recommendations are invaluable for picking up on special offers and interesting bottles, as are the ever-increasing number of blogs: far better than simply going to the supermarket and picking up whatever has the biggest discount.

Tableware

For interesting crockery, table linen and cutlery, you can't beat poking around antiques markets and charity shops (the more obscure the location, the better the finds: those in big cities tend to be picked clean). eBay is the online equivalent – if you know what you're looking for, of course. Sites like mydeco.com and etsy.com offer similarly unusual new products, and divertimenti.co.uk and johnlewis.com are a reliable source of more mainstream cookware and tableware.

Ingredients

If your local shops stump you, just about any ingredient under the sun is available for purchase online. For spices, I like the ones from steenbergs.co.uk, which come in smart little jars, and coolchile.co.uk for all things Mexican, while souschef.co.uk has dried rose petals which you may wish to use on the cake on pages 311–12, plus all those fancy professional ingredients bandied about on *MasterChef* – you won't need agar agar, green yuzu juice or a Himalayan salt plate for any recipe of mine, but still, it's useful to know that they're there. The rice wrappers for the Vietnamese summer rolls on page 304 are available from oriental suppliers like waiyeehong.com.

Acknowledgements

First of all, I'd like to thank Juliet Annan and Sophie Missing at Fig Tree, for being so boundlessly enthusiastic about this book, chocolate rabbits and all, and for the considerable advice and encouragement they've provided along the way (including memorably pointing out when a menu was 'too yellow'). I'm also grateful to Caroline Craig, Annie Lee, Bren Parkins-Knight and Ellie Smith for all the hard work they've put in.

Joe Woodhouse has my undying gratitude as the coolest, most relaxed photographer I've ever worked with – thank you for making it all so easy (it's amazing what you can find down the back of the sofa), and also to Nina Farrell for the beautiful illustrations and design.

Thanks to Sarah Ballard and Lara Hughes-Young at United Agents for pushing me not to rest on my laurels after *Perfect*, for their support, and for taking on all the serious stuff for me. Susan Smillie and Rick Peters at the *Guardian* also deserve a pat on the back: both for giving me a chance in the first place, and for making me laugh every week, even when I feel slightly less than perfect.

My housemates past, present and nearly, Alex, James, Lucinda, Jot and particularly Anna have put up with endless food mountains and force-feeding with very good humour, and I am truly grateful to you all for your patience, appetite and criticism. Thanks Ali for the recipe testing and email entertainment, and everyone who's come and eaten my food over the months, and the many friends I've neglected in favour of staying in and cooking instead.

Thanks to my family for all their support down the phone: and especially to Amelia and Seb for reassuring me the jam tarts were up to scratch, and Finlay, Harry and Sofia for sterling cake consumption.

I'm indebted to the entire online food community, bloggers, tweeters and Word of Mouth commenters for their inspiration, advice and for kindly claiming that my many blurry pictures of pulled pork look delicious. Likewise, all the chefs and other food writers I've leant on for advice along the way.

Lastly, Richard, I can't thank you enough for your patience, your kindness when I needed it most, and your miraculous ability with calming mugs of Horlicks. I really don't think I could have done it without you. Beans on toast from now on, promise.

Index

Page references for photographs are in bold